DELTA SCOUT

Published in 2008 by 30° South Publishers (Pty) Ltd.
28, Ninth Street, Newlands, 2092
Johannesburg, South Africa
www.30degreessouth.co.za
info@30degreessouth.co.za

Cover images by Craig Bone and Charlie Aust
Operational areas map by Richard Wood

Design and origination by 30° South Publishers (Pty) Ltd.

Printed and bound by Pinetown Printers, Durban

ISBN 978-1-920143-21-3

Anthony Trethowan

DELTA SCOUT

Ground Coverage operator

30° South Publishers

About the author

Tony Trethowan was born in England in 1955. His parents immigrated to Southern Rhodesia in 1958, where he grew up. He served in the BSA Police from 1974 to 1981 but resigned shortly after Zimbabwean independence. He has had three careers—policeman, educator & trainer and health & safety professional. He is presently studying for an MSSc in Occupational Safety and Health at Queens University in Belfast. His home is in Northern Ireland, but he is currently working for a large oil and gas company as an HSE consultant in Yemen. *Delta Scout* is his first book.

This book is dedicated with love to my wife, Janine, and my daughters, Nicolle and Leanne

Note from the publisher: The author's BSAP Ground Coverage call sign was in actuality 'Scouter Delta'. For the title of this book, we have taken the liberty of inverting the words for reasons of a more universal clarity.

Send no weapons no more money
Send no vengeance across the seas
Just the blessing of forgiveness for my new countryman and me
Missing brothers, martyred fellows, silent children in the ground
Could we but hear them could they not tell us
"Time to lay God's rifle down"
Who will say this far no further, oh Lord, if I die today

James Taylor
Belfast to Boston (God's Rifle)

Contents

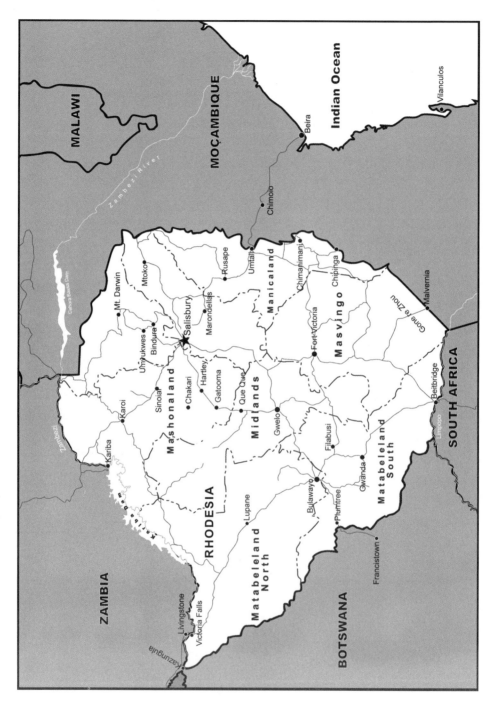

Map of Rhodesia

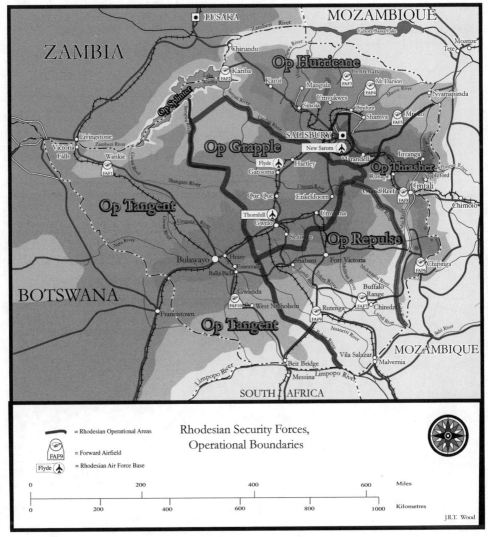

Rhodesian operational areas

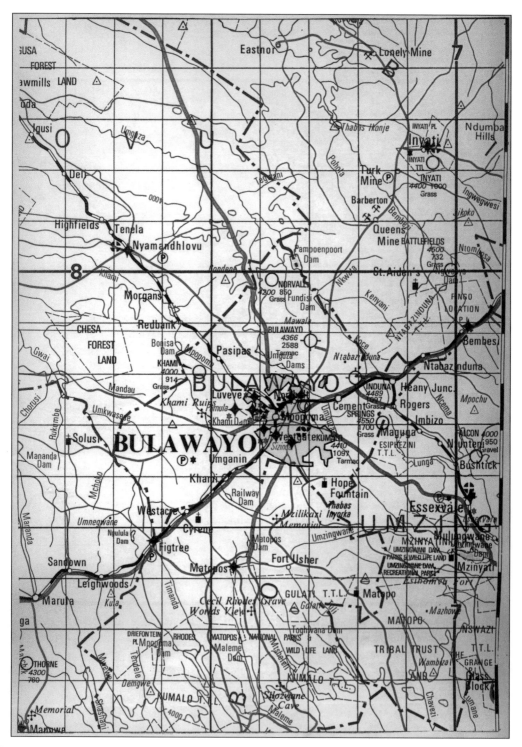

Bulawayo area

12

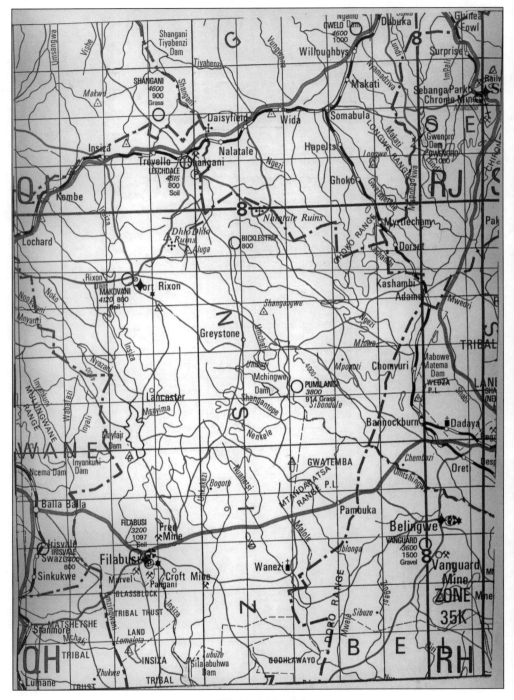

Filabusi North

13

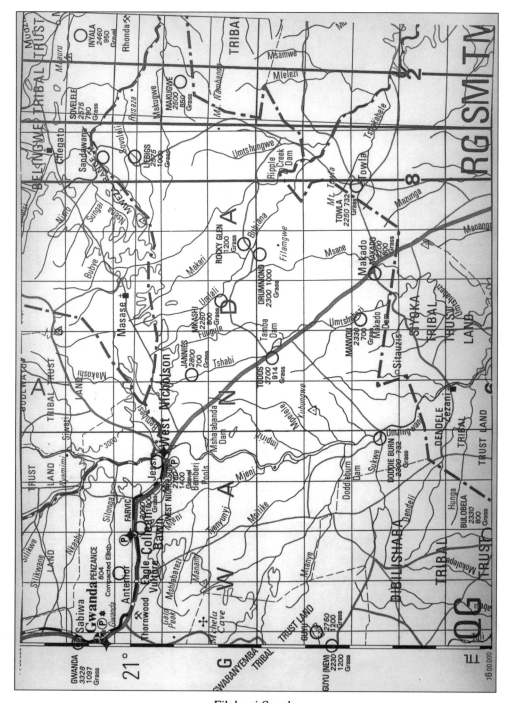

Filabusi South

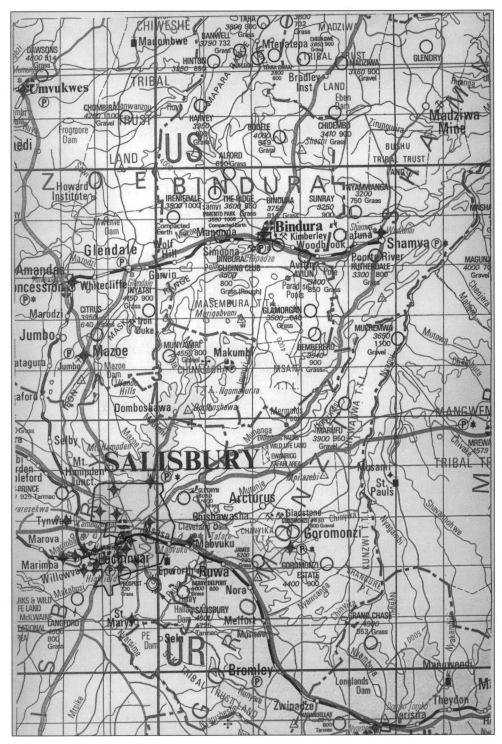

Salisbury North

Author's note

I thought that writing this book would entail little more than putting my thoughts down on paper. To the contrary, apart from writing it, it has been a long, hard journey involving much research, fact finding and verification and sourcing of photographs. I have contacted dozens of people, some old friends, some I barely knew, and many whom I haven't spoken to in thirty years— and without exception and without hesitation every single one has offered their unstinting help.

I would particularly like to thank the following:

Jane Lyle who took the time to read the manuscript and convinced me that I should get it published.

Will Leitch in Northern Ireland who went through every page of the manuscript and gave me some invaluable advice on how to write for a broader international readership. Thank you also for writing the foreword.

Neville Spurr for his critique and photographs—also for being such a great boss.

Colin Ross for the photographic work.

My nephew Paul who is a shining example of our legacy and who happened to say the right thing at the right time.

My brothers Ian and Brian for their photographs and stories that I have included in the narrative. Both have weathered severe storms in their lives and remain an inspiration to me.

My brother Paul for his support.

Allan Brent for his photographs and for being there for me.

John Benjamin for his encouragement.

My journey through my fifty-three years has not been taken alone. Some of the people who have shared parts of my life have left lasting memories that I will treasure forever. These are the people, some of whom are no longer with us, who have inspired and continue to inspire me:

Bev Layard—in spite of your disability, or perhaps because of it, you have demonstrated a courage that is an inspiration to all who know you.

Billy Glen, John Bebbington, George Venturus and Bobby Wilson—all who are no longer with us.

Wolf Fabiani who left us a few years ago—will you ever know how much you have helped me?

André Geldenhuys stands as a man among men—I feel so privileged to be able to call you my friend.

Steve Herman whose unique sense of humour always seems to calm even the most troubled waters.

The Kommetjie Men's Group, ably led by Ernest who provided a solid foundation and support.

There are those people whose stories appear in this book; in some cases I have used their real names and in others cases not. They know who they are and I thank them.

The staff of 30° South Publishers—Chris has been a patient and caring editor who pandered to this new author's rather fragile ego as he desperately clung to his manuscript, fearful of letting go. I don't quite know how he did it but he gently prised the manuscript away from me and with his knowledge and understanding of the subject gained my trust, which made for an easy working relationship.

Kerrin Cocks for designing the book and particularly the cover. I was adamant that I knew exactly what I wanted it to look like. Kerrin listened briefly to what I had to say and then presented me with something totally different— yet absolutely perfect.

Thanks to Craig Bone and Charlie Aust for allowing the use of their images on the cover. And to all those kind people who have supplied photographs—I have tried where possible to credit you in the photo sections.

In many ways I have been truly blessed but none more so than with my family—my wife Janine (Nin) and daughters Nicolle (Nic) and Leanne (Pooky). Together we have formed an unbreakable bond.

Nin—you have been married to one of the most difficult people I have ever met, for twenty-five years. I will never understand how you managed to keep our family together through times that would have torn most families apart. I love you so much.

Nic and Pooky—the two of you fill my life with absolute pleasure and make me so proud to be your dad.

Tony Trethowan
Belfast
March 2008

Foreword

Tony Trethowan is a remarkable man. Among the many people I meet and interview, he stood out immediately as someone different, and special. He simply never gives up. He has fierce integrity. He hates to see a mistake being made. So concerned was he about the international coverage of events in Zimbabwe some years ago that, one day, he contacted BBC Radio Ulster to point out our shortcomings very politely. I was the reporter on duty, and was duly dispatched to meet him and other 'Rhodies' now living in Northern Ireland.

In truth, where he saw a wrong to be righted that day, we simply saw a potential story. Yet from my first meeting with a new 'contact', from that first attempt to explain what is going on in Tony's former homeland, grew an unlikely friendship that has lasted.

Tony will throw little gems into a lunchtime chat without the slightest awareness that his stories far outstrip the experiences of most people sitting around him. From policing to bushcraft, from the culture of health and safety to the economics of the oil business, from his love for his former country, to his despair at its current difficulties, we'll chat about it all. After a couple of years of always letting him pay the bill, I felt I knew this man pretty well.

And then I read the manuscript of this book.

Not for the first time, I felt deeply uncomfortable at my profound ignorance, and that of many Europeans about what is happening in Africa. I knew I hadn't understood the first thing about what my friend had lived through. Britons and the Irish often find Africa unsettling. Britain struggles to come to terms with its colonial past, and generations of Irish missionaries bear witness to our fascination with the continent. Many hundreds of us still feel drawn to visit, to live and work there. Those of us who have stayed behind watch the television news, and some of us might even read more in the newspapers or keep up with events online, but the problems seem far away, and intractable. For what can come of wars where no one really wins? Where so many suffer and die?

And then I look up from my keyboard, across the trees to a white building shining in the late winter sun. Not a mile from where I am sitting, Irish Republicans and Ulster Unionists sit together at Stormont, nearing the end of their first full year in government. After three decades of bombs, bullets, and deep despair, few believed such a day could ever happen. History will record what happens next, but all observers agree we have seen sights and developments in the last twelve months that seemed almost too unlikely to take in.

I can see no such hope in Zimbabwe. Northern Ireland is wondering how to deal with the events of the past and how they impact on the present. Many of us have looked at South Africa's Truth and Reconciliation Commission, and wondered what such ideas might offer us. I firmly believe that reading about the events described in this book will go a long way to helping you understand what is happening in Zimbabwe now.

This is a true story from one of Africa's forgotten wars. While unions flexed their muscles in Britain, while oil prices rose, while Margaret Thatcher came to power, while men, women and children died on Irish streets, ordinary people were also fighting for their lives in a war in the Rhodesian bush. The word 'terrorism' is almost always very hard to define.

Tony's account of his police career made me laugh, it made me despair, it made me sit up half the night thinking about peace, politicians, and ordinary soldiers. I thought I'd done enough of that already, so it's a rare story that can make me start such a journey again.

Enjoy your journey.

Will Leitch
Belfast
March 2008

Will Leitch has been a BBC journalist for almost twenty years. He works now as a presenter and reporter for BBC Radio Ulster in Belfast, Northern Ireland.

Introduction

Why on earth would someone want to write about a series of events twenty-seven years after they happened?

This book is a narrative about a period in history (1974–1980) through the eyes of a young policeman serving in the Rhodesian police force—The British South Africa Police. It is not a definitive history and therefore will have some inaccuracies, although I have done my best to avoid these. Everything you read is the way I saw events and the opinions are mine alone. In order to be true to the narrative I have had to relive everything in order to be able to truly recount events, feelings and emotions the way I saw and experienced them. There were many times when it was not an easy thing to do and, as I relived these events and experienced the emotions, I went through many mood changes—from joyous laughter to sadness and, many times, despair.

I do not want the book to be seen to be about only me, although the narrative is in the first person. Many young men endured similar experiences, felt the same grief, witnessed similar tragedies and laughed, and cried, with their comrades. It is a brutally honest and open account about a people and a way of life about which so little has been written. It exposes truths, some of which will be hard to comprehend, but must be heard. It is, I hope, a thought-provoking account interspersed with humour, pathos, tragedy—and, perhaps, a hope for the future.

It is a record and commentary of those times that provide an insight for those who only had the merest glimpse or idea of what was happening in that little corner of Africa.

Although Rhodesia ceased to exist in 1980 its people remain today, scattered all over the world—the characters that they developed over many years now as much a part of them and their children as they ever were. This book attempts to explain the character of these people and in doing so becomes a celebration of a way of life.

A few years ago my eldest daughter Nicolle and I were watching a news broadcast on South African television. The news item was about a man who had committed a series of violent sexual assaults on young girls. The girl's mother identified the man who was then attacked and beaten to death by a crowd of angry residents, giving them the gratification and instant justice they sought. Nicolle sat quietly, then turned to me and said: "Gee dad, it must be great to kill someone." She was speaking of the satisfaction that supposedly comes from killing someone who 'needs' to die. I gave the sort of meaningless response fathers might typically give but her question continued to niggle me.

When the Truth and Reconciliation Commission hearings were taking place in South Africa I thought they served a purpose in that people were able to talk about things that had happened during the years of apartheid and, in doing so, go some way to coping with the trauma of it all. What disturbed me was the fact that soldiers who were eighteen or so at the time had to publicly apologize for what they had done under orders. They were made to feel guilty through the thoughts and actions of others—not their own.

Wars are often glorified by those who have fought in them in an attempt to make sense of what they have done. I can and do empathize with these people for reasons that will become apparent in this book. At the same time war has been sanitized by politicians to justify the decisions they make and often, in doing so, to hide their hidden agendas. These people need to understand the consequences of the decisions they make.

I became increasingly convinced that people just don't understand—I became increasingly aware that I must write about the way it really was, and is.

In the chapter 'Wendy Atkinson', I recall a life-changing incident that happened to me in 1976. I had been a policeman for over two years—I had seen people die and many dead bodies, usually victims of murder, traffic accidents and suicide. My attitude towards death was probably best described as one of 'callous indifference'—a clinical process in which a human being stopped breathing and became a mass of lifeless flesh and bone. Nothing more, nothing less.

As an individual I lacked empathy and understanding towards people. My whole attitude towards life was one of self-preservation. Life was about me, what mattered to me and me alone.

When I was with Wendy as she was dying it was the first time in my life that I was aware that someone really needed my help ... and that I could provide that help. I came to realize that being a policeman was all about providing a service to others without expecting anything in return; the satisfaction one gets from being alive is in what you can do for others.

I have had more than my fair share of turbulence in my life—but being aware of the needs of others, being able to focus on what I could do for them rather than myself, got me through some truly difficult times and situations that would otherwise have destroyed me.

The way I think and behave towards others stems from the experience I shared with Wendy. Without question I am undoubtedly a better person, father and husband for it.

And that's what this book is really all about.

About Rhodesia/Zimbabwe

The country today known as Zimbabwe lies in southern-central Africa between the Zambezi River to the north and the Limpopo to the south. Towards the end of the first millennium AD, Bantu peoples migrated southwards from the Congo Basin into central-southern Africa, displacing the indigenous Bushmen. Between AD 1300 and 1450, the empire of Great Zimbabwe was at its zenith, flourishing from trade with the Arab merchants of the east coast of Africa. Inexplicably, but probably as a result of a series of droughts, the empire disintegrated and split into two distinct groupings—the Torwa who migrated west to Khami and the Mwenemutapa who settled in the north along the Zambezi escarpment, to establish what became commonly known as the Kingdom of Monomatapa, consisting of a loose affiliation of clans.

The five main sub-groups, or tribes, of what was later referred to by the white colonizers as the 'Mashona' nation were, and still are, the Zezuru, Korekore, Ndau, Manyika and Karanga (the original inhabitants of Great Zimbabwe), the term 'Shona' deriving from the common language of chiShona, that was and is used in its various dialects by these five tribes. Other offshoots and 'non-Shona' tribes that inhabit the region are the Tonga in the Zambezi Valley and the Shangaan in the southeast.

Apart from limited Portuguese intervention, the region enjoyed a period of relative peace and prosperity until the Zulu general, Mzilikazi, established the Ndebele kingdom in Bulawayo in the late 1830s, having fled north from across the Limpopo to escape the ravages of alternately Shaka's Zulu impis, and the Boers. Under Mzilikazi, and latterly his son, King Lobengula, the martial Ndebele (also known as the Matabele) subjugated the Mashona tribes. Matabele impis roamed the country with impunity, pillaging and capturing and assimilating Mashona women and children into the Ndebele tribe. (Over a century later tribal friction would again erupt when the Mashona turned the tables on their old Matabele foes.)

This all came to an end when Cecil John Rhodes' British South Africa

Company (BSAC), under charter from Queen Victoria, occupied the region in 1890 and raised the Union Jack at Fort Salisbury. The colony became known as Rhodesia.

In 1893, the Matabele under Lobengula rebelled, taking the white occupiers by surprise. After some initial successes (e.g. destroying Major Alan Wilson's 'Shangani Patrol' to a man), the Matabele were ultimately defeated at the Battle of Bembesi by the white men and their Gatling guns. Three years later, the Mashona revolted in what became known as the first *Chimurenga* (war of liberation). In spite of inflicting some notable casualties on the settler population the Mashona were defeated and their leaders, the women spirit mediums Kaguvi and Nehanda, were hanged for their troubles.

Rhodesia grew and flourished. In 1923, with the BSAC making way for formal colonial administration, a referendum was held (whites-only franchise) with the electorate voting by a narrow margin to become a self-governing Crown colony rather than incorporation into the Union of South Africa. With the new colony of Northern Rhodesia across the Zambezi River, Rhodesia became Southern Rhodesia. During both World Wars, 'the Rhodesias' contributed considerable numbers of personnel (black and white) to the Allied war effort.

After World War Two, the two Rhodesias experienced a phenomenal period of growth and prosperity (mainly because of the copper boom in the north and tobacco in the south), with a large white immigration from post-war Britain. During this period, to consolidate political and economic control, the white colonial politicians led by Sir Roy Welensky formed The Federation of Rhodesia and Nyasaland. It was during this period of the 1950s that Black Nationalism began raising its head. An economically crippled post-war Britain, in unseeming haste to divest herself of her African colonies, began granting independence to her African colonies, starting with Ghana in 1957. This signalled the demise of The Federation which collapsed in 1963, with Nyasaland being granted independence as Malawi in 1963 and Northern Rhodesia as Zambia in 1964.

Southern Rhodesia dropped its prefix and the conservative white Rhodesian Front Party (RF) came to power in 1964 under Winston Field, followed shortly thereafter by Ian Smith. Joshua Nkomo became the leading Black Nationalist and with his Soviet-sponsored Zimbabwe African People's Union (ZAPU) fomented a national campaign of violent civil unrest. The ZAPU Shona faction broke away under Ndabaningi Sithole and formed the Chinese-sponsored Zimbabwe African National Union (ZANU). Both Nationalist parties began dispatching cadres overseas to the Eastern Bloc and China for military training in order to commence the second *Chimurenga*.

In the meantime, Prime Minister Ian Smith and the equally intransigent British Labour Prime Minister Harold Wilson were deadlocked in talks, with the British insisting upon immediate majority rule ('one man one vote') and Smith demanding a gradual phasing-in of the black franchise. In frustration, on 11 November 1965, Smith unilaterally declared the country independent (UDI). Britain immediately imposed international sanctions as the Nationalists seized their opportunity and began infiltrating guerrillas into the country. Robert Mugabe had by now wrested the ZANU leadership from Sithole.

So began a fifteen-year-period of stand-off and conflict with ZANLA (Zimbabwe African National Liberation Army, ZANU's military wing) operating out of Mozambique's Tete Province, supported by the Mozambican liberation movement Frelimo; and ZIPRA (Zimbabwe People's Revolutionary Army, ZAPU's military wing) operating out of Zambia.

The 'bush war', as it became known, consisted of three distinct phases: Phase 1, 1966 to 1971, saw armed incursions from across the Zambezi by both ZAPU and ZANU. These incursions were dealt with easily enough by the Rhodesian security forces in the harsh, sparsely populated terrain of the Zambezi Valley.

Phase 2, 1972 to 1975, saw the guerrillas, particularly ZANLA, changing tactics, using subversion and terror on the local tribespeople to gain local supremacy. The Rhodesians, caught by surprise, opened up Operation *Hurricane* in the northeast of the country, and gradually gained the ascendancy with the introduction of some novel military tactics such as the Fireforce concept. It was during this phase that two events, which were to signal the ultimate demise of the Rhodesians, occurred. In 1974, South African Prime Minister John Vorster, using his economic trump card (South Africa kept the Rhodesian economy and war effort afloat with fuel and arms supplies), forced Smith to accept his policy of African 'Détente' (effectively, compliant independent black states north of the Limpopo, including Rhodesia), which entailed a general ceasefire and release of all detained Nationalists. ZANLA, in particular, used the opportunity to lick its wounds and regrouped on the borders. 1975 saw the overnight withdrawal of the Portuguese from Mozambique, handing power to an astonished Samora Machel and Frelimo. In one fell swoop the Rhodesians now found themselves defending a further one thousand kilometres of hostile border—from the Zambezi to the Limpopo.

Phase 3, 1976 to independence in 1980, saw ZANLA and ZIPRA (to a lesser degree) flooding the country with guerrillas. With South African support dwindling and the country in dire economic straits, Smith and his black-moderate allies, Muzorewa, Chirau and Sithole, were forced to the negotiation table at Lancaster House. Mugabe and Nkomo, with both ZANLA and ZIPRA staring military defeat in the face, were likewise forced to attend the talks, as the 'Patriotic Front' (PF), an unholy alliance between the two tribal arch-enemies. To rid himself of the troublesome colony, the British mediator, Lord Carrington, bulldozed through a constitutional 'agreement', clearly biased in favour of Mugabe. A ceasefire was declared in December 1979 and general elections, that were not free or fair, were held in early 1980, which Mugabe's ZANU (PF) won overwhelmingly with the vast majority voting for Mugabe simply as a means to end the war.

On 18 April 1980, Mugabe became the first prime minister of Zimbabwe and was heralded by the world as a model of reconciliation and pragmatism. British expediency was therefore justified. However, it didn't take long for Mugabe to show his true colours. In 1983, using the pretext of a ZAPU insurrection, he sent in his notorious North Korean-trained Fifth Brigade to embark on a systematic programme of genocide against innocent Ndebele tribespeople in Matabeleland.

However, it was only in the late 1990s and early 2000s, with the bloody white-farm invasions, that the world slowly and finally began to appreciate the fact that Mugabe would remain forever a brutal tyrant, who would retain power at whatever cost—the ultimate victims being his own people who are today starving and dying in a country whose economy and infrastructure has totally collapsed.

Source: Chris Cocks

The British South Africa Police

The history of the police force commenced in 1889 with a recruiting campaign for the British South Africa Company Police to accompany the Pioneer Column. The force numbered five hundred men under the command of Lieutenant-Colonel Pennefather. In 1891 the Mashonaland Mounted Police came into being, followed by the Matabeleland Mounted Police, and a municipal force known as the Southern Rhodesia Constabulary. In 1896 the word 'company' was dropped from the name and in 1903 the force was reorganized and the first commissioner, Colonel Bodle CMG, was appointed. In 1909 all the above forces, together with the Bechuanaland Border Force, were amalgamated into one unified force—the British South Africa Police. Contingents of the BSAP served in the Anglo–Boer War and in the First World War.

Until 1953 there was no standing army with the police being the first line of defence, therefore being the senior uniformed force and holding the 'Right of Line' in any parade.

The BSAP rank structure was:

White ranks

Commissioner

Deputy Commissioner

Senior Assistant Commissioner

Assistant Commissioner

Chief Superintendent

Superintendent

Chief Inspector

Inspector

Section Officer

Patrol Officer

Black ranks

Sub-Inspector

Sergeant-Major

Senior Sergeant

Sergeant

Constable

Source: Encyclopaedia Rhodesia, *Peter Bridger, Margaret House et al (eds), College Press, Salisbury, Rhodesia 1973*

Chapter one

Wendy Atkinson

If you are very fortunate someone will come in to your life and change it forever. I am. The name of the person who changed my life was Wendy Atkinson.

On Monday 19 April 1976, I was the Duty Patrol Officer on what I thought would be another dull day. It was a public holiday (Easter Monday) and I had been detailed to set up a roadblock on the main Filabusi road.

At 1600 hours Constable Ncube loaded up our police Land Rover with the equipment we would need and we set off. As it was a hot day we wore our summer uniform—khaki shorts, grey short-sleeved shirt, cap, shoes and long socks.

I chose a point on the road that would give people ample time to see the roadblock and went about setting it up. It consisted of two pairs of whitewashed 44-gallon drums with gum poles running through them, one pair positioned in either lane and set about ten metres apart. If anyone tried to smash their way through the gum poles they would hit the spiked mats that had been placed behind the poles and have their tyres ripped to shreds.

(The best use these were ever put to was the time when an elderly patrol officer got the better of a carful of rowdy youths. A roadblock can be a long, boring duty. At best you get the public abusing you for inconveniencing them and at worst a fire fight.

This particular patrol officer was in charge of the roadblock team but was losing his sense of humour as the day wore on. The car with the youths in it came screaming up to the roadblock and the P/O dutifully put up his hand signalling the driver to halt. The driver, in trying to impress his buddies and hoping to scare the P/O, came to a halt mere inches away from him. It worked. The P/O got a heck of a fright, but put up with the ensuing abuse before calmly letting the car through. However, he'd ascertained where they were going and that they would be back later on in the day. So he had a chat with the other members of his team, then re-positioned himself in the other lane and waited.

Sure enough, the same car was later seen approaching in the distance. The P/O put up his hand to signal the car to halt. The driver had his eyes fixed on the P/O, his attention focused on trying to come to a halt close enough to give the P/O another fright. What he didn't notice was that the spiked mats had been placed behind the P/O but *in front* of the drums. As the driver hit his brakes the P/O stepped out of the way and the driver came to a messy halt on the mats. His front tyres were torn to shreds. A heated discussion ensued and only ended with the driver realizing the cops had got the better of him. No malice had been intended. The cops gave him and his buddies a lift home and it was left at that.)

As it was Easter Monday, the last day of Easter, I expected the cars to start queuing up with people returning to Bulawayo from camping trips at Kyle Dam near Fort Victoria. The occupants would be irritable, impatient and tired. Constable Ncube and I could soon expect a busy time.

The war had not yet started in the Filabusi area although there had been a few farm attacks and vehicle ambushes on civilian vehicles in adjacent districts. You could not travel anywhere in Rhodesia at the time without worrying about being ambushed or hitting a landmine. (As a result the public were becoming increasingly nervous and took to carrying all sorts of weapons with them in their cars. If they didn't have a firearm they would borrow one from friends. It didn't matter that they might have no idea how to use the weapon. The 'friend' would hand it over—loaded, safety catch off and ready to fire. All the person in the car needed to do was point the weapon in the right direction and pull the trigger. Much beyond that they had no idea what to do. The weapons gave them some comfort but presented more of a hazard through an accidental discharge than any terrorist attack ever would.)

Our job was simply to show a presence, reassure people and check for the odd vehicle defect, drunken driver or dangerous weapon that presented a threat to innocent civilians.

At about 1630 hours an old rusty *bakkie* (pick-up truck) stopped at the roadblock. The driver was a friendly, weather-beaten *madala* (old man), probably an agricultural foreman from the nearby farming area. I kidded with him about the condition of his vehicle but didn't give him a ticket. In Rhodesia spare parts were in chronically short-supply so you had to make allowances and help out where you could. I exchanged pleasantries with the driver and, as he drove off, he leaned out of the window, pointed behind him and in Ndebele said: "Three people have been killed back there." As what he said registered I called after him but he was well on his way and out of earshot. His warning could have meant anything—from a practical joke to a terrorist ambush.

Constable Ncube and I ran over to our Land Rover, jumped in and headed off in the direction indicated.

As I came over the crest of a hill I saw, in the distance at the bottom of a long, rolling hill on my side of the road, a pantechnicon truck horse and trailer. It had partially entered an access road and was stationary, leaning slightly over to its left side, the back protruding onto the main road.

I drove towards it and, as I came around to the other side, saw amidst a crowd of people a Renault 12 smashed beyond recognition. It was firmly embedded in the linkage between the horse and trailer.

I later established that the R12 and pantechnicon had both been driving in the direction of the roadblock, the R12 behind the pantechnicon. As they began coming down the long hill they built up speed. Then the driver of the pantechnicon had slowed down and started to move farther over to the left side of the road, his intention to make a right-hand turn into the access road that led to a mine. The driver of the R12 thought the truck driver had moved over to the left to allow him to overtake so he increased speed as he moved over to the right side of the road. By this time the pantechnicon had commenced its right turn the R12 driver suddenly realized that he was running out of the space he needed to pass the pantechnicon. He accelerated to full speed in a desperate attempt to try and get past the rig, but didn't stand a chance. He was fully committed to his attempt to overtake and at the moment the rig entered the side road he collided with it at high speed, smashing into the section between horse and trailer. The result was that the force of the impact shunted the fully laden rig three metres onto the side of the road. We estimated that the car had been travelling at about 140 kilometres per hour.

The truck driver and some helpers had removed the occupants from the R12 who were lying scattered and unattended on the hard ground.

Five people had been travelling in the car—Peter Atkinson was driving, his wife Wendy was sitting next to him and in the back seat were his daughter Michelle and his parents, Jill and Andrew.

I parked the Land Rover and walked over to the injured. Peter was lying on his side, unconscious with massive head and internal injuries. Andrew was sitting propped up against the front wheel of the R12 and was moaning softly. He had broken his collar bone, shoulder blade and jaw and was suffering serious internal injuries. Jill sat next to him, dazed and in shock. She had a few broken ribs. Michelle sat quietly next to Jill. She had a few minor cuts and grazes. Wendy was lying on her back with her head awkwardly propped up against the back seat of the car, which someone had taken from the car and placed on the ground nearby. Her eyes were closed and blood seeped from her mouth. She was very quiet.

The gaudy burgundy colour of the seat contrasted awkwardly with the reddish-brown clay earth and painted a macabre picture.

I knew the others were as comfortable as they could be under the circumstances so I moved across to attend to Wendy. As I knelt down on one knee next to her she seemed to sense my presence. She slowly turned her face towards me and opened her eyes. Her face was angelic, with clear white skin. Short, pitch-black hair fell in a fringe above her eyes which were incredibly dark, piercing and very much alive. As I looked into her eyes she held my gaze and without saying anything asked me to help her. No words were necessary; her eyes said it all—she was distressed and needed my help and she knew instinctively that I could give it to her.

Wendy was having trouble breathing so I softly cupped the back of her head in my left hand and ever so slowly raised it so as to elevate and support her. I then placed the middle and index fingers of my right hand between her lips, opened her mouth and gently started to remove congealed blood, broken teeth and bits of flesh from her mouth in an attempt to clear her airways. Her breathing became less laboured and she coughed. As she did so blood and goodness knows what else was vomited up, over my grey shirt and khaki shorts. Encouraged, I further coaxed Wendy and more contents were vomited up.

I had nothing to use to clean her up so I pulled the bottom of my shirt away from the inside of my shorts, tore it into strips and gently wiped away the blood and mess from around her mouth and face.

All this time she kept her eyes firmly focused on my face. It did not distract me; rather, Wendy in her own special way managed to calm and guide me.

I was hypersensitive to everything that was going on around me and was satisfied that the other injured were coping. My immediate concern must still be for Wendy. She coughed again—this time a shallow, throaty cough. I was still supporting the back of her head in my left hand. In order to make her more comfortable I positioned myself so that I was cradling her head in the crook of my right arm.

Again I became aware of her eyes. She did not speak, she could not speak, but instinctively I knew what to say. Almost in a whisper I spoke words of reassurance and comfort and as I spoke she became less distressed. And then her eyes, eyes that were so alive and bright, began to fade. The energy seemed to physically flow from her body and her body relaxed. Still staring intently into her eyes I watched them slowly close and open, close and open, gently, much like a child who is falling asleep. An incredible sense of peace came over Wendy and, as I looked into her eyes, the brightness continued to diminish. I gazed into them until I was aware that the bright life had dimmed and was gone. Wendy continued to breathe but I knew that her soul had left her.

Very gently I laid her against the car seat, stroking away strands of hair that had fallen over her eyes and, in ways that I did not understand, said goodbye. Wendy was at peace.

I was privileged; indeed I had been blessed. God had allowed me to be present when Wendy's spirit, her soul, had passed into Our Father's hands. From life to life.

I got up and went to attend to the others. Peter was still unconscious but stable. Andrew lay on his side moaning quietly. There was some more cleaning up to do so I tore up what was left of my shirt into strips and used these as best

I could. After making Andrew comfortable I went across to Jill and Michelle, talking quietly to them so as to give them the reassurance they needed and managed to settle them.

During this time the traffic had built up as I had expected. Constable Ncube was doing a good job of controlling the vehicles. Dozens of cars drove by. The drivers all slowed down to have a good look but no one stopped to help—they all just drove past. What they saw was absolute bedlam—three critically injured people lying among the wreckage and two sitting quietly hand in hand. They saw a black constable directing traffic and a white patrol officer tending to the injured—a young man shirtless and drenched in blood, others people's blood, from head to foot. To them we were merely a conversation piece, something to talk about in the car on the long way home, a story to tell.

An ambulance arrived from Filabusi and with it my member in charge, his wife who was a nurse and Patrol Officer Colin Craig.

The injured were gently placed in the ambulance. I had done all I could for them.

I stood and looked around at the scene before me. Someone placed a hand on my shoulder and asked me if I was okay. At that moment I became aware of what other people were seeing. I was not wearing a shirt and was quite literally covered in blood. Even the gold and onyx ring my sister had given me for my twenty-first birthday was blood-stained, the gold ring and black onyx contrasting with the brownish-red blood. I did not answer; I did not want to talk to anyone.

I then had to attend to the mopping-up which included making an inventory of everything at the accident. When I was satisfied that I had done all that was required of me I left the scene and drove back to Filabusi. I dropped off Constable Ncube, had a shower and left for the hospital. As I arrived the member in charge's wife came to meet me. While we stood in the dark under a bright security light she told me that Peter, Andrew, Jill and Michelle had been taken to Bulawayo by ambulance as Filabusi did not have the requisite medical facilities.

I asked after Wendy, but I knew the answer. Wendy did not leave for Bulawayo by ambulance. She left in a separate vehicle or rather her body did. She had died in Filabusi hospital at twenty past six that evening.

When the nursing sister left I stood alone for some time outside in the dark. This would be the first of many occasions when, as a policeman and a civilian, I would seek the solitude of darkness, alone with my thoughts, pondering a world that had gone completely mad.

Wendy and I had shared something special. In the brief time that I was with her she had taught me many valuable things. I did not understand it at the time but I am beginning to now.

As an aftermath, neither the truck driver nor Peter Atkinson was ever charged—and rightly so. Peter lay in a coma for twelve days before recovering, as did the others … at least from their physical injuries.

Chapter two

Morris Depot—police training

In 1973, during my last year of school, terrorist incursions into Rhodesia were on the increase. From 1972, when ZANLA terrorists began attacking farms in the northeast of the country it became apparent that more personnel were needed to bolster Rhodesia's armed forces. As a result the national-service (NS) period of conscription was increased from nine to twelve months, then to eighteen months in 1976, and later to two years. By the end of 1973 the situation had got to the point where national servicemen, who'd finished their time, were expected to serve six months a year as territorials in the TF (Territorial Force) units. Understandably potential employers were not keen on taking on able-bodied males when they knew that they could only have them in situ for half the year.

This left most school-leavers with few options on leaving school. One was to do your NS, then look for a job and try and make the system work for you. The other was to sign up for a three-, five- or ten-year contract with a regular unit i.e. army, police or air force and 'enjoy' the benefits of a regular serving member. The third, assuming you had the wherewithal, was admission to a foreign university and effectively avoidance of military service—at least until you returned to the country (many did not return with the result that legislation was instituted that national service became compulsory *prior* to university). There was a fourth option—that of leaving the country and avoiding NS altogether but I only know of one person who did this. Of course, there was always the unthinkable—becoming a conscientious objector.

Few of us had any interest in the politics of the country. Although Ian Smith had declared UDI back in November 1965 I only had a vague idea of what it meant. To us, a land we had grown up in and loved was being threatened by. The fact that the enemy were predominantly black Africans meant little to us. We had grown up with blacks and were to fight alongside them. The enemy was characterized by their evil intentions not by the colour of their skin. Apartheid was a word we didn't believe applied to Rhodesia, or so we thought. We were fighting not to eliminate blacks but to coexist with them as we had done all our lives.

I quite liked the idea of being a policeman so I signed up with the British South Africa Police (the BSAP, or 'The Force' as it was referred to by its members) for three years and on 8 January 1974 reported to Morris Depot, the police training depot, in Salisbury.

Training took five months; slightly longer if your squad did equitation—this meant remaining behind after the others squads had passed out, to handle ceremonial parades which would continue until the next squad was ready to take over.

The first few days were spent running around in a total state of utter confusion, from place to place, getting measured for uniforms, belts, trousers and shirts. While running from place to place and being yelled at by people who demanded to know "what the hell are you are doing here" we were issued with everything from socks to caps, whistles to lanyards and trench coats to goggles.

The big occasion came when we met our squad instructor—Staff Lance Section Officer Mike Lambourne. I have never in my life come anywhere near to being more terrified of anyone than I was of Mike. He was a giant of a man—at least six foot six and, as luck would have it, he also had a black belt in judo and, to top it all he was the national hammer-throwing champion. When Mike yelled the whole of Salisbury came to a standstill. He was terrifying in the extreme and scared us witless.

Mike's job was to shepherd us through our training, discipline us and take us for PT and instruct us in the intricacies of drill.

The day started at 0530 hours with roll call followed by PT. Mike always set the pace as he was much fitter than any of us. No matter how fit you thought you were he would run you into the ground. As our fitness levels increased he decided to get us to carry some weight to make things that much more difficult. You would think this meant giving us packs to carry. No way—Mike divided us into groups of six (four groups per squad of twenty-four) and each group was given a telephone pole to carry on our shoulders—around and around the police golf course. Of course not everyone was the same height so the tactic of any shirker was to position himself in the middle of the group so that, with the taller men at each end shouldering the pole, all the shirker had to do was hold on to the pole and pretend he was carrying it. When Mike saw that this was happening in our group he called us to a halt and made us carry the shirker on top of the pole. We were livid at the injustice of it all but said nothing and did as ordered. When we had carried him about two hundred metres Mike again called us to a halt. He then told the little bugger to carry the telephone pole all the way back to Depot by himself and, if he was not there for the next session after breakfast, he would be charged … and he was.

Part of PT involved swimming. For all but one man in the squad, Richard, this was no problem. Richard had joined the BSAP direct from university in England. On the day of our first lesson we all arrived at the pool in our short swimming costumes, our Speedos. Richard had obviously had too much of the good life at university. At the pool he removed his towel and there he was— in all his splendour—skin as white as our bed sheets, standing 'at ease' with his pot belly protruding from above his swimming trunks, which looked like the boxer shorts that bantamweights wear—you could barely see his knees. Richard had told Mike from the very start that he could not swim. This was unusual because every other person in Morris Depot could. None of us could quite understand why so we put it down to the fact that he was English.

While the rest of us swam length after endless length, Mike let Richard paddle about in the shallow end, wading from one side to the other like a child. For any of the rest of us this would have been a mortifying experience but Richard couldn't have been happier. He walked rather than swam across the pool, every so often calling across to us and waving delightedly as we were put through our paces.

But it had to come to an end—Richard's elation was not to last. Mike told all of us, including Richard, to get out of the pool and line up at the bottom of the three-metre diving board. We were told one by one to climb the steps, walk to the end of the board and somersault into the pool. Richard was clearly not happy with this. Not only was he unable to swim but he was also scared of heights. He raised his concerns to Mike about his ability to do what "has been asked of me".

Mike's response was: "I did not ask anything of you; I am ordering you to jump off the bloody board. Now do it!"

Richard knew there was no way out so he made his way to the bottom of the steps. As he stood there quaking two squad members were told to jump into the pool and tread water—to rescue him when he jumped.

All of us were studying Richard with some concern. Ever so slowly, head bowed, he laboriously made his way to the top of the steps all the while clutching onto the handrail with both hands, knuckles white. When he got to the top he let out a huge sigh of relief, I suppose much like Edmund Hilary did when he got to the top of Mt Everest. He then looked out into the distance until his eyes focused on the end of the board, all of six metres away. That walk was going to take forever. With both hands desperately clutching the handrail he inched his way along the diving board all the while muttering, "Oh my dear, oh my dear!" The handrails only extended so far and then it was open diving board and a frightening three-metre drop to the water so very far below. With us cheering Richard on he let go of the handrail, closed his eyes and took a step forward. When he opened his eyes he realized where he was, took a step back, grabbed on to the handrails and shuffled back to the start of the board.

As Mike cursed him from below we cheered him on, the process being repeated over and over again. At last Richard, to his credit, got to the end of the board and looked at the surface of the pool far below. That's when he froze. This was a tricky situation, which any one of us would have had some difficulty dealing with—but not Mike. As we all looked to Mike he came up with the perfect solution. He ran up the stairs leading to the diving board, got to the top and screaming at the top of his voice charged at Richard. Richard had a quick glance over his shoulder, did a double-take and saw this giant of a man bearing down on him. Facing Mike was not an option so he resigned himself to his fate, took a step forward and fell, hands clasped by his side, ramrod-straight into water where he was grasped by willing hands and shepherded to the security of the edge of the pool. Not even Mike could hide his grin.

That episode was one of the moments that helped us bond as a squad ... and Mike knew it.

The training included various courses. One of these was police law in which we were taught crime investigation, statute law and common law with particular emphasis on the essential elements of the crime. We needed to know these because if you knew what to look for when investigating a crime and were able to prove each element you would invariably get a conviction in court.

The interest in police law varied depending on the subject being taught at the time. Statutory law was boring. Common law was interesting when we were discussing murders and assaults but became boring again when we got to crimes such as fraud, forgery and uttering. With abduction and kidnapping our interest increased and then faded when complexities of theft (*contrectatio*) were taught.

When the instructor came to the sexual crimes he got our undivided attention. These subjects were made all the more interesting with the recruits throwing in all sorts of 'what ifs'. Some of the more gruelling cases are worthy of censorship but my favourite was from the recruit who, after much thought and deciding to impress the class with his knowledge, raised his hand and said: "Sir, in view of the fact that oral sex involves no more than the exchange of a few words, a mere discussion if you like, how can carrying it out in a public place be considered an indecent act?"

Janet taught us that other essential skill a policemen needs to know—how to type. Janet had something of a 'reputation' which to most of us was all the prompting we needed to attend the class. We began by gazing in bemusement at the ancient Remington typewriter in front of us, desperately trying to work out why all the keys were not in alphabetical order. Why on earth does the T key come between the Y and R and whose idea was it to place the C between the X and V? All the time we watched a screen as letters were highlighted and we duly punched the correct, or incorrect, letter. As we progressed and progressed from sorry attempts to touch-type to two-fingered typing, a piece of cloth was placed over our hands thereby hiding the keyboard beneath. An ingenious idea you might think but one that didn't work because you cannot type with two fingers without displacing the cloth and exposing the keyboard. Ultimately we got to the point where we actually began to enjoy the lessons. Our arms would be raised above our heads and on Janet's command would come crashing down to pound away at the keys like a frantic pianist in a Disney comedy churning out six, seven or even eight words a minute.

We embarked on riot-squad training where we wore our riot gear, consisting of not much more than wooden batons, aluminium shields (with holes in to see through), an awkward type of helmet not dissimilar to a World War Two German 'coal scuttle', a breathing mask and an assortment of riot guns. All in all—extremely uncomfortable.

Part of our training was to assemble on the parade ground, with half of us putting on our gear, taking up our shields and facing the 'rioters' while the other half threw lead-weighted wooden blocks at the riot squad which were, ideally, fended off by the shields. The shields, being aluminium, were not very effective and it only took one blow from a wooden block to realize that the best option was to duck or get the hell out of the way. More than one recruit suffered a broken arm from trying to parry a wooden block. When playing the role of a rioter we found that the best way to hit one of the 'cops' was to toss the block up into the sky rather than at them—the confusion caused was immeasurable.

During a riot the classic formation was to line up in ranks and wait while the rioters threw abuse and anything else they could find at the policemen. If a rioter was particularly troublesome the person in charge, usually an inspector, would command one of the cops in the front rank to aim "at the person in the red shirt". The riot gun we used fired a one-and-a-half-inch cartridge filled with tear gas. The drill was to aim at "the person in the red shirt" and fire at the ground, about three or four metres to his front—the idea being that the cartridge would explode and splatter him with tear gas.

The reality was slightly different. First, we never waited for an instruction and, secondly, there was only one way the tear gas was going to effectively neutralize the rioter and that was when it was fired it directly at him. If you hit him in the chest he got dumped on his back. If you hit him on any other part of his body—then it hurt. Either way— neutralized.

When the tear-gas cartridges were at a later stage replaced with tear-gas grenades (fired from a gun) it became more exciting. The grenade would be fired into a crowd; when it landed it would let out a hissing sound for a couple of seconds and then explode, spewing tear gas all over the place. It never ceased to amaze us how, without fail, one of the rioters, instead of running away, would dash to the tear-gas grenade and try to douse it with sand. Inevitably he would be bent over it when it exploded, get covered in gas and pass out for a few seconds. This happened every time; it never failed.

In training we experienced just exactly how effective tear gas can be. Our instructor would hand out gas masks and tell us to put them on. In full riot gear we would be told to run around in circles, so that we could get used to the masks—or so we thought. The harder you worked the more you inhaled and the more difficult it became to inhale because of the strain on the internal valve. When we had worked up a good sweat we were told to fall in in our squad formation. With the perspiration flowing four tear-gas canisters were ignited and as a squad we marched into the midst of the swirling gas. We were told to remove the masks and wait—to experience how effective the masks were. In seconds the tear gas attacked every bit of sweat it could find. Eyes and the back and the front of the neck were exposed and took the full force. Even though we were wearing long trousers it managed to get into our armpits and groin areas. We weren't permitted to move and only broke ranks when finally told to do so. Then it was straight to the nearest horse trough where we doused ourselves with water.

After this we repeated the exercise, only this time running around without tear-gas masks. Instead of tear gas two 'puke-gas' canisters were ignited. This was bad stuff. Most of us thought the best bet was to hold our breath. Of course, all this did was to make us inhale even deeper when we did eventually take a breath. As soon as the puke gas got into our lungs we spewed our guts out. Then it was back to the barracks for a shower.

When I was eventually put on riot-squad duty we were sent to soccer matches played at the large stadiums in the Bulawayo townships. Surprisingly enough our main task was not to subdue potential rioters but to protect the referee! When a game was drawn the whole crowd would go after the ref. If one side lost then only half of the crowd would bay for his blood. The refs were briefed to position themselves near the exit just before they blew the final whistle, then blow the whistle and dash through the tunnel to our awaiting Land Rover for a speedy getaway.

On one occasion the ref delayed his exit and in no time at all we were surrounded by a crowd twenty to thirty deep, demanding we hand over the ref. We thought about it for a second, refused, and they started throwing rocks at us. It was frightening. Although we were well armed with two Land Rovers full of cops, we were unlikely to get through the crowd unscathed. The section officer in charge had been through this before. He instructed us to get into our Land Rovers and on his command drive directly through the crowd at speed. Before he gave the command he fired one round in the air. The crowd, momentarily shocked, parted and we made a successful getaway.

Musketry is all about weapon training. We were taught how to strip, assemble and use various weapons, their characteristics and safety features before heading off to the range where we fired thousands upon thousands of rounds into the butts. It was also during musketry training that we were issued with our personal rifles—to be ours for the duration of our service. This was the FN 7.62mm, a wonderful weapon that features heavily later on in the narrative. We became so adept at stripping and assembling our rifles that we could it blindfolded (and in fact did).

Each weapon has its own characteristics, which we came to know intimately.

Being issued with a rifle and taking ownership of it ("It's really mine!") was a huge event in our lives. It is no exaggeration to say that our lives came to depend on the proper functioning of our rifles. The clichéd analogy of 'treat her like a lady and she will look after you' could not have been truer.

The big day came when we were driven to the range. Lying in the prone position with the butt tucked into your shoulder, nestled securely against your right cheek, you got the target lined up between the front and rear sights and gently squeezed the trigger. And then, Bang! The sound of the first round you ever fired was ear-splitting; the recoil whacked the butt into your cheek leaving you with a lovely red bruise at the end of the day's range-practice—and the smell of cordite was something you never forgot. It became addictive—back to the range over and over again, firing in all three different positions (prone, lying and standing), walking away with our ears ringing, our cheeks bruised … but loving every minute of it.

Our counter-insurgency training (COIN) was a ten-day course. During this we were taught a range of immediate action (IA) drills, including how to set up an ambush and what to do when ambushed. We were taught patrol formations, hand signals, map-reading, helicopter drills and the correct radio procedures to use when communicating with aircraft. We spent time on the range getting graded. If you achieved a certain score you qualified as a 'marksman' and got to wear the prestigious crossed-rifle emblem on the sleeve of your police jacket.

It rained so heavily during my COIN course that we spent most of the time in our tent, drenched to the bone, with water running in a continuous stream—in one side, through our sleeping bags and out the other. As a result many of the exercises were cancelled. With four people cramped in a tent conversation soon faded until we came up with a song that everyone knew the lyrics to. The only one we knew was Gilbert O'Sullivan's *Alone again, naturally* which was sung over and over again, *ad nauseam*. When I hear it now I tend to either become somewhat melancholic or want to smash the sound system to pieces.

One day of the course was devoted to 'chopper' drill—that is, learning how to quickly and efficiently get in and out of a helicopter during a deployment. After we had finished the dry-runs using a mock-up of an Alouette III cabin we moved onto the real thing. The pilots at the nearby air force base must have drawn straws to see who got to do the flying. On the first trip the chopper landed, we emplaned (got in) and it did a circuit. When it landed again we deplaned (got out) and ran to our pre-arranged defensive positions.

For the second 'voyage', the chopper landed, we emplaned, the pilot did a circuit and then came to a stop, hovering above elephant grass which the chopper technician told us was about four-feet high. The idea was to plunge ("Step away from the chopper—do NOT jump—if you do the chopper blades will take your head clean off"), land and assume defensive positions. Elephant grass can grow to ten feet or more in height and is so dense that you cannot see its base and therefore have no idea when you are going to hit the ground. As the pilot came to a hover above the grass, the first man in the 'stick' of five was given the signal by the chopper tech and 'stepped out', then the second, third and fourth. I was fifth, the last; however, each time someone deplaned the helicopter rose another foot or so. By the time my turn came we were at least twelve feet above the ground and I was given the signal to jump.

I vigorously shook my head and said: "No way, it's too high. Go down!"

The chopper tech almost fell out in surprise. He yelled at me and told me that as each person jumped out the chopper naturally rose because it was lighter. If that were true then I should be flying the damned thing—at least I'd make the requisite adjustments. In any event no one argues with a tech so I stepped out into space and as I hit the ground I twisted my ankle with an ugly ripping sound. In truth I experienced such an adrenaline rush that I barely felt a thing.

We learned first aid. The course lasted three days and focused on attending to injuries that might occur when we were on operations. At first glance some of the content matter appeared to be more devoted to sex education than the more serious subject of bush warfare. I am referring to the use of tampons, condoms and the subject of Tender Loving Care otherwise referred to as TLC. As it transpired we were taught that tampons are excellent at plugging gunshot wounds, condoms when placed over the barrel of your rifle keep the rain and grit out and, when all hope is lost, you cannot go wrong by giving the casualty plenty of TLC.

Drill was part of the whole discipline process and took up an inordinate amount of time. To have Mike as our drill instructor was an unforgettable experience. The squad would form up on the parade square in drill kit and wait 'at ease' for Mike. You heard him before he arrived—the *clack, clack, clack* of his studded drill boots as he marched across the drill square and then the high-pitched scream of a banshee as you were called to "Atteeenshun!"

Drill was endless. We were taught at first how to march and then how to turn to the left and turn to the right. Mike demonstrated each move in steps to us which we repeated over and over until we got it right. We were instructed how to stand at ease, stand to attention, how to march, execute left, right and about turns and how to come to a halt—and then the same drills again, but as a squad with all sorts of wonderful combinations and permutations—quick marching, slow marching and funeral drill. Although we were petrified of Mike we slowly we began to appreciate what he was trying to achieve. Getting shouted at and abused was the way things were done and although no one ever really took it personally you never forgot it—nor the steps …

The squad is marching happily along; you are all perfectly synchronized with each foot hitting the hard-standing of the drill square as one, arms swinging in perfect rhythm by your side and then "Squaaad … halt!" Our boots come crashing down together and as one the squad comes to a halt, everyone standing rigidly to attention, every head facing forward, eyes not daring to move and every one of us thinking: "What the hell have I done now? Please God, don't let it be me." You know that someone has screwed up and is about to get an almighty bollocking. The question is who?

Mike marches up to you. You know this because you can hear the sound of his boots getting louder and louder and then, he stands just behind you … and pauses. The hairs on the back of your neck are also standing to attention. You sense Mike towering over you and even though you can't see him you can feel his breath as he lowers his head until it is an inch from your left ear. You close your eyes as you hear him inhale and wait for the blast. He then he takes a half step forward and screams—at the recruit in front of you. The poor guy wasn't expecting it and involuntarily hunches his shoulders as he takes in the vocal assault. You are tempted to breathe a sigh of relief but can't because you haven't exhaled for the past three minutes. Instead the relief of it all causes your knees to wobble while the poor fellow in front of you almost collapses in a gibbering heap.

Mike screams and yells and curses. When it's your turn you learn things about your parents that you never even suspected which you will certainly want to discuss with them. You learn that you have been deformed from birth and that you will probably be battered to death in the next few seconds with one of your arms that Mike has long since ripped from your shoulder. You also learn that Mike is the only person on the planet who can hit you so hard on the top of your head that your teeth will fall from their sockets and appear, in a very short time, in your underpants. You also learn that your chances of having children may be seriously jeopardized, and this is indeed worrying.

Room inspections were a nightmare. Two recruits shared a room and did their best to keep it clean. We were told the day before that an inspection would take place "after PT" the following morning. That meant PT, shower, breakfast and then back to your room for the inspection. Grif, my roommate, and I made our beds the night before and slept on the floor so as not to crease the bed sheets. We scrubbed and polished the floors, dusted down the shelves, polished the window latches and cleaned the windows, inside and out. Anticipating Mike's every move we even upended our beds and dusted down the springs. But nothing we did was ever enough.

On the morning of the inspection we are standing at ease outside our bedroom. As Mike approaches we come to attention. He ignores us, enters the room and starts an examination that would leave a forensic scientist awestruck. Just when we begin to relax, thinking we might just have scraped through, we see him run his hands along the top of the window pelmet. We look at each other in total surprise as our shoulders drop and we hear him say: "You boy, what's this?" He is holding up his right index finger, palm facing towards us. On the tip of the finger we see, to our absolute horror, dust. Mike has managed to find dust in the one place we'd never considered—Mike has won this round. He glares at me, says "See me after parade", and walks out.

The first thing I think is "Why not Grif?" and then "This should be fun; I have two hours of drill ahead of me and then I have to report to Mike outside the drill instructors' office. Man, am I going to get hammered."

In the way of things all recruits *will* get disciplined at one time or another. It could be anything from a minute speck of dust found on a window pelmet to going AWOL—now it's my turn.

After lunch I make my way to the assembly point outside the instructors' office. There I meet three other recruits all standing at ease. As I arrive we ask of each other the names of our squad instructors.

"Mine's Pop Ellis."

"Mine's Mike Watt."

"Hey Tony, which squad are you from?"

"Five of Seventy-four," I reply.

"That's Mike Lambourne's squad, isn't it?" With this they shuffle a few inches away from me and look at me as if I have just announced that I have just being diagnosed with terminal prostate cancer … that's contagious.

We wait, and wait. The offices are the old 'terrapins'—rounded asbestos roofs, wooden walls and floors. The instructors get up one by one and make their way along the corridor. Then Mike gets up from his chair. It makes a loud scraping noise and I swear I can hear the cushions sigh with relief. He makes his way along the corridor. The sound of his drill boots crashing down on the wooden floors makes the other squad instructors' boots sound like the pitter-patter of tiny feet. As he gets to the exit he looks straight ahead (but I can see him looking at me out of the corner of his eye), turns, descends the steps and comes marching toward me. I come to attention and look up at him. His peaked cap, in the fashion of most drill instructors, is pulled down over his eyes in such a way that it makes me wonder how he can see where he is going. "Maybe that's why he needs to stand so close," I think to myself. To add to the overall dramatic effect Mike glares at me with a look of such utter contempt, pulls back his shoulders and takes a deep breath. He seems to have tripled in size in the space of fifteen seconds and I think "Here it comes" and boy! does it ever.

I am standing to attention. I have broken out in a sweat and my ears are literally burning from Mike's hot breath as he screams at me, his mouth no more than two inches from my face. Again I am forced to wonder who my parents really are. I think about my younger brother who I have begun to have suspicions about because he shaves every day and I don't. I decide I will definitely have a chat with my dad and, quietly but diplomatically, so as not to raise any suspicions, ask to see a diagram of the family tree. Come to think of it, a copy of my birth certificate might also prove useful. As Mike continues lambasting me I am also prompted to think what it really must be like to be beaten over the head with the wet end of my left arm and I resign myself to never being able to have sex, let alone children.

Mike stops. Heck! I think he is hyperventilating. "What am I to do with you, boy?" he snaps.

I instinctively know I am not supposed to answer but have been considering this very dilemma for the last five minutes and want to say something that will, in some way, prevent me from being what?—fed to the lions, strung up against a tree and *sjamboked* (whipped)? Do they send recruits to prison?

I open my mouth and start to speak but instead of an eloquent speech imploring Mike to spare me, all that is emitted is a squelchy sound like air being let out of a car tyre.

Mike yells: "Shut up!"

Okay, so speaking was not such a good idea.

"Confined to barracks this weekend," he barks, then turns and walks away.

It was all healthy stuff and, without knowing it, largely because of Mike, you evolve from being a nervous schoolboy to a confident young man. By the time the pass-out parade comes along you are ready to take on the responsibilities of a policeman.

Although the food in Depot was pretty good rumours circulated that the instructors put copper sulphate in the tea urns. The idea behind this was to lessen our sex drive. I couldn't help wondering what a fat lot of good that would do—most of us were still virgins and unlikely to even see a female in the months ahead. However, curiosity getting the better of us, in next to no time one of us was despatched to discreetly lift the lid off the tea urn and have quick peek.

Sure enough, the recruit came back to the table, saying: "There's a frothy blue scum on the surface of the tea."

That did it … no sex for six months.

On one occasion, when we were about to be granted a weekend pass, Mike told us to assemble in one of the classrooms. When we arrived he handed us over to Pop Edwards who gave us a lecture on safe sex. That meant condoms, which most of us had never seen and, even if we had, wouldn't have the vaguest idea where to get them from. Of course we weren't going to admit this. We were told to be wary of glamorous women who would take advantage of us by seducing us and then relieving us of all or money. As my monthly wage was 182 dollars I thought this was a wonderful idea and looked forward to *any* seduction. He then said that these same women might accuse us of rape and during the trial would appear in court in school uniforms looking like sixteen-year-olds, thus garnering the magistrate's sympathy. That part wasn't so wonderful, so back to square one.

Pop's final words were: "When you leave here I want you to behave like gentlemen," and then, with a knowing grin on his face, "and fuck like gentlemen."

There was a general murmur as we all agreed with this, looking around, nodding at each other like Muppets.

The odd night we did get away from Depot was spent on a pub crawl. That meant Flanagan's pub, downing draught beer and getting drunk and severely hung over. I have never really taken to beer but had no idea what else to order. I tried all sorts of exotic drinks so that I might appear more a Man of the World. Drinks like cane and lemonade, ouzo and Coke, whisky and Fanta (I was set up!) and combinations of vodka and anything. It all tasted vile so I went back to beer. (My favourite drink now is Southern Comfort and tonic water which goes to show how I've overcome the vileness of old.)

A pass-out parade is a momentous event. Six squads all fallen in, ready to march past the visiting dignitary as our escort takes the salute. At my pass-out parade the person is charge of the entire parade is ... Mike. Who else?

All the preparations are complete. Exams have been written and passed, drills honed to perfection and end -of-course parties held. At roll call the morning before the event Mike gives us a final briefing. He explains how hot it will be and that we will be standing to attention for hours on end.

He issues a stern warning to every recruit in a low, moderated tone that makes you wish he would start yelling: "This is a *police* pass-out parade [as opposed to army]. If any of you feel like fainting you will give it some serious thought before doing so. Dizziness and the blurring of eyes means that a faint is imminent and you will soon start to fall over. I don't want any of this poncy getting-down-on-one-knee with hand-on-forehead while you wait for someone to come to your assistance. No! You will fall from the vertical to the horizontal in one fluid movement with arms held firmly by your sides. You will *not* flinch on your way down to the horizontal. When you hit the ground you will stay there and will not move your body until I have detailed someone off to come to your aid ... Do you understand?"

"YES SIR!" we replied, as one.

We were in no doubt that should this happen we would be lying face-down in the horizontal position, the only object on the deserted parade square, long after everyone had left.

The pass-out parade is now a blur, but it went off without hitch. We were very proud.

Years later when I was a confident Detective Section Officer in Special Branch, Mike walked into a pub where I was drinking and I almost had to stop myself from leaping out the window to avoid him. And still, years later when I was on holiday with my wife at Victoria Falls we met Mike on a path while walking through the rain forest. I thought I handled things pretty well but my wife says I acted like a fawning schoolgirl around the local high-school jock.

Mike had a profound influence on me—certainly he is one of the most memorable characters I've ever met.

After the parade I had a few drinks with my parents and then boarded a train with other newly graduated policemen for the overnight trip to Bulawayo.

I had been posted to Mzilikazi police station.

Chapter three

Mzilikazi—first posting

Mzilikazi is a police station situated on the outskirts of Bulawayo on the edge of four predominantly 'black' townships. A township, in the context of Rhodesia was a 'suburb' comprised of thousands of low-cost, mostly single-storey houses, among a scattered hotchpotch of hostels, business centres, beer halls and—to service all the townships—the vast Mpilo Hospital.

Mzilikazi was a southern African king who founded the Matabele, or Ndebele, nation. Originally one of Shaka's lieutenants he fell out with Shaka and, facing ritual execution, fled north with his tribe via Swaziland and Mozambique where he devastated all that he came across, absorbing many tribes into what become known as the Ndebele. His battles took him to the Transvaal highveld where he came up against the Boers. In a series of bloody wars he was finally defeated at the battle of Vegkop in 1835 and once again fled north, this time over the Limpopo River into the southeastern portion of what was to become Southern Rhodesia, where he established his capital at Bulawayo (place of the killing) in 1840.

I was attached to the shift known as 'Two Relief' and assigned to charge office duties, which included receiving and attending to reports ranging from minor theft to murder—interspersed with sudden deaths, traffic accidents, assaults, control of civil disturbances—everything and anything. Each shift comprised a section officer who was in charge of the shift, a senior patrol officer (i.e. a P/O who had served three years or more; also known as a 'two-bar' P/O), three or four patrol officers, a sergeant-major, two sergeants and twelve or more constables.

In the days of the BSAP the most junior-ranking white policeman was a patrol officer and the most senior-ranking black policeman a sub-inspector. A P/O was senior to a sub-inspector although only on paper (racial discrimination affected all the services and was only addressed in the late 1970s). The reality was that a sub-inspector had as much training, experience and ability as any high-ranking white policeman. They were highly thought of and accorded the respect they deserved.

The Member in Charge (MIC) Mzilikazi was a chief inspector whose second-in-command was an inspector. The latter's responsibility was to oversee the investigation of all cases—he was also known as the Member in Charge Enquiries. The entire station complement consisted of between sixty and seventy personnel.

Day shift was from 0600 to 1400 hours; afternoon shift from 1400 to 2200 hours; and night shift from 2200 to 0600 hours. It took a while to get used to night shift but the thrill of being a policeman stationed at Mzilikazi was such that I was hardly ever aware of the time of day, let alone what shift it was. We were given 'time-off' after a week on each shift, which we willingly took but would quite happily have done without.

I have never been comfortable classifying people by the colour of their skin. It only seems to apply to Africa. We talk of 'blacks' and 'whites' in southern Africa. 'Coloured' applies to people of mixed race (i.e. mixed black and white) and is not to be confused with US nomenclature of 'African American'.

We use terms like 'black' and 'white' governments, 'black politics', 'white-controlled' this and 'black-controlled' that. Every time these terms are used there is a negative connotation attached to them, exacerbated and perpetuated by post-independence, 'black'-legislated 'affirmative action'.

I am labouring this point because such terminology is unfair and misleading, however, I use these terms in the context of the times. When I joined the police I, like most of my generation, was blithely unaware of any black–white tensions, perhaps naïvely so—after all there was a so-called 'war of liberation' unfolding. The more enlightened white politicians were advocating a removal of segregation; the white right-wing was advocating an entrenchment of racial discrimination; and the black nationalists were using the colour card to advance their own ends.

Friday night was the busiest time because most of the people were paid their weekly wages on Friday afternoon and went straight to one of the many beer halls. A few drinks inside them inevitably led to arguments, which in turn led to fights. The local criminals targeted anyone they suspected of carrying their weekly wages, usually robbing them on their way home from work or, if they were foolish enough to keep their wages with them, at the beer halls. Domestic disputes between husbands and wives, relatives and siblings often resulted in violence ranging from lightly domestic to very serious.

The policy of the BSAP was that we were not allowed to get involved in domestic disputes unless there was a danger to life. A woman coming in and sounding off about her husband was not really an issue. A woman coming in with blood streaming down her face from a six-inch wound in her skull caused by her husband cracking her with a knobkerrie, was. More often than not it was a concerned neighbour who would phone in and ask us to attend to the dispute.

Up front I have to state that I have a great deal of empathy for 'coloureds'. With a white government in power they are classified as 'black' and therefore marginalized. With a black government in power they are classified as 'white' or not-quite-black and also ignored. The situation remains this way today. The result is that coloured folk have fallen between two posts and their well-being effectively cast aside. Because of a lack of government interest in their welfare, there is an appallingly slow rate of social development in these communities. For decades they have been pushed to the back of the employment queue with relatively few coloureds in formal jobs. As the years have gone by their motivation to work has deteriorated to the point where they have given up even trying to find a job. They deserve better.

The social service systems in southern Africa are manned, in the main, by competent people who do a fine job with the meagre financial resources available to them. As with most African governments, when economies start deteriorating, financial resources are plundered from the welfare sector to fund the military—which is certainly the case in what is today Zimbabwe.

It's a downward spiral from there. Military support is crucial for most African regimes. To quote George Bernard Shaw: "A government which robs Peter to pay Paul can always depend on the support of Paul." Whichever way it is, it is the poor and the coloureds at the bottom of the food chain.

Having said this, largely due to their frustrations domestic disputes were a way of life in the coloured community. What little money they could scrape together became something to fight over. I was called to a 'domestic' where a coloured woman had thrown a kettle of boiling water at her husband. In retaliation he picked up a pot of chips cooking in boiling oil and threw the contents at her, hitting her in the face. When I got to her she had stopped screaming and had gone into shock. All I could do was wrap her in a blanket and take her to Mpilo Hospital.

Mpilo is a large hospital that caters for the hundreds of thousands of predominantly black people who live in the western townships of Bulawayo (referred to as 'high-density' suburbs) including Mzilikazi, Ngubyenja, Western Commonage, Thornycroft (a coloured suburb) and others. The staff at Mpilo Hospital were a dedicated, highly efficient group of people. On any night they were kept busy but on Friday nights, pay day, they were stretched to their absolute limit. The staff implemented a triage system to cope with the casualties. If one of us happened to go to Mpilo, and inevitably we did, we were dispatched to the casualty section where we hoped that the sight of our uniforms would go some way in helping to control the crowds—there were hundreds of people all milling about, all anxious.

Among the impoverished life is cheap. An argument over a ten-cent coin resulted in a person being stabbed in a beer hall. The victim was taken to Mpilo and died in one of the casualty wards. A drunk kicked a heavily pregnant woman in the stomach and she bled to death on the spot. Heads smashed open with knobkerries, disembowelment from carving knives and stab wounds to the heart were common occurrences.

Aside from crowd control we helped the nurses lift and carry casualties from the waiting area to surgery where their wounds were cleaned up and stitched. The casualty wards were literally awash with blood. At a glance you knew who the seriously injured were. They sat there with their eyes following your every move and never said a word. The less seriously injured moaned a bit; those with minor injuries a bit more and the uninjured or those with only a few scratches or bruises screamed and wailed, constantly demanding attention.

Every so often I would hear a voice say, "Hey you!" I'd look up from what I was doing and focus on a doctor bent over a patient whose bloody wound he was trying to stitch up on his own, indicating with a flick of his head for me to come and assist him. This was not a place for the squeamish. You did what was asked of you and just hoped that in some small way you had helped alleviate the medical staff's workload.

Most doctors, I believe, didn't have much time for cops. They felt that we were callous, indifferent individuals who couldn't care less about their patients. This just wasn't true. Like them we dealt with the carnage of human tragedy every day. Unlike them we had to go in among violent or rioting people to retrieve the wounded. Of course we got angry sometimes—our lives were being endangered unnecessarily because of someone else's self-centred actions and complete indifference to our own well-being. No sooner had we transported a victim from the scene of an assault or vehicle accident and deposited him or her at Mpilo Casualty than we were off again—back to attend to some new carnage.

And so it went on ... and on. No one complained or even thought of doing so—that was our job. A quiet word of encouragement every so often from a medic would have gone a long way to making us feel our efforts were worthwhile.

I came across an old man who was having a very bad epileptic fit. When it had passed I wrapped him in a blanket, put him in my Land Rover and took him to Mpilo. Rather than the doctor on duty thanking me for the care and consideration I had shown he turned on me and accused me of being "a typical cop who doesn't give a damn about people".

Sometimes you just can't win.

Sooner or later every cop has to pay his first visit to a mortuary. You hear tales in Depot, while training, of what these are like and the horror stories follow you to your first posting. It's best to get it over with on your first shift. I was fortunate as my first visit was clinical and painless. Others not so. At Mzilikazi the P/Os would suss out each new recruit. If he was a particularly nervous sort someone would quietly mention morgues and suggest that the first visit be postponed for a few shifts. More stories, each gorier than the previous, would follow and the poor lad would become increasingly apprehensive. When the selected night shift occurred the set-up would fall into place. Typically this would happen:

A call would be received to attend a sudden death, in this case a suicide. Patrol Officer Brown would be taken to the scene. The property at 44 Ngube Road was one of many mass-produced, brick-under-corrugated-iron, two-roomed houses in Mzilikazi Township. Relatives are seen gathered outside, grieving. P/O Brown is led through the front door and into a darkened room. He looks but cannot see anything and then, with a start, realizes he is looking at a man suspended from the rafters, feet dangling inches above a wooden stool. Others are looking for a suicide note or anything to indicate nefarious activities. This case is quite straightforward. The deceased had decided to hang himself. He had taken a stool from the dining area, placed it below the rafters and stood on it. With some two-strand plastic-coated electrical cord he tied one end around the rafter and the other around his neck. His last conscious act was to kick the stool from under him.

Death by hanging is anything but sudden. In this case the weight of the deceased caused the cord to cut through the neck muscles below his lower jaw and come to rest against the windpipe, thus cutting off the air supply to his lungs. A slow, painful death by strangulation followed.

P/O Brown stands on the chair and unties the cord from the rafter. He has been told *not* to detach the cord tied around the deceased's neck, as this would interfere with the pathologist's examination.

From there the body is put in the body box, placed in a Land Rover and he and P/O White drive to Mpilo Hospital. P/O White collects the keys from hospital reception and drives to the morgue. The morgue is situated at the back of the hospital in an unlit, dark and forbidding area.

P/O White then tells P/O Brown that he has "to go and get some forms" from reception. He hands P/O Brown the keys and tells him that he should open the door to the morgue, switch on the lights and wait for him to return. P/O Brown does not like the sound of this but is reassured when P/O White tells him that all he needs to do is "put the key in the door, open it, step inside and the light switch is at eye level immediately on your right". This doesn't sound any better but no way is P/O Brown going to let on that he is in fact terrified. P/O White then leaves.

But P/O White doesn't go to reception to get the forms. He has everything he needs with him and doubles back to wait in the dark from where he can watch the ensuing fun. P/O Brown hesitates. Faced with being left in the dark with a dead body or entering the morgue and at least being in the light he gingerly approaches the door, puts the key in the lock, turns it, slowly nudges the door open, takes a half-step in and reaches for the light on his right-hand side at eye level. His hand doesn't come in to contact with it. A gentle reach for the switch turns in to a hasty and frantic attempt to find it. Nothing happens so he takes another step and enters the morgue proper. As he does the door shuts. *Clang!* Panic turns to sheer terror as a pair of hands grabs him around the throat. He screams and the lights come on. He sees two other P/Os from the station who had sneaked in ahead of him and set the whole thing up with P/O White in cahoots. When they have stopped laughing they calm him down and they all have a good laugh.

After that no morgue anywhere will ever even begin to faze him.

People who work with corpses are often accused of being disrespectful towards the dead. In view of what these people are dealing with, levity is not meant as a sign of disrespect but as a coping mechanism.

You always wonder what your first arrest will be. "Will I arrest a serial killer, maybe a spy or someone who has gone mad and is shooting up an embassy, perhaps an international gem thief?" No such luck. I made my first arrest in Mzilikazi in 1974.

A common form of transport in the townships at the time was a 'scotch cart'—a two-wheeled carriage drawn by a donkey. The driver sits on a seat just behind the donkey on the edge of the carriage and controls the donkey with the reigns and sharp cracks from a whip. At the time I was with a two-bar P/O patrolling the townships when I saw a scotch cart parked by the side of the road.

The donkey was quietly grazing on the grass growing on the edge of the road. It had a severe infection where the harness had chafed away its fur through the outer layers of skin into muscle. As I was looking at the wounds the owner of the scotch cart approached, saw me and ran for it. While the two-bar P/O watched I ran after him. I chased him for a couple of hundred metres before he realized he could not outrun me, so he stopped. After all what was I really going to do to him? The very most he could expect was a caution. That was what he thought. What he didn't know and something that I was very conscious of was that this was my 'first arrest' in the offing. What I should have done was stopped, walked up to him and had a quiet chat. But no! With my first arrest at the forefront of my mind I continued running towards him. He probably thought, "Oh no! A new guy," and made a half-hearted attempt to run away. By now it was all coming together for me—the viscous criminal about to escape and me, rookie P/O that I was, about to save a donkey in distress by capturing this mad lunatic and saving the world. I increased my pace and in a textbook manner that any Springbok rugby player would have been proud of I tackled the villain, brought him crashing to the ground, put him in handcuffs and marched him off to my Land Rover.

My first arrest—what a feeling!

A 'sudden death' was a term applied to someone who had died from causes other than assault, murder or vehicle accident and every day we were despatched to at least one incident. Most of them were suicides.

A body had been found hanging from a tree in the bush area on the outskirts of Mzilikazi. When I got to the scene I saw that the deceased had climbed up into the tree and then along a horizontal branch. He had tied one end of a length of rope to the branch, the other around his neck and then deliberately fell from the branch. To get him down I had to park my Land Rover beneath the body, climb the tree, untie the rope and lower him into the body box which had been put on the roof of the Land Rover. It all went according to plan and I drove back to Mzilikazi where I parked the Land Rover with the body still in the body box on the roof and went off to have some breakfast. My intention was to have my breakfast, return to the station and take the body to the mortuary at Mpilo.

During breakfast I got a call to return to the station and see the member in charge. This was never a good thing. I went to his office and was told to stand at attention. As I stood there as he gave me a severe reprimand for parking directly beneath his office window. The body was badly decomposed and stank. The smell had drifted its way through the station causing people to evacuate their offices.

That was not the only time I got into trouble. On another occasion I attended a case where an adult had severely beaten a child and I'd been summoned to court to give evidence. Between the date of the crime and court case I had been sent for motor-cycle training and had managed to break my collar bone and get concussion. After a period of recuperation in Salisbury I returned to Bulawayo and on the date of the trial was lying in my bed strapped up with a broken collar bone feeling pretty grim.

At about 1100 hours P/O Martin, the court orderly banged on my door, told me I had missed the court session and instructed to get to Number 2 Court immediately. I had completely forgotten about the case.

When I arrived at Number 2 Court I waited outside until my name was called and, on entering, proceeded to the witness box where I was sworn in.

I had really drawn the shortest straw this time. Milton Boys' High School had chosen that particular day and that particular courtroom to take their sixth-formers to court as part of a careers development programme. The pupils, much the same age as me, were all dressed in their school uniform and looked to me to make some sort of an impact. I did not disappoint them. The magistrate, a Mr Bartlett, was clearly pissed off. He asked me to explain why I was late. When I started telling him he stopped me in mid-sentence and then gave me one serious dressing-down in front of all the pupils. He told me that my behaviour was "typical of today's policeman", that I was a "disgrace to the Public Service" and so on.

As abruptly as he had started he stopped and said: "What do you have to say in your defence?"

Now I know this guy was the magistrate and I also know that he must have been aware who the accused was. I wanted to say, "Your Worship, the accused is on the other side of the court; ask *him* what his defence is." Instead, stunned, I mumbled, "Nothing your Worship."

He paused, then in a somewhat petulant tone, continued, "You must have *something* to say in mitigation. Come on what is it?"

The word 'mitigation' got to me. You were only asked to plead in mitigation when you were about to be sentenced. As far as I was aware, other than being late for court, I hadn't done anything wrong. Not according to Mr Bartlett. I realized I was in a tight spot and thought I better say something and quickly.

As I began he cut me down and said, "As a result of your disgraceful behaviour I now fine you ten dollars or five days in prison for contempt of court."

I stood there totally dumbfounded, not knowing what to say or do. One minute I am a policeman giving evidence and the next an accused—and a convicted one at that! I felt a friendly court orderly nudge me and I left the courtroom.

When I got outside the public prosecutor (PP) met me. It turned out that he and I were at the same high school, he being a couple of years my senior. He approached me: "This is a first. I have never heard of anything like this happening before!" (How many times would I hear this in my life?) And then told me that he would get hold of the magistrate's notes and find out exactly what he had written. He said he had a hunch that the senior public prosecutor must have had something to do with my reprimand as he was known to despise policemen. The court orderly then advised me that I should report immediately to my member in charge.

I returned to Mzilikazi and reported to the MIC who already knew what had transpired. By now I was angry and not in any frame of mind to listen to his paternal advice.

"There really is no need to worry about this."

"I will *not* pay the fine, sir."

He, thinking I was broke, said, "Not to worry, I'll take care of that."

"I mean it, sir. I am *not* paying the fine and I will choose to go to prison for five days."

No cop in his right mind would say such a thing so I can only think the painkillers had started to kick in. The MIC told me to go back to single quarters and "We will talk about this later".

We never did. I never paid the fine and, other than in this narrative, never thought about it again.

It turned out that Mr Bartlett was an ex-cop who had got his degree and left the force to become a full-time lawyer before becoming a magistrate. For some reason he had chosen that day to let all his frustrations come out and took them out on me. As for 'giving evidence' an 'expert witness' was needed to give an opinion on the sort of instrument used to inflict the injuries on the complainant. Clearly the 'expert witness' was not me—I was therefore never needed in court in the first place. Mr Bartlett surely must have known this.

A few months later I got my own back, albeit unintentionally and not on Mr Bartlett but on the senior public prosecutor when I arrested him for drunken driving (nearly as good!). I was on patrol when I spotted his vehicle passing me, driving erratically at high speed. I gave chase and signalled to the driver to pull over to the side of the road and stop. When I asked the driver for his driving licence he showed me his ID card. Up until then I had no idea what the SPP looked like. A quick look at the words 'Court Official Senior Public Prosecutor' registered and I thought, "Ah ha! The game's on!" I went overboard by making him get out of the car, 'officially' arresting him and taking him to Bulawayo Central police station where I insisted he be charged—whereas in normal circumstances a quiet caution would have sufficed. In all truthfulness I don't really think he was that drunk.

It was another Friday night. For reasons that I cannot quite remember my boss, a section officer, had left me as the only white policeman in the charge office. This made me the most senior policeman—on paper. The reality was that everyone else, from sub-inspector to constable, had been in the force longer than me; they knew perfectly well how to do their job without any interference from what they saw as a young white upstart.

I was sitting at a single desk three metres behind the long charge-office counter, watching what was going on and observing how everyone was doing their job. In typical Friday-night fashion at Mzilikazi complainants were arriving at the counter all vying for the attention of someone in uniform. Some of the complainants were drunk, very few were sober and most of them seemed to be covered in blood. The one thing they all had in common was that they were all angry, shouting to make themselves heard above the noise.

Some accused who had been arrested were being escorted in quietly, others were swearing and a few fighting like cornered cats. If under control they were finger-printed; if abusive or aggressive they were thrown in the cage (a sort of open holding cell in the centre of the detention cells surrounded by strong iron bars) and hosed down with jets of water from a fire hydrant.

Amid the pandemonium a very large, obese African woman waddled into the charge office. I only noticed her because of her size and the fact that she had a look of thunder on her face. She shoved and jostled her way to the counter. When she found a place at the counter she glared at a constable who happened to catch her eye as she slammed what looked like a bundle wrapped in newspaper on the counter.

All went dead quiet while everyone nervously looked at her.

She said that she had a serious complaint to make—she had been to her butcher and had asked for a pound of beef. The butcher went into a backroom and had returned with the pound of 'beef' neatly wrapped in a few sheets of newspaper. The woman paid him and left. While walking home she'd peeled back the newspaper to inspect her purchase. When she saw the contents, she'd let out an angry grunt and changed course—to the Mzilikazi charge office.

The constable, obviously irritated with such petty issues, whipped off the newspaper, exposing the beef inside. Only it wasn't beef—it was a large puff adder. The charge office erupted into absolute bedlam. Everyone jumped over, under or into something, screaming and shouting "*Mai weeeeh, mai weeeeh*" or "*Aieeeeee, ee, eeee*". I have never seen such a large room vacated so quickly, leaving only a few African policemen cowering under the counter or under my desk. I couldn't see the serious side of all this and remained sitting at my desk, laughing my head off with tears streaming down my face.

The room was deathly quiet so I thought I'd better do something. I went to the counter and looked at the snake. It was a beautiful specimen but very dead, looking like it had died peacefully in its sleep, with not a mark on it or a scale out of place.

As I picked up the snake further shrieks and wails erupted. I put it down and they stopped. Picked it up again and they started. Put down—silence. Pick up—wails.

With assurances to all around that the snake was very dead I wrapped it in its newspaper and put it in the desk drawer.

A short while later everything was back to normal—the Friday-night mayhem had resumed.

My section officer returned a while later and I told him what had happened. He thought about it for a while. "Do you want a quiet night?" he asked.

"Yes, of course," I replied.

After briefing the African staff he took the snake and went outside. He put the snake on one of the steps leading to the door of the charge office and turned off the entrance lights.

Not another soul entered the charge office until we knocked off at six o'clock the next morning. We would be sitting waiting behind the counter and hear the *clop, clop, clop* of someone making their way up the stairs. Then silence as someone would spot the snake, followed by more screaming and the sound of panicked footsteps fleeing.

Before knocking off I told one of the P/Os, Ray, who was coming on duty what had happened. He asked if he could have the snake so I shrugged and gave it to him before I left. A couple of nights later Ray was on night shift, still with the snake in his possession.

We had a big problem with 'pirate taxis' that operated illegally in the townships. These were either VW Combis or Toyota minibuses—the type with double doors at the back that open outwards. Pirate taxis were not registered and as such 'stole' potential passengers from the bus companies operating legally in the townships. This led to threats against the taxi operators, followed by counter-threats and shortly thereafter, violence. The risk was to human life and we had to stop it.

Our task was to approach a taxi, signal the driver to pull over and then issue him a ticket. It was an exercise in futility as most of the information supplied was false so we could never trace a driver and in any case the volume of tickets was so high that it would have diverted much-needed manpower from other more serious investigations. Nor could we fine the passengers because they simply jumped out and ran away. For the drivers we were nothing more than a minor inconvenience. It was a game of cat and mouse—only in this case the mice were the winners.

We decided one night that we'd deal with the taxis once and for all—in our own way.

In a Land Rover we'd follow a taxi and indicate for him to stop. As he slowed down and came to a halt we would drive right up to the vehicle with our fender nudging the back doors, preventing the passengers from opening the doors and running away.

On a couple of occasions there were mishaps and I know of one P/O (me) who mistimed his approach. An instant before he got to the doors a passenger opened a door and stuck his arm outside. As the Land Rover made contact the poor man's arm got caught between the doors and snapped in two. The man was more concerned about being fined than anything else so I graciously let him off with a caution and sent him on his way.

Ray used this tactic in a somewhat insensitive manner. He had the snake with him and as the taxi stopped with everyone trapped inside he lobbed the snake through one of the windows. Ray merely wanted to give them all a fright. Instead they erupted in white rage and turned on him. He was lucky to escape by jumping in his Land Rover and making a hasty and undignified getaway.

While stationed at Mzilikazi I was sent off for driver training. We were first taught how to drive Land Rovers and when we had passed that driving test we were taught how to ride motorcycles. Each course lasted two weeks and comprised four students.

One of the students on my course was 'Gumby' who had been driving for years but had never passed his driving tests. Knowing it all he spent the entire fortnight sitting in the back of the Land Rover passing useless advice to the student in the front.

After learning the theory we were shown around a Land Rover before setting off on our first trip. The training Land Rovers had dual controls—pedals and steering wheel—and we shared the gear lever. The student being instructed sat in the front on the right-hand side with his instructor sitting next him and the other three students sat in the back.

The course was a lot of fun and Mel, our instructor, had a permanent twinkle in his eye—I guess a sense of humour was a prerequisite for his job. The first few days were spent at the driving school learning to start the vehicle with the following instruction repeated over and over again: "Clutch in; put it in first gear and slowly let the clutch out." With that we dropped the clutch and the vehicle shot forward and came to a dead stop. This was followed by "You moron/idiot/imbecile! What the hell are you trying to do? Kill me?" This process was repeated *ad nauseam* until we were able to move forward a few metres—and even then the vehicle bunny hopped along, severely testing the shock absorbers and the ability of Mel's dentures to stay in his mouth.

With the basics behind us and having the mastered the art of changing gears we were sent off on long trips to the Matopos—a spectacular range of hills just south of Bulawayo where Cecil John Rhodes is buried at 'World's View'.

With our confidence increasing we started driving around the suburbs of Bulawayo. This was where we came across threatening creatures that stood sentinel-like at intersections, positioned in such a way so as to intimidate and frighten us. It became a battle of minds between these creatures and the students. The creatures had names like 'Give way' and 'Stop'. The more devious had coded messages on them which we had to decipher. When translated the codes meant anything from 'Caution overhead bridge clearance ten feet' to

'Beware loose gravel'. It was all very confusing but we never gave up although we were occasionally forced to subdue the creatures by driving into them, all unintentionally of course.

We drove all over the Matopos, up *kopjes*, through gullies and down dry riverbeds. We learned how to use four-wheel drive, how to avoid getting stuck in sand and how to dig ourselves out of it when we did. We learned how to drive on wet dirt roads where the slightest mishandling of the brakes could cause an uncontrolled skid. We continued to grow in confidence until Mel felt we were ready for our final driving test.

We were driving along a suburban road with Kevin, my co-student, at the wheel. The instructor waited for him to get to within two hundred metres of a particular intersection.

"Okay, Kevin," he said. "T-junction coming up. When you get to it, take a left turn."

Simple enough, no?

Kevin hunched his shoulders, ducking his head slightly, focusing all his attention on the 'Give way' sign that had been deliberately put there to confuse him and exacerbate his stress levels. There was silence in the back, apart from Gumby of course who was giving his unending useless advice, as we observed, waiting to see how he would deal with the enormity of the task at hand.

As Kevin got to within a hundred metres of the intersection the vehicle started drifting over to the left. Mel was ready to take control as he realized Kevin was so fixated on the 'Give Way' sign that a collision with it was imminent. He steadied his hand on his steering wheel and said to Kevin, "Okay, Kevin. Let go, I have control."

Kevin did not let go and a struggle ensued as they wrestled against each other for control of the vehicle and then ... *kadunk!* Problem dealt with—at least in part as the 'Give way' sign was destroyed.

We jumped out, pulled the fender away from the wheel, jumped back in and, with a change of driver, continued on our merry way.

Then it was on to motorcycles—with a change in instructors—Ken taking over from Mel.

We arrived for the first lesson in shirt, shorts, shoes and socks. The motorcycles we were learning to ride were 350cc Yamahas—big and heavy. The exhaust ran horizontally along the right side of the bike at a level just above your ankle where your socks, which had dropped to just below your ankle, now exposed the skin. It didn't take long for the exhaust to heat up and burn your skin until it blistered and hardened. All four of us students had minor burns just above our right ankle, which came to signify that we were attending driving school, a sort of emblem.

We progressed fairly quickly. The first day we learned to start the bikes and drove around in circles—stopping, starting, falling off, picking up the bike and repeating the process over again until we got it right. Then off to Matopos for long rides through the hills, stopping every so often at a roadside café to get a Coke.

Then the instructor would say: "Alright, that's it for the day. Make your own way back to the driving school for the day's debrief."

Inevitably one of us would run out of fuel. In my case this happened eight kilometres from Bulawayo on a stretch of open road. Ordinarily the solution was to lean down, flick the fuel-change level from main to reserve, restart the bike and continue with the journey. Unfortunately, either by neglect or, I am sure, by design no one had mentioned to me that the bike had a reserve tank. Not being terribly technically minded and in an effort to try and find out if there was perhaps another reason why the bike would not start, I tapped the headlight, tweaked the accelerator, made a *vroom vroom* sound, switched the lights on and off and sounded the horn. None of this made any difference so, left with no other option, I pushed the 350cc Yamaha all the way back to the driving school where Ken was waiting for me, smiling. The more technically minded reader might suggest that if I had opened the cap of the petrol tank and looked inside I would have seen petrol in the tank and perhaps considered that there was a reserve switch. I would concur.

I got my own back on Ken by giving him a fright when we went to the Falls Road scramble track and began doing circuits of it. Around and around we went, going up and over and through the various obstacles until Ken signalled to us to stop and change direction. I stopped, turned the bike around, opened up the throttle and headed toward a ramp. At that instant the throttle stuck, the revs rocketed and the bike took off. I am told that when I hit the ramp the bike and I went nine feet up in the air as rider and machine parted company causing me to come crashing down onto my left shoulder. The end result was a total write-off for the bike and for me—a broken collar bone, concussion and five days in hospital.

Chapter four

Just George

It was at Mzilikazi where I met George Beaver. George is one of life's loveable eccentrics—a short, tubby little guy with a round, slightly balding head and a wicked sense of humour. Whereas most of us collected copies of *Playboy*, daydreamed about women and spent most of our time chasing after them, George collected copies of the Bulawayo Museum's *Journal of Reptiles*, daydreamed about snakes and spent his off-duty hours catching frogs and lizards with which to feed his pet snakes. His was obsessed with the creatures.

All the single policemen lived in a single quarters in a hostel known as Stops Camp. The quarters were a five-storey building comprising fifty-two single rooms. The camp consisted of a mess hall, offices, and sports facilities which included a swimming pool. Every day would see George hunting among the rockery by the swimming pool, stalking lizards, pouncing on them, stuffing them in his pocket and gleefully taking them back to his room where he would feed them to his pet snakes.

George's room was on the bottom floor. All rooms were subjected to surprise inspections by the Officer Commanding Camp, expect George's—because the OC was petrified of snakes. George was told he was not allowed "to keep snakes" and was thus ordered to have them removed from his room. He figured out that this meant he was not allowed, by definition, to keep more than *one* snake. With this in mind he promised the OC to abide by his orders, released his mamba and mole snake and kept the night adder.

Needless to say the OC carried out his surprise inspection, saw the snake in its glass cage, nearly fainted, cursed George and never went near his room again.

Talking about cursing, like all these establishments, we had the local camp bully—a big dim-witted moron called Paul. Paul was too thick to do anything else so they put him in the Crime Protection Unit (CPU) which meant being allowed to dress in civvies and to wander about Bulawayo—in his case not really doing anything constructive but keeping out of everyone's way.

Paul was also petrified of snakes and had threatened to beat George to death if he ever saw or even suspected that there was a snake in the hostel.

George managed to keep out of Paul's way until the night he decided to play a practical joke on his good buddy Mike Kernick—a big loveable rogue who was always getting into trouble. George and he were inseparable with George being the brains behind their relationship and Mike the muscle. Mike was also petrified of snakes. The understanding between them was that George could do whatever he liked so long as he never allowed any of his snakes near Mike.

George used to work part-time at the snake park on the outskirts of Bulawayo. Usually on a Saturday afternoon when off-duty he would make his way to the snake park on his motorcycle. He wore an old lumber jacket secured at the waist and zipped up to the neck. Stuffed in between the jacket and his shirt were hundreds of frogs, lizards and rats that he had caught to feed the snakes.

Can you imagine if he'd had a vehicle accident? The medics arrive, George is lying on the road, the medics unzip his jacket and all these beasties dash out. The medic would think he had been caught in a scene out of the *Alien* movie, leave George where he was and commence therapy immediately.

George had come back from the snake park with a dead python which he was going to afford a proper burial—in the rockery—next to the pool. As he arrived back late everyone had already gone out on the town and George was on his own. He knew that Mike would be coming home drunk so he made a cunning plan. He waited until he saw Mike's car coming up the driveway, went the few doors down to his room, opened the door (we hardly ever locked our rooms), put the dead python next to Mike's bed, shut the door and waited in his own room.

Unfortunately it was not Mike that arrived back that night drunk but Paul and his heavies. George lay there thinking: "Not too bad, Mike will be back soon. Just as well I put the snake in *his* room." … and then … "Hang on; is Mike in room nine or eleven?" … "Oh shit! He's in room nine! I put the damn snake in Paul's room!"

George lay frozen beneath the sheet, the blanket pulled up to his neck as he listened to the *clippity-clop* of shoes scuffing down the corridor towards Paul's room. Then the sound of Paul's door being opened … silence … and then a high-pitched scream from four terrified men as they saw the snake. This was followed by the sound of thuds and "Kill it, kill it man, or it will strangle us to death" and "Let's get outa here!" The snake was being pulverized.

Then and eerie silence, followed by, "Beeeaaaveeerrrr, I'm gonna kill you!"

As his room was on the ground floor George managed to jump out of his window and escaped. Fortunately for him there was no way Paul was going back into his room until the snake had been removed and only George could do this. A compromise was negotiated by the OC, who'd heard the ruckus and had beatled over to the hostel, agreement was reached and George removed the python.

I was off duty the day George got bitten by his night adder.

These are small snakes but highly venomous. George had captured a lizard and had been dangling it in front of the snake much like you would a piece of string in front of a kitten. Like a kitten the snake went for the lizard, missed and bit George on his finger. George came rushing into my room and told me he had been bitten. Like most Rhodesians I knew something about snakes and knew that as night-adder poison was fast-acting I had to get him to hospital quickly.

Another off-duty cop, Ralph, and I put George in my car and we set off for Bulawayo Central Hospital. George was lying on the back seat insisting that Ralph take notes as the symptoms manifested themselves so that he could refer to these later "when I write a paper for the herpetological society".

We arrived at casualty, grabbed a gurney and loaded George on it. The doctor on call asked George what had happened and not only did George tell him but insisted on telling him exactly what treatment he should give.

The doctor humoured him but when George started demanding to know the doctor's qualifications, experience and a general breakdown of his work ethic ("Do you like snakes?"), his sense of humour began to wane. The necessary treatment was given and an orderly called to take George to Ward D1 for overnight observation.

The doctor had briefed the orderly and told George that the reason for overnight observation (which George felt was not necessary) was to watch over him, as there was a chance he could die. This smartly shut George up.

As he was wheeled to the ward the orderly took a slight detour which Ralph and I knew would take us past the mortuary. Even in George's drowsy state he was able to recognize the room of death and the sight of it confirmed his innermost fears. He asked us in a quiet, pitiful voice why we were going to the morgue. Cops being as they are, full of compassion for each other, are not going to miss such an opportunity.

"Cos you're gonna die and the doc reckons it best to put you straight into the morgue so they don't have to move you later on," Ralph stated matter of factly.

Maybe it was a combination of the sedative and sheer fright that caused George to quietly pass out. In keeping with our caring manner, without a word Ralph pulled the bed sheet over George's face and that was how he was wheeled, much to the consternation of those patients still alive, into Ward D1.

There is one last story about George that I must relate. We were on foot patrol in Bulawayo when George picked up an empty matchbox. Normally this is nothing to write home about but in this case it was.

George had been thinking about joining Special Branch. He thought that to do this you needed to be a serious code-breaker so he'd read up on the subject. Anything more than half a page of notes unrelated to snakes was too much for George's brain to handle so he didn't really absorb very much.

He studied the picture on the matchbox which was of a lion (hence Lion matches) lying on top of some grass. The 'grass' on the box was no more than a series of squiggles. George came to the conclusion that the individual blades of grass were actually a form of Arabic script and, "as all Arabs are spies" (George was also an avid James Bond fan), he was convinced it was a secret message left for another agent to pick up. George had however trumped them all by spotting the matchbox and therefore capturing the code before the 'spy' could get at it. There was nothing I could do to convince George otherwise and nothing I really wanted to do—it was all too much fun.

George called for a patrol car to pick us up and take us back to the police station where he went directly to the inspector in charge of the shift. They spent the next three hours together with George trying to convince the inspector of the value of his find and the inspector trying to explain how this could not possibly be so—the obvious explanation being that "there are thousands of matchboxes printed every day, Patrol Officer Beaver, all with exactly the same picture on them, which would surely indicate that if we follow your argument then there are more spies roaming around Bulawayo than anyone else", only served to further raise George's suspicions. Needless to say his application to join Special Branch was turned down.

Chapter five

Lunatics and whores

George was a breath of fresh air, but there was the other side of police work where the harsh reality of what you do sinks in.

Having to accompany a man from the sanitation department to unblock a sewer system was one such unsavoury task. The location was a major sewage-pipe junction. Opening the manhole, I watched as human foetuses were fished out, and put in a wire basket to be dumped later at the morgue.

Another distasteful duty was trying to comprehend why a three-month-old baby had been brutally raped by her father before, mercifully, succumbing. The father, with no idea what the fuss was all about, simply stated: "It's my child; what business is it of yours?"

Or being scared witless by a woman who had lost her mind and was trying to break free from her shackles. I was called out to such an old woman who was known to be insane. Her family had been coping reasonably but when she started showing signs of violence we were called in. She looked so old and frail. When a constable tried to escort her to my Land Rover she started swatting his hands away and cursing him. He thought she was a *nganga*, a witchdoctor, and backed off—afraid. I moved over to her and while gently holding her by the elbow guided her to my vehicle. She turned on me, grabbing my arms, hissing like a witch as her razor-sharp fingernails tore into my skin. I managed to get away and she lunged at me. Before she could grab me I hit her full in the face but, other than driving her backward, my blow had little effect. In desperation I hit her again, this time with the full force of my weight behind the punch. She reeled backward and came at me again ... so I hit her, again and again until she lay exhausted, sprawled on the ground with a bloody, pummelled face and a broken jaw, unmoving.

My constables quickly pinned her arms behind her back and handcuffed her.

On the trip to Mpilo she emitted a series of eerie wails like a banshee. Then there was an ugly sound, like the tearing of flesh, followed by kicking and struggling ... and then silence. I stopped and got out to have a look at her in the back. I will never know how, and quite honestly don't ever want to know, but lying there with her handcuffed arms now in front of her in an impossibly grotesque angle, she had bitten a two- or three-inch gash in her lip, virtually severing the bottom lip. The back of the vehicle was awash with the blood that had spurted all over the place.

It still wasn't over. We arrived at Mpilo and informed the doctor on call what had happened. He brought a gurney up to the Land Rover and called for our assistance. The woman was dragged onto the gurney on her back. Four of us— fit, strong men—were told to hook our legs under one side of the gurney and lean over her so that she was trapped under our chests, locking our arms under the other side at the same time. The doctor prepared a syringe, advising us that he was going to jab it into her backside. He told us that she might jerk a bit so we should hold on with all our strength. I thought I had seen enough to know what to expect but was in for a surprise. As the needle penetrated the skin the old woman jerked upward in a flash and the two men who were lying on her stomach and pelvic area were thrown off with the force of a rocket. I was lying with my body just below her chin and all I could think about was that she would bite me as her head thrashed from side to side. I held on for dear life but, thankfully, within seconds the sedative took effect and she settled down.

Another unhappy duty was trying desperately to get to a dying man—the victim a pedestrian who had been knocked over by a speeding car in a serious road-traffic accident. By the time I arrived at the scene the crowd of onlookers was about twelve deep. The crowd were calling to me to attend to the injured pedestrian and pointing towards him but no one was letting me through. Eventually, in sheer frustration, I lost my temper and with strength I didn't know I had I shoved people roughly aside before finally reaching the victim. He was lying on his back and I knew that he was moments away from death.

Someone pushed me and I started to worry that the crowd might turn on me. I was tempted to run and get as far away from the mob as I could. But I had no option. I tried calmly to assert my authority, speaking what little Ndebele I knew, firmly but without shouting, while I was thinking to myself, "Where the hell are my constables?"

The crowd backed off and I turned toward the injured man. My first glance told me that he was dead. I didn't want the crowd to know this so I started acting like I was treating him, attending to his wounds by applying field dressings. All I wanted to do was buy time until the ambulance arrived. I could hear the wail of sirens in the distance and I knew that help was on its way. When the ambulance arrived at the scene the crowd that had prevented me from getting to the injured man allowed the medics through and I was able to thankfully take my leave.

Rescuing a badly beaten young prostitute from a whorehouse is not a nice task. Prostitution was illegal but that's not the only reason why we got involved. The prostitutes were young girls. We intervened because their pimps would steal their money and if the girls tried to recover it they were mercilessly beaten. The girls could not tell anyone because they knew their parents would beat them just as badly, so who could they turn to?

On receiving an anonymous report we went to the whorehouse and found the girls cowering in a corner in a dreadful state—clothes torn; gaudy make-up and blood smeared over their faces; eyes swollen almost shut.

The pimps were lounging about outside with arms folded, looking at us with smirks on their faces. They knew full well that the girls would not a say a word that might incriminate them for fear of further beatings. They were right—we could not arrest them but that didn't stop me, on more than one occasion, dishing out the same sort of treatment to the scum that they were—in the hope that if they reported me the complaint would get no further than the charge-office counter.

The girls were taken to Mpilo where the empathetic and understanding staff detained them for a few days until they had recovered. And then they went back to their pimps and it would start all over again.

The scenes I was attending were no different to any of those that hundreds of other policemen were attending in the many townships scattered across Rhodesia.

Nowadays, at the drop of a hat, policemen, and others, take weeks and months off work and receive massive compensation for stress-related illnesses they claim is due to the nature of their work. What made us different and how was it that we, as eighteen- or nineteen-year-olds, were able to cope?

I could never understand the fear and concern that our parents tried vainly to hide when we went off to do our duty. At the time we were filled with all the self-assurance of youth, believing we were invincible. It was not about putting your life on the line—it was an adventure to look forward to.

Yet, in spite of the bravado of youth, or perhaps because of it, I think the answer is partly because, like nursing or teaching, being a policeman was a vocation (I hope it still is). We did the job because we were passionate about our work and not driven by monetary incentive. We genuinely wanted to make some kind of difference. Within this group of people, my peers, and I were blessed with a built-in support system that had been developed over many years—people with whom I lived, worked and played—we were always there for each other, in good times and in bad.

It was only after I had left the BSA Police that I realized such a support system even existed.

In mid-1975, after ten months at Mzilikazi, I was transferred to Bulawayo Central.

Chapter six

Bulawayo Central

Sooner or later every policeman has to do the sort of duties one does at a large police station. Coming from a station where I'd had a semblance of autonomy to a charge-office environment at Bulawayo Central police station was a big let-down. I was immediately assigned to charge-office duties which meant standing behind a counter for hours on end, taking reports and dealing with complaints from members of the public. It was all very dull stuff and in my own way I started to rebel.

Shifts at Central began with an inspection. I am the first to admit that I was not the most neatly dressed cop in the force and having to stand at attention while our shift inspector checked to see if our caps were on straight, shoes polished and buttons all done up was a bit too much for me. Part of our uniform was a blue lanyard that we wore over our left shoulder. The end of the lanyard had a whistle attached to it, which was tucked away in the left breast jacket pocket. When I was told that Inspector Flynn would inspect our whistles (which we never used) to see if they were working properly I swapped mine for a red and white plastic whistle that had popped out of a Christmas cracker. As Inspector Flynn came and stood before me he instructed me to produce the whistle and when I did he blew his top. Everyone else could see the joke which, as it turned out, worked in my favour.

After a while Inspector Flynn became so fed up with me that he ordered me to report to a patrol-car driver to become a full-time observer. Patrol cars were known as B-Cars or 'Bee Cars', why, I've no idea. One theory was that the siren sounded like "*beee caar, beee caar*" and the other that the South African police referred to their patrol cars as 'Wasp Cars' and as ours were that much smaller they were lumped with the title 'Bee Car'.

Our B-Cars were originally Austin Westminsters in the 1960s, and latterly

Peugeot 404s and Alfa Romeo 1300s during the seventies—clearly the French and the Italians didn't take sanctions quite so seriously as the British.

In those days my ambition was to become a B-Car driver. To do this you had to first serve a stint as an observer and then, assuming you were selected, attend the B-Car course.

Being an observer was great fun. The observer sat next to the driver, answered the radio and attended scenes but really as back-up to the driver who was the senior partner. This was wonderful because you really didn't have too much to think about. When we got back to the station the driver had to complete all the paperwork while the observer went off to the canteen for a cup of coffee.

One incident that affected me was when, in the early hours of the morning, I spotted an old green Morris Minor parked just off the verge of a side road. At first glance this did not warrant further inspection as there might be any number of perfectly good reasons why it was there. We drove on by, but returning two hours later, we decided that as the car was still there, we should check it out.

We stopped behind the car as I got out and walked up to it. Sitting in the driver's seat was a boy no older than fourteen who could barely reach the pedals. Next to him was a girl of about nine, his sister, and in the back a boy of two or three years of age—the little brother. When I asked what was going on the boy put up a brave front and started getting a bit bolshy, purely as a form of defence. A quiet, non-aggressive approach was needed and very soon the two older children were in tears. It turned out that the elder brother and sister had been abused for months by their mother who herself was subjected to continual beatings from an alcoholic husband. The boy, who had never driven before, had put his sister and baby brother in the Morris Minor and driven all the way from Salisbury to Bulawayo—a distance of some five hundred kilometres!

From a legal point of view what he did of course was wrong but I admired his courage no end. I put them in the B-Car while I followed in the Morris Minor to Central where they were given lots of TLC (tender loving care) by our very special W/P/Os (women patrol officers) before being handed over to Social Welfare.

I eventually became a patrol-car driver. The day-time shifts and evening shifts up till midnight were exciting, but the hours from midnight till dawn were deadly dull. With six patrol cars on the road in the city at any one time, with two-way radios and young, fertile imaginations, we soon found a way to overcome the tedium. One driver would set off in his car and the other would chase him. Officially, if caught, we were testing our 'chase skills'. In reality we were playing tag—and what fun it was too.

We each had our own patrol area and would choose one of these in which to play tag. Mac, my friend and another B-Car driver, and I chose the suburb of Killarney. This was my regular patrol area, with which Mac was unfamiliar. It had been raining for days, making the road surfaces wet and slippery which only added to the excitement. It was Mac's turn to chase me. He managed to keep up with me for quite some time until I shrugged him off as I went tearing down a long stretch of road. I slowed down, turned into a cul-de-sac, switched off my lights and waited. Mac's solution, fearing that he would lose me, was to accelerate in an effort to catch up. What he didn't know was that the 'long stretch of road' was also a cul-de-sac. In my rear-view mirror I saw him flashing past. Before Mac realized what had happened the road came to an abrupt halt.

The only option he had was to aim his car at the first available driveway, enter it, turn the car around and make his getaway. The driveway he chose was a circular driveway which bisected a lush green lawn, in the middle of which was a pristine suburban swimming pool. Mac entered the driveway and then, with a thud, ramped the verge. He hit his breaks, skidded to a halt and did a spectacular one-eighty-degree turn before coming to a stop in front of the house, metres from the pool. As the house lights came on he switched off his headlights and 'wheelied' out, spraying a fountain of mud into the pool, before exiting the property like a rocket.

All our radio transmissions were monitored by Central's control room so when you heard a short hissing sound coming over the radio it meant you had to change to a prearranged channel so that another patrol-car driver could talk without fear of Central hearing the conversation. Mac and I signalled each other thus and rendezvoused a few roads down from 'the scene of the crime'. We agreed on a cover story and waited to see what would happen. Sure enough, a call came in from Central instructing me to proceed to an address in my patrol area to attend a case of vandalism. It was the house where Mac had 'done his thing'. He had made a real mess of the place but all credit to his driving skills in getting out of there and not getting bogged down. The complainant had tried vainly to identify the vehicle. The fact that he was unable to do so might have been due to one or two misleading things that I might have said to him. I did, however, commiserate and promised to keep a sharp look-out for drunken revellers. I made my report back at Central, leaving out any essential details and the whole thing was written off in the report book as NSND (No Suspect No Docket).

Hillside Dam is a lovely tranquil spot situated in the southern Bulawayo suburb of Hillside. It is a popular picnic resort set in a range of picturesque *kopjes*. It was also within our patrol area and a great place to have some fun. On nights when nothing was happening we would drive out to the dam and stop in the parking area. Sometimes lovers would be seen doing what they do best. When they saw our patrol cars approaching they would think we had come to check up on their safety and would bring their proceedings to, we hoped, a not-too-abrupt halt before driving off. The way was now clear for us to have some fun.

Positioning our cars in the centre of the car park we would bring up the revs, put the flashing blue light on, release the clutch and execute three-sixty-degree hand-break turns. The effect of the blue strobe light bouncing off the surrounding hills was spectacular though if you did it for too long it left you totally disorientated. It was like driving a car through a disco.

That left us with the siren. 'Going red' was the term we used to put on the blue light *and* the siren. To do so we had to get permission from the duty inspector at Central. Going red was especially effective when trying to make your way through traffic to a scene where you were urgently needed. It was also great to scare lazy drivers. When someone was spotted dozing at the wheel waiting in heavy traffic we would position ourselves next to him, request permission to 'go red' and then switch on the blue light and siren. It was amazing how many people got such a fright that they instinctively switched off their ignition. I still can't make sense of that—a bit like trying to douse a tear-gas grenade—no logic.

Bulawayo has two training colleges for which members of the entire BSA Police will be forever grateful. One was the Teachers' Training College (TTC) and the other the Nurses' School. The TTC was situated in Hillside. As the students were the same age as us we got to know them well and had some good parties. Folk music by the likes of Gordon Lightfoot, Joan Baez and Bob Dylan was popular, so the TTC girls used to organize 'folk evenings' which were held in the students' lounge and to which we were extended an open invitation.

As the evening kicked off the lights were switched off and a single coffee table, with candles lit at either end providing the only light, was placed at one end of the lounge. Cushions were scattered around the lounge—all very cosy. When you arrived you found a place to sit and began chatting to the people around you, while, unprompted, someone would stand up, guitar in hand, walk over to the coffee table, sit down cross-legged next to it and begin strumming.

You would think that a room filled with horny young adults would produce a different sort of vibe but it didn't. There were other times for that. Those nights were a time when the angst of boy–girl relationships was set aside while the music took priority. You might be sitting there lost in your thoughts, allowing the lyrics to conjure up their own images and become aware that a girl you didn't know was resting her head on your shoulder, also lost in the music. Not a word was said; you absorbed the atmosphere and made the most of a special opportunity to relax and unwind.

At the end of the evening some of us would get together and go for a cup of coffee at a late-night joint or a friend's house. These were peaceful times. They taught me that you can have a platonic relationship with a woman without her feeling threatened—and that it is possible to be yourself around a woman.

There was one cop though who tried to take things a little bit further. There's always one, isn't there?

Speedy thought he was God's gift to women, aided, he believed, by the Triumph 3 sports car and motorbike he owned. He was a South African who came from a wealthy family and had joined the force with the sole intention of becoming a motorcycle traffic cop.

When he qualified he was posted to Bulawayo Central Traffic Section and spent his days riding around on his bike issuing traffic tickets. Before setting off for his shift there was much preparation to do. He began by putting on his jodhpurs, followed by his shirt which had been tailored in such a way that it showed off his V-shaped torso, then his freshly ironed tie (he also had his own iron) neatly secured with a Winchester knot. With this in place he put on his patent-leather belt followed by his patent-leather boots followed by his patent-leather leggings, before lifting his uniform jacket from the coat hanger and leaving for work.

Compared to the rest of us he did look pretty smart but then very few of us were traffic cops.

Speedy's MO (*modus operandi*) had been worked out to the n'th degree. On one particular occasion he spotted three TTC students walking past the Central post office. He worked out that if he circled the building he could approach them from behind, get a few metres in front of them, take a left turn into a motorcycle parking bay and, in one fluid movement, kick down the bike stand situated just below his left foot, stop, hop off the bike and present himself in all his glory to the girls. Simple.

There he was, back ramrod-straight, hands held out gripping the handlebars, Zip Nolan wraparound sunglasses in place and police issue cap which he had spent hours and hours (completely against regulations) shaping to look like a World War Two fighter pilot's.

Now … to pull off the manoeuvre. Everything was going according to plan. He has the girls in his sights and cruises by; they notice him, he does a slight left-hand turn into the parking bay, kicks down the stand, stops and in one fluid movement attempts to dismount.

Unfortunately the stand has a return spring, causing it to spring back into place which causes the bike to crashing down on top of Speedy, trapping him underneath, peaked fighter-pilot cap and Zip Nolan sunglasses seriously squashed. The girls come to his assistance and lift the bike off him.

If this had happened to any one of us we would have gone AWOL, never to be seen again. As only Speedy could, he managed to elicit the girls' sympathy and ended up taking them all out for a night on the town.

This is the same man who would arrive at TTC, walk into the lounge looking for a date, stand there, click his fingers and have two of three students grab his hand and disappear. The rest of us would have been bombarded with anything from cushions to teacups to abuse.

Probably the most distressing of duties we had to perform was delivering death messages. On receipt of the telex the duty inspector would give us the details and tell us where to go. Bear in mind that, over and above the 'normal' deaths from motor vehicle accidents and natural causes, the war was intensifying and members of the security forces and the public were getting killed every day, so sadly, it was a common enough task.

A policeman and a policewoman were required to deliver a message together. In the normal arrogant way of males we assumed that being the tougher (supposedly) of the two sexes we would 'serve' the message but it never worked out like that.

When I got to the front door of a house I never knew what to expect. No one knows how they will react when they are told that a person they love dearly has been killed. They may turn around and walk away, quietly weep, get angry or even hysterical. Delivering the death message is one thing; dealing with the recipient's grief is another and this is where the women cops came into their own. Inevitably, after delivering the death message the male cop stood awkwardly while the woman cop provided a shoulder to cry on, made tea and always seemed to say the right things.

The truth be told, when we left to return to the station and got into the car, the grief that we had just witnessed in fact affected all us men in some way. Again the women cops came to the fore. Without in any way making you feel awkward they somehow managed to make you feel you had actually done a good job. But as we got back to the station we reverted to form with nonsense like: "Ja, I handled it fine but W/P/O Jones cracked up so I had to sort her out; you know what women are like!"

I once received a telephone call from someone who said he was the Member in Charge Fort Rixon, a police station out 'in the sticks'. He gave me his name and told me to proceed to such and such an address and tell a Miss Debra Brown that her brother had been killed in action while on operations.

I went to the house, rang the bell and someone, whom I presumed and later confirmed was the deceased's father, answered the door. I was aware of a lady standing in the background whom I assumed was his daughter. I passed on the sad news and told him what had happened. He was stunned. The girl went hysterical so much so that we both had to restrain her.

"When did you say he was killed?" the father asked while grappling with the sobbing girl.

"Yesterday afternoon," I replied.

"But, he was de-mobbed yesterday afternoon and spoke to us from the barracks!"

"What! Huh?"

Seeing my concern and confusion he managed to get a phone call through to the 'deceased person' and confirmed that he was in fact very much alive. With a thousand apologies I left and promised to get to the bottom of the débâcle. The whole thing was a hoax. The girl was not the 'deceased's' sister. She was in fact his fiancée who had been staying with her future father-in-law while her fiancé was in the army. I had been set up by a jealous previous boyfriend. It didn't take much in the way of serious investigation to find out who the culprit was. In our own way he was 'dealt with'.

The Johannesburg branch of the Hell's Angels had come to town. This was in the days when these guys were held in absolute awe. Their leader was someone named Perreira and was something of a legend. As they arrived on the outskirts of Bulawayo they were met by the officer commanding and told that they were welcome to stay but must deposit any weapons they had in their possession at Bulawayo Central police station for safe-keeping. After that they could make their way to a campsite situated on a farm just outside Bulawayo where they could enjoy themselves and do what they did at their leisure. They duly arrived at Bulawayo Central and dumped a small armoury on the counter.

I was on duty and almost speechless with excitement when I saw them—all beards, moustaches, leather jackets and looking about as macho as you can get. There were hundreds of stories about how ruthless and violent they were and how they drove around Johannesburg terrorizing people and flogging cars with chrome-plated chains. The fact of the matter is they were a wonderful group of people—rather than uneducated thugs many of them were professional, upstanding members of the community. But I did not know this at the time.

Night shift started at 2200 hours and ended at 0600 hours. 'Breakfast' was held in Stops Camp, a five-minute drive from the station, between 2300 hours and 0100 hours. Normally I caught a lift with a patrol-car driver but on that particular night I missed my lift. The duty inspector told me to "take the Vesper". A Vesper is a small scooter that no man with an ounce of self-respect would dare to be seen upon. They were for the women patrol officers—not us. I had two choices—either miss breakfast and go hungry—or take the Vesper and lose my self-respect. I mulled over the dilemma for a few minutes. I figured that after midnight the streets of Bulawayo would be deserted and I would likely not be spotted—my dignity would be intact and my belly full …

I'd never ridden a scooter so it took me a while to work out how to start it. I decided not to wear a crash helmet in case anyone saw me leaving the station and presumed I was a wimp. Instead I rode wearing my police cap.

It was the middle of summer. I was making my way along Main Street enjoying the ride, gently weaving from one side of the road to the other, with not a soul in sight—I may even have been humming a tune.

Then I heard a roar of thunder. At least I thought it was thunder. I looked up, the sky was still cloudless but the thunder was intensifying, alarmingly so. I looked behind and did a double-take. What I saw to my absolute horror about two hundred metres behind me and rapidly approaching was a phalanx of Hell's Angels taking up the entire road from side to side.

My instinct was to accelerate and hide but I didn't. As luck would have it I came to a traffic-light intersection and hoped I could make it through while the lights were still green. However, as I reached the intersection the lights turned red and, being the conscientious policeman that I was, stopped. Foolishly. Quite why, I will never know.

The roar of thunder got louder as the sound of their engines reverberated off the walls and shop fronts. In next to no time the Angels were behind me and then all around me, showering me with insults and abuse for riding a scooter.

"By the way *oke*, where is your helmet, hey?" they taunted.

I tried to disappear into myself by lowering my head and hunching my shoulders. With head bowed I cautiously looked left and right but no, dammit! they were still there and I hadn't disappeared.

After what seemed like hours the lights turned green. It was probably delayed shock that made me cackle with laughter and give the Angels a 'twos-up' (the two fingers, an inverted 'V') as I revved the scooter, released the brakes and screeched away, my cap flying off in the process. I was doing fine for about three metres when I stalled the damned thing and almost fell off. I released whatever it is that makes scooters stall, madly kick-started it and slowly made my getaway. It probably would have been quicker had I picked up the wretched scooter and ran with it.

Although the Angels were by now paralytic with laughter one of them decided to follow me. Not knowing what he would do if, God forbid, he caught me I ducked into the nearest alleyway, sped through it with my shoulders hunched over the handlebars like a racing cyclist's to reduce wind resistance, and came out on another large street. I kept repeating the process from one alley to the next until I dared look over my shoulder and realized I had lost him, somewhere near the magistrates' court.

At the time I felt like all the demons on the planet were chasing me whereas it was simply one guy chugging along behind me on his Harley Davidson, more from amusement than any evil intention. The image of an eagle chasing a fly comes to mind.

The end result was that I lost all self-respect and never had my breakfast. My cap was returned to the station the next day by one of the kindly Hell's Angels. Hardly 'cap in hand' so to speak.

Two W/P/Os had their counselling skills tested to the limit when they teamed up as observer and patrol-car driver to patrol the streets of Bulawayo.

There is a small dam virtually in the centre of the town. It has a smallish parking area that gently slopes towards the water's edge and is frequented by people who want to be alone—in other words horny young couples.

The two W/P/Os were driving past when a naked man ran in front of their car and waved them down. The poor man was too upset to talk and kept pointing to the dam. They did the only thing they could—wrapped him in blanket, stuffed him in the B-Car and took him back to Central. When they arrived, he at last managed to stutter that his girlfriend had died in the dam. At first no one believed him. However, when all the details were pieced together the police sub-aqua team was called out and, sure enough, retrieved a body the dam.

What had happened was that the couple had driven to the dam, parked the car, with handbrake on and got stuck in to some serious sex. But in the throes of passion the handbrake was accidently released, causing the car to slowly roll down the slope towards the water's edge.

It had been raining and with the muddy surface providing little friction for the wheels to grip there was nothing to stop the car's inexorable progress to the bank. It reached the edge of the dam, a sharp drop-off, and then plunged into the water to a depth of eight feet. With water pouring in they tried desperately to escape. The water pressure, even at eight feet, made it almost impossible to open the doors but eventually the man was able to extricate himself. He swam to the bank and ran for help. His girlfriend's fate was, however, sealed.

Tragic as it was, the newspapers had a field day.

I have never understood why the public are so anti-policemen.

I was called to a burglary in one of Bulawayo's affluent suburbs and on arrival approached the front door and rang the bell. The owner answered. I was about to step inside when the owner told me haughtily that I should go round to the back door as "that is the servants' entrance". Here was a woman who had asked for my help and was now treating me like an intruder.

All policemen have had this sort of thing happen to them. As long as people are in trouble we are needed. When things are going okay we are the bad guys.

A policeman stops someone to do a vehicle check and the driver turns on him with well-worn clichés such as "I pay your salary; if it wasn't for me you wouldn't have a job" and "How dare you ask me for my name; that's an invasion of my civil rights" and from someone too drunk to stand, waving his finger at you saying, "When I get to the police station I will report you to your officer commanding."

Male cops tended not to let another man get away with a thing. With women it was slightly different—a well-rehearsed tear, a light touch on your shoulder or an extra button undone would have the most dedicated policeman backing down.

There are four words that have been terrifying men since the female of the species was able to string her first sentence together. No sooner are these uttered than every one of us males is sent scrambling for the hills, looking desperately about for the nearest exit before running like hell.

Picture this—a woman driver is hauled over for driving recklessly. She gets out of the car. You ask her what is wrong and she says: "It's a woman problem." That's it. No more need be said. In a flash the most horrendous images are conjured up in your mind, you apologise profusely, get down on your knees, beg for forgiveness and run. You cannot help thinking "What if she reports me?" and "My God, what have I done; what did I say?" and "Do I need therapy?"

I have a wife and two daughters both of whom know this tactic well and use it.

One of my not-so-pleasant memories is of getting beaten up in the charge office.

A patrol-car driver had made an arrest and brought to the station someone who had been hurling abuse at him. Like all accused he was taken to the detention room, in his case shouting and swearing at the arresting officer.

I was told to go and "detain him as he may be some trouble". I looked at the duty inspector and thought, "Might be trouble? He's a scrawny little bugger; how can he be any trouble to me?"

The procedure was for the person being detained to remove his belt, shoes, tie and anything else he might use to strangle or injure himself, or others. It was a straightforward procedure. I walked into the detention room expecting, as was the norm, a constable to accompany me in case of any trouble but no one followed me in.

What I did not know was that the duty inspector had wryly observed that I was an over-confident, cocky sort and, knowing the detainee's character, decided to let me sort things out myself.

When I told the accused to remove his belt he told me to "get stuffed". I told him again and received the same response. Like any young man, I was looking for an opportunity to assert my authority and here was an opportunity presenting itself to me on a platter. I summed up the accused, knew that I could easily overpower him and approached him to grab him by the scruff of his neck and let him know who was boss.

As I put out my arms to man-handle him he head-butted me and I hit the floor.

That next thing I remember is coming round with this lunatic on top of me and two constables attempting to restrain him as he tried to struggle loose and punch me in the face. They managed to get him off me and pinned him to the ground on his back, his arms firmly in their grip. In my dazed state I stood up and thought that if I fell over his legs he wouldn't be able to move and we could cuff him easily enough. Not the brightest thing I have ever done. As I dropped onto his legs he kicked out, hitting me square in the jaw—I was 'lights out' in an instant. When I eventually came to, I noticed he'd been successfully manacled and dragged off to a cell.

The duty inspector had known of the accused's violent nature for many years—he'd been in and out of prison for various petty offences and was notorious for beating up prison wardens. I'm sure the duty inspector allowed himself the hint of a smile after my episode. Certainly, from then on, I was more wary of suspects, regardless of what they looked like.

But my time at Bulawayo Central wasn't all that that bad.

I have memories of coming on duty at six o'clock in the morning and being the first to the bakery for fresh doughnuts. Even in a city, strategically parked and waiting for a call, an African sunrise can be spectacular. Or listening to another driver telling you how he'd just seen a "huge eagle owl near the quarry at Hillside" and, as I approached, saw it totally fixated by my headlights. At the last second it gently took off, its wings brushing against my windshield. When I met up with the cop later he said: "You see! I promise you, if it was any bigger you wouldn't have had to take avoiding action; you could've just driven between its legs."

Chapter seven

A cheeky magistrate

The bane of any policeman's life has to be the plethora of petty crimes that people report. Often the 'crimes' are reported for no other reason than to boost the fragile ego of the complainant (person reporting). In Rhodesia the report process of a stolen bicycle, for example, would go something like this:

The complaint is received, usually by phone, and a patrol car despatched to attend. On arrival at the scene of the crime the policeman interviews the complainant and any witnesses, carries out an on-site investigation, take notes and hopefully arrests the accused. On return to the police station a 'Crime Attendance Form' is completed and handed to the shift duty inspector who sends it to the Enquiries Section. Enquiries complete the investigation and prepare a docket for court. When this is signed off by the Member in Charge Enquiries it is sent to the Office of the Senior Public Prosecutor where it is then handed it to a public prosecutor for trial. A court date is set and summons issued.

There was a well-know magistrate whom I shall call Jim. A professional to the absolute core, his antics made him a legend among members of the BSA Police. Jim had been sitting through case after case of these petty crimes and had had enough. He decided to bring things to end and this is how he did it:

The complainant in this particular case was the owner of a café, a 'corner-shop', a small shop that sells cigarettes, newspapers, sweets, milk and basic foodstuffs—much like a British newsagent. Instead of being sold in packets, cigarettes could be purchased singly or in pairs.

The 'defendant' was a humble *madala* (old man) who had come to Bulawayo from his home in the rural area and who had walked into the shop and bought two cigarettes to the value of six cents. He could not understand or speak a word of English.

After purchasing the two cigarettes the *madala* was standing outside having a smoke when a patrol car arrived to arrest him—the café-owner had phoned in a report of theft, claiming the *madala* had not paid for the cigarettes. The story was highly unlikely but it came down to his word against the accused's. But a crime and been reported and the wheels of justice had to turn, although it was clear that the complainant had fabricated the report in an effort to deter would-be shoplifters and other thieves who plague such corner-shops.

When the case got to trial Jim read through the docket and listened to the public prosecutor and the witnesses presenting their arguments and testimonies. It were a case he knew he could easily enough have it thrown out for any number of reasons. But he had other plans ... he told the court that they would adjourn for thirty minutes while he considered the verdict and sentence, if any. In his rooms he told the PP, the translator and court orderly what he would do.

On returning to the courtroom he went through the whole, long-winded preamble, saying he had reviewed the case and found the defendant guilty. This was relayed to the defendant by the translator as: "The magistrate says you are not guilty." The defendant did not say a word nor change his blank facial expression.

The complainant, who was sitting expectantly on a bench in the front of the courtroom, smiled on hearing the verdict and looked at the defendant as if to say "I told you so; this is the way I get people to deal with things". He then sat back, waiting to hear what the sentence would be.

"I take cases like this very seriously," Jim continued "and today, after much consideration, I have decided that in order to put an end to this type of theft I will pass down the maximum sentence that this court allows me to do."

This was translated to the defendant as "The magistrate says he hopes your wife and cattle are well and that you have good crops this year."

The complainant had a smirk of grim satisfaction on his face, expecting Jim to issue a fine of five dollars.

Jim then nodded to a court orderly who took out a black cloth bag that Jim had given him earlier, walked across to the defendant and placed the hood over his head.

The translator then said to the defendant: "The magistrate wants to buy you a hat and we will measure your head for size by putting a bag over your head." The defendant was quite happy with this.

There was a pause. The complainant's look of grim satisfaction had changed to one of silent desperation, all colour gone from his face and his mouth opening and closing like a goldfish—but not a sound came from his mouth.

"I now sentence you to death—take him away!" Jim's gavel sounded like a bullet.

This was translated as "Does it fit?" and, from under the hood the muffled sound of "*Yebo*" was heard.

This was now too much for the complainant. Never imagining anything like this could happen he was mortified, knowing that his self-serving pettiness had resulted in an innocent man being sentenced to death. Looking down at the complainant Jim noticed that he had fainted.

There is another wonderful story that also involves Jim …

In this case he was the regional magistrate for an area in the northeast of the country. Part of his job involved visiting police stations and sitting in on trials that were conducted *in situ*, for areas without a magistrate's court.

The particular location was a small town called Mtoko, a dusty village, but with one of the largest military concentrations in the country, including army, air force, Special Branch, Ground Coverage, Internal Affairs etc. The military camp also boasted a CID office for the resident detective patrol officers. One of the D/P/Os was full of the self-importance that CID personnel sometimes acquire—a way perhaps of disguising their inferiority to their far superior colleagues in Special Branch.

This D/P/O, whom I shall call Tim, had assumed the role of a super-sleuth and was forever scurrying hither and thither to gather 'hot int' (hot intelligence) of foul deeds being perpetrated. However, as he rarely stepped foot outside the perimeter of the camp, he only ever stumbled upon petty crimes and other incidents of little consequence.

Add to this he had adopted an annoyingly pious demeanour. He continually prattled on about "family values", how he had the perfect marriage and how "Jen and I will always be together because our relationship is based on trust and I would never do anything to upset her." He pontificated about swearing, drinking and, heavens forbid! pornography! He believed that reading pornography was the worst thing anyone could do as it poisoned the soul and was a guaranteed one-way ticket to hell.

All things considered he was perfect for a set-up.

When it was learned that Jim was going to be in the area a bunch of guys got together and briefed Jim on their plan. Jim, of course, happily bought into the arrangement. During a conversation in the mess, Jim casually let slip to those around him, including Tim, who coincidentally happened to be in earshot, that he was going to come down hard on anyone found with pornography—that he would use the full force of the law to deal with such perverts. Tim couldn't believe his luck and assured Jim he would get "some undercover people in place" as "such evil needed to be purged from men's hearts".

Two days later Tim's boss, Detective Inspector Syd Browne, told Tim that he wanted a surprise inspection carried out of all accommodation to search for pornography. Tim fell right into the trap even volunteering to have his room searched first "just so the others can see that I am no different from anyone else and will willingly suffer the same inconveniences".

With that Syd and Tim started walking towards Tim's room. As if purely by coincidence the air force camp commandant joined them, followed by the army commander.

Tim's chest swelled as he showed them his room, the bed perfectly made with the mandatory photo of wife on the bedside table. With everyone watching, Syd had a look inside the cupboard and under the bed.

"You see, sir," Tim said, "I told you; nothing to worry about. Let's go and look for the real criminals."

As they made to leave the air force commandant said, "One more thing if you don't mind," went to Tim's bed and ran his hand under the mattress. "Hello what's this?"

Tim, in a rush to catch the real villains, said, "Probably bread crumbs, sir. Come on, let's go."

"Weeeell, I think I've found something," the air force commandant retorted and with that pulled out four pornographic magazines—planted beforehand by someone from CID.

A deadly hush ensued before Syd said quietly, "This is a punishable offence, Tim. You and I need to talk."

At that very moment Jim made his appearance (on cue) and asked what was going on. On being told that porn had been found under Tim's mattress, he suggested, "Why delay? I am here so let's have the trial first thing tomorrow morning."

All the officers agreed. Tim was confined to his room and instructed to report to the makeshift courtroom at 0900 hours the following morning.

Poor Tim must have spent that night sweating blood. He couldn't even phone his wife to pour his heart out as all the phone lines were down.

The next morning he was duly escorted to the courtroom by two constables. He arrived in the packed courtroom a completely broken man as he took his place in the dock. He hadn't slept a wink, his face was tear-stained and he was barely able to talk.

Jim looked at him and said solemnly: "Detective Patrol Officer, before this trial commences there is something that I must ask you."

Tim nodded, his Adam's apple bobbing furiously.

"My question is Tim: are you aware that this has been a set-up—a bit of fun and games?"

There was no response from Tim who had by now decided that his life was totally ruined and nothing else mattered. I am told that it took a while for the message to sink in. Shortly thereafter, Tim requested a transfer, which was granted with unseemly haste.

In the meantime, I was about to leave Bulawayo Central. I'd been transferred to Filabusi in rather unusual—and sudden—circumstances.

Chapter eight

Into 'Districts'—Filabusi

Filabusi in 1976 was a small, dusty village situated about one hundred and twenty kilometres southeast of Bulawayo. It still is. 'Filabusi' is an Ndebele word that means either 'the face of a dead goat' or 'struck in the face by a man-made weapon' depending on which source you choose.

One of the delights of living in Rhodesia was that all the vernacular place names and tribal names can be translated into English and mean something. The boring colonial way of naming a town after a prominent figurehead simply didn't apply. Instead of Salisbury being named after Lord Salisbury you would have Lalapanzi which in Ndebele means 'lie down' and there would be a story to it. Bulawayo means 'the place of killing' (there is still a huge tree on the outskirts of Bulawayo beneath which King Lobengula executed criminals and malcontents). 'Ngwenya' means crocodile, 'ndhlovu' means elephant, 'nyama' is meat therefore the town of Nyamandhlovu means 'meat of the elephant'.

Filabusi has the unique distinction of being the place where the only stagecoach robbery ever occurred in Rhodesia. It happened sometime in the late 1920s. The stagecoach was carrying gold from Killarney Mine to Bulawayo when it was stopped and held up by a man on a horse. At gunpoint he demanded and took from the occupants their hard-earned gold and headed off in a cloud of dust. Unfortunately for him our stagecoach robber never thought to wear a mask of any sort and, as he had lived in the area for some time, was well known to his victims. The police were notified and he was arrested in quick time—by his colleagues—he was to our eternal shame an off-duty member of the BSA Police stationed at Filabusi. If this was the best he could do in committing a crime one can only wonder what his standard of investigation was like.

I'd never had any intention of becoming a district policeman and would never have applied for the post were it not for the fact that I had got myself into trouble with a lady while stationed in Bulawayo as a B-Car driver.

It isn't as bad as it sounds, but typical of the sort of thing that happens to me. Someone in a block of flats had phoned in, complaining about noisy neighbours. I got the call to attend and while interviewing the tenants met Jackie. I suppose, largely because I was wearing a uniform, I impressed her no end—so much so that I was soon not wearing my uniform and had my wicked way with her. I dressed into my uniform and left, deed done and that was the end of it … or so I assumed. I am unsure how or even if I told her I that I didn't want to take things further. At the time diplomacy was not a strong point of mine so I am assuming I was not terribly empathetic or understanding. I was just being 'a man', or so I told myself.

Jackie, however, had other ideas. She started stalking me—phoning me, sending messages and leaving notes on my windscreen jammed in the wipers. She even got my younger brother to come to Bulawayo from Salisbury and have a chat with me. Apparently she told him things about me that simply were not true and Brian, being the absolute gentleman, believed her. I am never going to live that down and Brian has never let me forget it. Like most men I thought I was God's gift to women, so I could understand her persistence but then things started getting out of hand.

I had gone out with a group of friends to see a movie in town. I was still fairly shy and disliked being the centre of attention or doing anything that might draw attention to me. At the interval I went to the foyer and was standing having a Coke and chatting to my mates when I became aware that the crowd was looking towards the main entrance doors. I turned and followed their gaze. What I saw, to my horror, was a glowering Jackie striding purposefully into the foyer. She seemed to fill the doorway (although I hasten to add she was petite and had a great body—I have to mention this because this is what got me into trouble in the first place) and was in a terrible rage. She had, in her right hand a reddish-black jersey (a colour I later came to identify as burgundy) that my mother had knitted for me and which I had forgotten at her house. I had intended to collect it from her.

It never occurred to me that I could be the cause of her anger but it soon became apparent as she advanced towards me.

"You bastard! How you could do this to me!" she screamed and threw the jersey at me.

It hit me in the face as I stood there paralyzed with embarrassment. I had no idea what to do. I thought of hiding in the toilets but I didn't know where they were and in the state I was in doubted if I could distinguish between the male and female signs. I decided discretion was the better part of confrontation and skulked back into the cinema and crept into my seat. I wanted to crawl under it and quietly disappear forever.

As people started filing back in after the interval women looked towards me with contempt in their eyes, nudging their escorts and muttering things to them. Their boyfriends knew that, by simply being male, they were guilty by association, so there was no way I could look to them for any moral support.

The movie ended and I waited until everyone, including ushers, had left (not just the cinema but the whole building), before I summoned up the courage to leave. I half-expected to be confronted with a gauntlet of angry she-devils, all brandishing ugly-coloured jerseys with studs in them, through which I would have to run. But the coast was clear.

When I got to my car I found another note, rather an epistle, stuck behind the windscreen wipers. It must have been seventeen pages long and contained many nasty things about me. I did try to read through the whole thing but must confess that I gave up after the fourth or fifth paragraph when it became apparent that I wasn't in line for any Christmas cards from her.

Jackie's campaign of terror had begun. The phone calls, letters, notes continued. It got to the stage where I was afraid to go out on my own and only ever felt safe when I was on duty surrounded by other policemen.

In desperation I applied for whatever posting came up. Everything from the Police Anti-Terrorist Unit (PATU) to the Criminal Investigation Department (CID) to bush postings—anything to get away. The police came to my rescue. They had a clear, albeit unwritten, policy when it came to dealing with members who had "got themselves into trouble". By now I had become an expert at filling in applications for postings, my latest one being for obscure bush work in the Mount Darwin area.

As was normal procedure I was summoned to the officer commanding to be interviewed for the post. I stood at attention in his office, head held high, eyes fixed on a point six inches above the top of his head. I recited my well-rehearsed reasons for wanting the transfer. I had all the answers and was the perfect candidate for the posting, or so I thought. I was well into my routine when I glanced down and became aware that the OC was not taking me terribly seriously. He was gazing out of the window into space while absent-mindedly playing with a rubber band, obviously not hearing a word I was saying.

I finished my recitation and waited.

He let out a deep sigh and asked if I had anything more to say. This was standard procedure so I rattled off a few better-chosen phrases while he continued to play with his rubber band.

"Is that all?"

"Yes sir."

He then looked up at me, slowly put his rubber band down on the desk and asked me what the *real* reason was for my wanting the posting. Although I hadn't expected this I realized that I had to be totally honest with him and this was probably the best chance I had of getting out of Bulawayo.

I took a deep breath and said, "Sir, I am in the shit."

He didn't appear in the least bit surprised and said, "Tell me about it."

I told him what had happened, without any embellishment.

"Okay, you know the procedure."

I didn't have any idea what the 'procedure' was but I said I did.

He saw I clearly didn't and so explained that if I agreed I would be posted as soon as possible to a remote police station and to all but members of my immediate family the police would deny any knowledge of me. I would have no choice as to which station I would be posted and would go unconditionally. I thought 'unconditionally' applied only to people who were surrendering so I felt it must be pretty serious stuff. Anyway, I agreed and was dismissed.

Two days later I arrived in Filabusi and my life was to change forever.

The village of Filabusi was spread out over a fairly large area linked by two access roads to the main Shabani–Balla Balla road. At one end of the village were a general store and a butcher and at the other the Filabusi Club which consisted of a bar, a recreation lounge and some tennis courts. To get to the centre of the village from the general store you crossed a bridge over the Insiza River, where you then discovered the police station and the District Commissioners' office and staff accommodation, next to which was a small post office. The village also boasted a small primary school with a large swimming pool.

On the outskirts of Filabusi were a golf course and a small airfield. The fairways were mostly 'roughs' and the greens were sand not grass. While most people attempted to play golf on the golf course others used the airfield to indulge their own form of drag-racing.

In a small village like Filabusi the most important people (depending on who you talked to) were the member in charge of the police station, the District Commissioner, the local doctor and the mine manager.

Immediately upon my arrival in Filabusi I got a message to go and see the mine manager's wife.

"I have something to show you," she said as she opened the front door and produced a cat. But this was no ordinary cat. Normally cats are cute, fluffy bundles of fur. Not this one which had not a hair on its body and looked as ugly as sin. As I had been summoned by the mine manager's wife I was expecting some sort of a complaint and assumed that the cat was the result of some unfortunate inbreeding. Thinking she wanted me to dispose of it I grabbed it by the scruff of the neck and started to walk away. The mine manager's wife screamed at me, asking me what I was going to do with her cat.

"Kill it, ma'am," I said.

Oh dear! Drama, accusations of cruelty to animals and grovelling apologies on my part followed. It later became clear that this hairless thing was in fact a special breed, her prized possession and she'd merely wanted to show it off to me.

The police station at Filabusi had on its strength:

1 x member in charge—an inspector

1 x section officer

4 x patrol officers

1 x sergeant-major

3 x sergeants

18 constables

A district policeman is unique. Until a policeman has been to 'District' he has not really been a cop—my own opinion which will undoubtedly irritate many town policemen who never left the urban areas. Town cops either attended or investigated scenes. They did the initial paperwork before the dockets were passed from clerk to bureaucrat to department for endorsement before being sent to the public prosecutor for prosecution. Other policemen did any one of a hundred different things—from filling in reports received to taking fingerprints to detaining suspects and putting bodies in the morgue. As a town cop you were a very small cog in a very large wheel.

In 'District' you were the whole wheel. District cops received the report, attended the scene, which often entailed four or five hours of driving along bush roads, then carried out an investigation that involved taking measurements, photographing and collecting evidence and then driving all the way back to your remote station.

The scene you attended could be anything from a petty theft to a complicated murder. If it was an assault you also took care of the victim by using the first aid skills you'd been taught.

I once attended a murder where someone had been clubbed to death with a knobkerrie on the banks of the Umzingwane River. To get there I drove four hours along dirt roads, another hour or so through the bush and then a four-hour walk with a body box to the scene. The body box was seven feet long and made of reinforced aluminium. It was heavy enough without a corpse and awkward to carry as it did not have any handles. My constable and I loaded the body into the box, carried it all the way back to our Land Rover and returned to the station.

All crimes were investigated and the docket submitted to the nearest public prosecutor for prosecution. If the case wasn't too serious one of the station patrol officers would prosecute in a spare room converted into a temporary courtroom at the Filabusi police station. In our case this was our station pub. The regional magistrate would arrive on the Tuesday of every other week, listen to the cases, pass sentence, have a beer and move on to the next little *dorp*, or village.

As a district cop we did it all and on our own.

District cops also had to attend post mortems in case the doctor performing the PM removed a part of the body to be sent to Salisbury for further examination. We were there to confirm that the brain, heart or whatever other body part had been removed from that particular body and in doing so complete the chain of evidence. Often the doctor was in no mood to perform the PM and was as put off by the body as we were. He would mistake our presence for enthusiasm and order us to assist by "holding this" and "cutting that". I attended many PMs and never enjoyed them as such—at first morbidly fascinated and then intellectually captivated. Dr van Wyk would start the external examination talking into his tape recorder and making notes on a post mortem form as he went along. When he realized that I was genuinely interested he would explain what he was doing and why.

At Filabusi the post mortem room was a tiled room, about the size of a bathroom, in the centre of which was a ceramic, slightly concave table which was raised at one end. It was one of the local doctor's duties (in our case Doc van Wyk) to carry out PMs. Because the PM room was so small there was no hanging back, no matter how off-putting the procedure and Doc van Wyk wouldn't tolerate anything other than total co-operation from the attending P/O. As far as he was concerned you were there so you were therefore part of the process.

The instruments used for carrying out PMs looked like rejects from a medieval torture chamber—absolutely grotesque. He would hand you one, for example a huge carving knife, and tell you to "hold this", "cut here", "pay attention you fool!" and then, as he cut open the stomach to examine the contents, hold it open for you before saying "Put your nose here, boy, and smell this—it's alcohol the man has been drinking." An appropriate comment was then expected.

"Ag, disgusting, man!" was not one.

The body would be placed on the slab, head at the raised end so that blood and body fluids could flow down through a plug and into a bucket placed beneath the table. There was nothing particularly distasteful while the contents of the chest and abdomen were exposed and examined. When it came to the head, things were quite different. In order to examine the brain an incision was made from one ear up over the scalp to the other ear. One part of the scalp above the forehead was pulled down over the eyes and the other part pulled down to the back of the neck exposing the skull. A type of metal ring with four screws evenly positioned was placed over the exposed skull and the screws tightened until the ring and screws gripped the skull. The doctor then sawed away at the skull and, when he felt he had gone deep enough, took a chisel, positioned it in the groove made by the saw and tapped the end of the chisel with a mallet. The top of the skull came away with a dull, hollow thud and the brain was exposed for all to see. Once you had seen and heard that nothing else was ever quite as grotesque.

One reasons I never had any qualms around dead bodies was that I always knew, without really understanding, that the soul had left the body and that I was looking at nothing more than a lifeless lump of flesh and bone. A human being is comprised of a body, a mind (the brain) and a soul. Each is interdependent of the other and together they form a living being. When the being dies the brain and body will decompose and eventually disappear. That leaves the soul. As the soul is a one-dimensional entity it cannot die. Something must happen to it and to my way of thinking the soul moves on. This is as good an explanation of 'life after life' that I can muster.

Sometimes the soul does not leave the body immediately. Anyone who has been around dead bodies for some time can tell you when this has happened. There is nothing spooky about it—it's just common sense and like so many issues that appear beyond our comprehension, the more complex the issue the simpler the explanation. We just have to look in the right place.

I would like to say that I settled in at Filabusi straight away, but I didn't. The truth is that at first I hated everything about District that I later came to love—the rural patrols, the thrill and intellectual challenge of working my way through a complicated investigation and having to use all my powers of reasoning and logic to solve it, taking statements, questioning suspects, long nights putting it all together and all the time growing within myself.

At one stage my member in charge, Inspector Morrish, felt I would not make the grade and recommended I be transferred back to Bulawayo. Shortly before the report was published Inspector Morrish left and a new member in charge arrived—his name was Reginald Graham. What a man. Reg taught me what it was to respect someone, not for his position in life but because of who he was. Reg, at six feet two, was slightly taller than me. He was a good-looking man with dark hair, bushy eyebrows and a Scottish accent. When he got angry with me, which initially was quite often, he would yell and I would lose track of what he was saying. He would scream at me and, as he was rounding off, would say "Do you understand?" I would with trembling knees say "Yes, sir!" and hope to God he hadn't given me any instructions. I would then walk outside and ask any of the other P/Os what he had said as the whole station could hear him even with his office door closed. Reg was a firm but fair man. I believe he recognised in me a quality and saw potential that others did not. He would let me have my say and would give me some leeway but only so much. He would however, never let anyone under his command overstep the line—we always knew where we stood with him.

The life of a District cop was special. On your average pre-war day (i.e. pre-1977, when the bush war came to the Filabusi area in earnest), you woke up, had a light breakfast and walked across to the station. The duty P/O attended to all incoming complaints. If Reg did not have something specific for you to do then your case investigations determined where you went. This could involve a trip to the white farming area, an African Purchase Area (APA) or a Tribal Trust Land (TTL). (TTLs were the traditional communal tribal areas, whereas black farmers who'd earned a government 'Master Farmer' certificate could own tenure of plots of fifty to a hundred acres, in an APA. Purchase Area farmers were supplied seeds, crop chemicals and fertilizer by Agritex (Department of

Agricultural Extension) and visited regularly by trained agronomists. In the main these farmers were incredibly hard-working and successful—until of course they became targets of the ZANLA and ZIPRA 'freedom fighters' and the whole scheme sadly disintegrated.)

When we were out on enquiries we would sometimes link up with each other and use the time to swap stories and catch up with each other's investigations. Lunch was eaten on the road and we were normally back at the station by 1700 hours. After hours we might gather at the station pub, have a few drinks with Reg or play a game of tennis or a round of golf at the nearby country club, which was pivotal to our social lives.

For months we waited in eager anticipation for a squash court to be built. When it was finally finished it was officially opened by the club chairman and the first match took place. It soon became apparent at the inaugural match that the players were capable of pulling off shots never before seen on a squash court. The shots were so good that they even deceived the person playing the shot. When it was discovered that the sidewalls of the court were slightly convex the match was abandoned and everyone went off for a drink. The court had to be rebuilt.

Evenings were spent watching TV and on weekends perhaps a trip to Bulawayo or an afternoon playing tennis and the subsequent evening drinking session at the club.

On most Saturday nights and certainly Sunday evenings the P/Os and their girlfriends (if at all) and a dozen or so people of our own age gathered in the single quarters, ate snacks and talked. We talked about everything. We joked, ridiculed each other, boosted someone who was feeling down and in the process built up an unforgettable camaraderie.

Two P/Os, Mike Franklin and Peter Godwin (the now-acclaimed author) were excellent guitar players. Pete and been trained as a classical guitarist and Mike a self-taught folk guitarist. Pete could read music and Mike had the voice.

There was a song that we sometimes caught on the radio, a song by Max Meritt and the Meteors called *Baby I've been watching you*. It was a catchy tune but one of those songs you could never quite put together in your head. Mike and Pete surprised us one day. They were sitting in the lounge when the

DJ announced that he was about to play this particular song. Mike grabbed a pencil and piece of paper and as Pete called out the notes he wrote them down. They then went off to Mike's room and put the song together. That evening, as we were having our normal Sunday-evening session with the usual crowd, Pete and Mike bought out their guitars and started playing. They covered the song absolutely perfectly, with every word and every note in place. I haven't heard the song for years but when I do it takes me right back to those times.

Once in a while a farmer would ask us to come and shoot baboons that had come down from the hills and were destroying his maize crops. This was not a wholly satisfying job but one that needed to be done. Baboons are clever animals. Traps don't work and because they can sense your mood they run off whenever they know you are up to something. To shoot them you infiltrate the area they are raiding and lie in ambush on slightly elevated ground. The males come down from the *kopjes* and when they are sure the coast is clear the rest of the troop follow. Each mealie stalk has two or three cobs on it. Baboons make their way through a field, ripping off a cob, taking a bite out of it and then tossing it away, leaving a trail of wasted maize behind them. When three or four had gathered in one place you took your shot.

Another crop invader was bush pigs. They'd come into a freshly planted land, pick a row and then proceed to vacuum out each and every mealie pip before it had a chance to germinate. Or, when the maize was cobbing, like baboons, they'd come into a land and rip off the immature cobs.

We had a grouchy old farmer, a Mr Levy, who was having trouble with bush pigs which were destroying his maize crops. I was on patrol one day when he asked me to come out and shoot a few.

"Ja, no problem," I said. "I'll come on Saturday."

When he asked me if I had ever shot one I told him "of course I have". The conversation ended with a deep-throated "as long as you understand what you're doing" before I was 'dismissed'.

I hadn't ever shot a bush pig; in fact I didn't even know what they looked like.

I was guessing they were little piglet-like creatures.

I told Reg what I was going to do, expecting him to give me some advice. Reg, in the way of all caring members in charge confronted with a cocky P/O, asked me what sort of weapon I would take. Because I thought I was only going to shoot a couple of piglets and not wanting to go for an 'overkill', I told him I would take an antiquated P1 9mm pistol. The calibre might have been correct but unless you are very, very close to your target a P1 9mm pistol has very limited hitting power. As I am not very accurate with a pistol anyway I needed to get very close to the target. After all, what were a couple of piglets going to do to me? When he asked me if I was going to take anyone with me I said no as I wanted to do this on my own—a real man of the bush in the making. Reg turned away and walked off without a word. Still the penny didn't drop.

I arrived at Mr Levy's house and asked him to take me to where "the bush pigs were last seen". My idea was to pick up their spoor, track them down and then quietly, clinically take them out one by one, much like Dirty Harry.

Mr Levy drove out to the farmlands with me following in my Land Rover. On a muddy dirt road at the edge of a maize field he stopped, alighted and waited. I got out, with an expansive 'let me at 'em' attitude, ready for my vermin-control duty.

"Where is your weapon?" he asked.

"Here," I tapped my holster.

Again, as was his way, he nodded.

"Okay, sir. You can go now; leave this to me. I will sort it out."

But he didn't go. Instead he folded his arms, leaned against his car door and studied me. By now the village idiot would have realized that something was not right. I hadn't. Adopting the posture of a seasoned tracker I commenced a quick search of the area, looking for spoor. I was expecting to find a set of typical cloven-hoof tracks about an inch and a half in diameter. When I found the spoor I knelt down on one knee, again in typical tracker pose, to examine it more closely. As my highly attuned tracker eyes focused on the cloven-hoof tracks I was horrified to find that that they were a lot larger than I'd expected. I looked across to Mr Levy as if to say "What the hell is this!"

But there was no backing down now. The ground was damp and the spoor prints so clear that a blind man could have followed them. I could not back out by saying "unable to track due to lost spoor, will have to come back later" (with a battalion of troops) so I got on with the job.

My problems had only just begun and Mr Levy knew it. I followed the spoor into a thick stand of mealies; pistol held out in front but unlike a real tracker anymore, more like a cheesy version of Don Johnson in *Miami Vice*. The truth is the bush pigs had trampled a path through the mealies for all the world to see. I then heard ominous crunching sounds—if only I had asked someone about these creatures, I would have known that they are vicious, that they have two tusks that curl upward and are razor sharp, that when cornered they come out fighting, charging their enemy, tossing their heads in such a way that their scimitar-like tusks rip to shreds anything they make contact with. They have been known to decimate entire packs of hunting dogs that got too close to them.

A bush pig snorted and emerged from the mealies in a short mock charge. It looked about the size of a baby elephant. I noticed the curved razor-sharp tusks, glinting evilly in the sun, set to tear my quivering body to pieces. My immediate reaction was to run like hell but instead I opened fire in the general direction of the bush pig. While emptying the magazine I heard a single, much louder shot from behind me as the pig dropped. I looked around and I saw Mr Levy standing at my shoulder, lowering a .308 rifle. I hadn't even noticed he was there. It was his single shot that had killed the bush pig.

Without a word he moved in front of me and I followed. As he stood over the pig he quietly started talking about them, their habits, their habitats, their nature and the like.

I looked at the pig and realized that I had just learned another valuable lesson—I didn't know it all, and this man, rather than chastising me, had instead taken time out to educate me.

This fine man, who had done so much for the upliftment of the area, was killed in a terrorist ambush three years later on the Shabani road, along with Dick Kenny, a local mine owner.

Chapter nine

Rural life

Because I was now stationed in rural Matebeleland one of the things I needed to do was learn the local language—Ndebele, or more correctly, isiNdebele. There was no question of going off and attending language courses. My member in charge's solution was to send me on a two-week rural patrol with an elderly constable who was a few months away from retirement. Constable Noah was instructed not to speak a word of English to me and all communication between us was to be in Ndebele. I thought it was a novel idea but did not seriously expect it to progress much further than a few attempts interspersed with a few laughs before reverting to English. However, a two-week rural patrol is all about communication—with chiefs and kraal heads, talking to the locals, following up investigations, attending to scenes—generally one large public-relations exercise. And it wasn't only about learning to speak the language. In order to communicate with the tribesmen I had to learn the processes involved in greetings, the customs associated with eating, the different dialects and specific mannerisms of each area.

Although I'd grown up in Rhodesia I'd only ever lived in large towns and had never had anything to do with rural tribespeople. In the cities and suburban areas the Africans learned our ways; in the rural areas we had to learn theirs. No matter how well you knew someone, or how urgent was your enquiry, when you met him in his kraal you had to follow a well-defined etiquette. The conversation would start with a greeting, a shake of hands and you would then be invited to sit. You would ask after the man's wives, the state of his crops, how were his cattle and goats, and then, pause. Only then, when he asked you a question, were you given the go-ahead to ask the questions you wanted. If you tried to bypass this protocol the person you were talking to would stop and a blank look would come over his face. The best you could do was to offer your most profuse apologies and take your leave, promising to come back another time.

I made a half-hearted attempt to learn the language. Realizing I was not making much progress I tried introducing a bit of humour. Constable Noah would have none of it and rebuffed me. I sulked and decided that if I didn't talk to Noah he would soon have to talk to me—in English. Again, that didn't work. Noah took his task very seriously. One of us would soon give in and start speaking the other's language and it was certainly not going to be Noah. I realized that I'd better start listening and I did. In a very short time I was able to understand the meaning of several single words, and then began to associate them with other words. Monosyllabic conversations with Noah progressed when I began putting a couple of words together which surprisingly developed into short sentences. When Noah noted that I was genuinely interested and trying my best he started conversing with me. In two weeks I was able to hold a basic conversation in Ndebele and began to understand their tribal ways. It grew from there and within a year I was a fluent Ndebele speaker. But during that trip, I listened and observed—keenly. It stood me in good stead.

The Filabusi police area, and therefore my patrol area, was over three thousand square kilometres. It consisted of two Tribal Trust Lands, Sibasa and Avoca; two African Purchase Areas, Godhlwayo and Gwatemba; numerous commercial (i.e. white-owned) cattle ranches; a large asbestos mine at Pangani and a thriving nickel mine, Epoch Mine. There were numerous small gold mines, scheelite (a tungsten ore) mines and other small diggings.

The Tribal Trust Lands were the traditional communal lands. Each TTL was presided over by a chief, after whom the TTL was normally named—e.g. Chief Sibasa and Chief Avoca. Answerable to the chiefs were *indunas*, or kraal heads, who presided over the kraal lines. A kraal line consisted of two or three hundred kraals, each kraal being a small village comprising of a dozen or so round, thatched, pole and *dagga* huts (wattle and daub). Aside from the huts each village kept a few cows (*mombes*), goats and sheep for milk or meat, a variety of poultry and cultivated a couple of acres of crops—maize, sorghum, millet and vegetables. The harvested maize was kept in granaries in the village and ground by pestle and mortar to make mealie meal (*sadza*)—the staple diet in most of Africa. Sorghum and millet were used for the brewing of traditional beer.

The chickens were a breed apart. When I was on rural patrol I used to take with me an old three-legged cast-iron pot—a *potjie* (Afrikaans for a little pot). Sooner or later the need for fresh meat would overcome us and my constable and I would agree that the time had come to catch and slaughter a chicken. The chicken's family strata comprised a bunch of tatty old hens serviced by one cockerel. These were wily old creatures that could run the legs off a cheetah. They were forever running backward and forward, going nowhere really.

After lengthy commercial negotiations with the village headman, he'd grant his permission for us to catch one chicken—but it had to be a cockerel. When I spotted the one I wanted the game was on. We would leap from the Land Rover and for some insane reason keep calling the fowl as if it would ever understand us—they also appeared to know that if caught they'd end up in the pot. Eventually, after running ourselves to a standstill one of us would finally rugby-tackle the chicken, smother it and swiftly break its neck. That was the easy part.

These creatures were as tough as old rope and much culinary preparation was needed. That night I would light a fire, fill the pot with water and add my herbs and spices (basil, paprika, a dash of salt and pepper), onions and carrots. The gutted chicken was cut into portions, put in the pot and the water brought to a gentle simmer, which was maintained for eight to ten hours with the cook continually topping up the herbs and water level. Any less and you ended up eating chicken with the texture of old car tyres and tasting a lot worse. When I eventually sat down to my meal I was always aware of other chickens moving about, scraping away the loose soil with their feet for grubs or seeds. I always felt I was being censured for eating their local stud. It was uncanny.

Scattered around the kraal were scrawny mongrels that would run away with their tails between their legs whenever you came near them. They lived off scraps and were used as playthings by the *piccanins*. (I use the word '*piccanin*' in its original inoffensive form. Derived from the Portugese *pequeno*, meaning 'small', it filtered into most southern Bantu languages during the late nineteenth century with the development of the Witwatersrand goldfields and the resultant migrant labour influx from all over central and southern Africa.)

The sheep were the biggest nuisance in that they would wander into the centre of the road and simply stand there, unmoving. I would come screaming around a corner in a cloud of dust, see the flock at the last second, frantically brake, skid twenty or thirty metres, come to a halt and find myself surrounded by sheep all baa-ing and bleating as if I had done something wrong and giving me a piece of their mind. It'd take forever to get them off the road so I could pass. I think they were a lot cleverer than they made out. Occasionally, from sheer frustration, I would try and run one over but I never could. I think this was due to the fact that because they were so idle they stored up their energy for when danger was imminent and could escape like a turbo-charged rocket.

The rural African's chief mode of transport was a donkey-drawn scotch cart. Generally the animals were well looked after but if there were any abuse the culprit would be reported to his *induna* and be punished accordingly. A scotch cart could carry a good load, which later proved to be to their disadvantage when terrorists started laying landmines in the road. Although meant for security-force vehicles the scotch carts would detonate the mines with messy and tragic consequences.

The chiefs commanded a great deal of respect and, out of respect for them, your first visit to a TTL was to the chief. The chief presided over tribal courts which dealt mostly with domestic issues and acted not only as a means for ensuring peace and stability within his area, but also as a forum for solving domestic disputes and dealing with anything from the theft of chickens to marital and spiritual affairs. Cases went to the tribal courts on the recommendation of the kraal head who had a role similar to, but not anywhere near as senior as, the chief.

Among tribal folk and especially the chiefs and kraal heads there were formalities that had to be observed before any form of business discussion could take place. I would arrive at the chief's kraal, alight from my Land Rover and wait until a 'chief's messenger' approached me and invited me into the kraal. He would then escort me to the hut in which the chief lived. As I approached the chief would exit his hut and extend his hand in greeting. We would shake hands; I would tell him who I was and ask if we could speak. He would nod his assent and invite me into his hut.

Once seated I would ask the chief about the welfare of his wives, his crop, his cattle and probably discuss the recent rains. One of the chief's wives would then approach, head bowed in deference, proffering a bowl of food. This usually consisted of cold *sadza*, sour goat's milk and a leaf of rape. It wasn't a great combination as far as a typical Western diet goes as the *sadza* was cold and tasted bland, the milk was sour and the rape leaf bitter. But to refuse would have been considered a sign of disrespect. The sweet tea that was served with the meal did, however, make it easier on the palate.

The chief and I would eat in silence with the only words emanating from me as I complimented him on the meal. When the meal was finished the chief would look at me in silence and indicate that we could talk about the matters I had come to discuss. Virtually anything could be put on the table except politics as the chiefs were in every way apolitical and matters of state were of no concern to them. Before leaving I would thank the chief for his time, wish him well and promise to attend to any matters he had raised.

The chief's messenger was a man appointed by the chief to carry messages, either verbal or written, to kraal heads, the District Commissioner, the police and others. They were usually elderly gentlemen who took their work very seriously.

Quite often a kraal head would arrest someone and the chief would task his messenger with taking the suspect to the nearest police station. The person arrested could be anyone from a petty thief to an armed terrorist. The villain's hands would be tightly bound with the handcuffs the police had given to the chief and he would be escorted by rural bus to the station. The only weapon the messenger carried was a knobkerrie and God help the villain should he try to escape—he'd be given a sound thrashing. The wily old messengers were as tough as anyone half their age and would not tolerate any form of disrespect towards them or the chief.

Within the TTLs were small business centres (BCs). A typical business centre would comprise half a dozen or so single-roomed shops that sold cooking oil, boiled sweets, mealie meal, tinned goods, cheap ballpoint pens, notepads, cheap shirts and warm Cokes and Fantas. There would also usually be a bicycle-repair shop and a butchery. The word 'butchery' is stretching the definition somewhat. On entering the BC you could not fail to miss the butchery. Typically it was a single room with a corrugated-iron roof and a door covered with wire mesh to keep the flies at bay—theoretically. Entering the butchery the smell hit you like a punch in the throat. Hanging from wooden poles would be the carcass of a freshly slaughtered cow or goat with flies swarming all over it. You chose the portion you wanted and paid 25c a pound with no fat. I loved it. My favourite meal, a great delicacy, was rump steak fried with onions, baked beans and chicken-flavoured Tastic Rice (imported from South Africa, so not freely available).

On the border of the TTL and APA, on the main road running from Belingwe to the town of Colleen Bawn lived a wonderful old man called Bekezela. He was well into his eighties and completely blind. Like most blind folk he had a stick, in his case a big thick stick that he would wave about in front of him much like an ant's antenna so that he could 'see' where he was going. In his youth he had been one of Cecil John Rhodes's herd boys. Bekezela owned a butchery—only this one was high class in that it had a counter. Sure it was stained with blood and animal fat but it did have a strip of metal trim along the front that made it look quite flash. I used to help him out by slaughtering cows for him. All it took was one round from my 9mm pistol.

Bekezela lived in a round hut made of brick and cement. There was very little furniture inside. When he heard my Land Rover he would send one of his sons over to greet me and I would be escorted to his hut. As I entered the hut Bekezela would roar with pleasure at my presence and start waving his pole about like a madman in order to find me, thrashing it about in all directions. The more I tried to stay out of his way the more frantic the waving became and sooner or later it would hit me with a loud, solid *thwack* which for him indicated where I was standing. He would then hit me a few more times just to make sure

I was there. Half-winded I would reach out and shake his outstretched hand. He would then sit down, order me to sit down, bark orders at his sons to bring tea and say "Tell me, tell me, and tell me." Memories I have now are of a dimly lit room, the only light coming from the natural light that squeezed through the doorway and the thatched roof. The acrid smell of smoke generated by a small oven fire permeated the walls and combined with the smell of damp straw to create a rather pleasant odour.

In this hut we would sit and talk for hours. Our conversation would range from the condition of his cattle to news of travellers who had stopped at his butchery to buy meat. We would speak of how the rains had caused the water level in the nearby dam to rise and flow over the dam wall causing the Umzingwane River to start flowing with increasing speed.

This meant trouble for the tribal folk who lived further downstream as their only means of crossing the Umzingwane was via a ferry. By a 'ferry' I do not mean anything terribly elaborate. It consisted of a raft made up of metal plates welded to 44-gallon drums. A half-inch steel cable was slung across the river from one bank to the other and secured at waist height on metal posts. To get across you drove onto the ferry—very carefully as any sudden movement would cause it to move away from the front wheels and you'd end up nose-first in the river. The next step was to grip the metal rope and slowly pull the raft across. Disembarking was equally hazardous as any jerky movement of the vehicle would cause the raft too shoot backwards back into the river and leave the rear end of the vehicle stuck in the mud.

Most rural folk had never left the remote area of their immediate homes. While on patrol in the southernmost corner of Filabusi I once followed a road which soon deteriorated into path before petering out altogether. Ahead was bush so my only option was to engage four-wheel drive on the Land Rover and 'bundu-bash' until I came to something that resembled a track.

I noticed a kraal in some open ground and drove towards it. As I approached, terrified teenagers and younger children started running away into the bush, screaming. My first thought was that terrorists were in the kraal. As it turned out there weren't any terrorists; it was my Land Rover. The youngsters had never seen a vehicle in their lives and the sight of one had scared them half to death.

"How can they be so scared? It's just a car?" I asked my sergeant.

"Well, how would white children in the cities react if a bull came into their kitchen?" he replied dryly.

African folklore is full of rich animal tales. Growing up in the suburbs with black maids and gardeners, we as white children came to learn many of these wonderful stories.

When I was out on patrol I would ask the constable or sergeant with me to recount their tribal histories. I loved the way they were told. Africans are great raconteurs and tell a story in such a way that the narration is filled with theatrical histrionics. The hand movements that describe the terrain where the animal lives or the strutting limb movements describing how a *leguaan* (monitor lizard) walks are simply delightful. And then there are the sounds— the throaty roar of a lion, the staccato *chuk, chuk, chuk* of a Guinea fowl, the plaintive screech of a fish eagle or the snorted warning call of a startled impala. (In time I was to pass these stories onto my children—it was a marvellous way to teach them about wildlife.)

One story goes that God had decided to let everyone live. He sent the chameleon to tell the people but being very slow the chameleon took too long to deliver the message and everyone died. The Ndebele people therefore consider the chameleon to be an unlucky and untrustworthy animal which they go to extraordinary lengths to avoid.

Witches and sorcerers are thought to ride hyenas and can even turn into one. To see an owl during the day brings bad luck and seeing an owl perched in one position for a great length of time means death is close at hand—not unlike Native American beliefs.

Getting to know these stories was useful because it helped me understand the Africans. Fobbing them off as fairy tales would have been a sign of great disrespect which would have only alienated the very people I was trying to get close to.

Tourists spend a lot of money on African carvings. But the carvings, exquisitely shaped from *mopane, mukwa* or leadwood, are themselves symbolic of a rich African folklore. African women are expert weavers and make the most beautiful beadwork and colourful fabrics. I am forever blessed that I witnessed first-hand such a wonderfully diverse and creative culture.

Vast commercial cattle ranches fell under my jurisdiction. The ranch owners and managers were a mixed bunch. While on patrol they would welcome you, give you something to eat and let you sleep in a barn or one of the outbuildings. I spent one memorable night sleeping in an old butchery filled with rats that spent the entire night crawling all over me and trying to get in to my backpack.

Some of the farmers were cantankerous old folk—people like Jack Rush who was the patriarch of the area. He would not lower himself to speak to anyone but the member in charge. If you dared arrive without paying him the respect he felt was his due then he would raise merry hell and chase you off his ranch. We got to know these people, their mannerisms and idiosyncrasies, and always had plenty to gossip about back at the station.

The farmers' children didn't spend much time on the farm because they were usually away at boarding school or university. When they came home during the holidays was the time all the single cops eagerly went off on patrol. A young cop arriving at a farmhouse would usually be greeted by the farmer, with his daughters standing in the background, eagerly watching to see which of the young bucks was visiting. The idea was to get the greeting over with, hope you were asked to join them for dinner and then impress the heck out of the girls by relating your impressive 'bush stories' and telling them about all the villains you had arrested. From then on the way things developed were in the hands of the gods. We all used to come back from patrol with exaggerated stories of our conquests.

Also on 'my beat' were several mines—Pangani Mine, one of the biggest, was an old asbestos mine comprising some six hundred workers, black and white, who lived in their own mine compound. The other big mine in the area, Epoch Mine, was a relatively new mine whose employees were housed in Filabusi.

There were a lot of smaller mines in the area—mostly gold, some scheelite and an assortment of other metals. Every so often I would see a miner in the post office taking out an old handkerchief containing a small conical piece of refined gold—the result of a month's hard work which had safely been squirreled away until his next visit 'to town'.

The most successful mine was a scheelite (calcium tungstate, used as a metal hardener) mine owned by John Tulley. John had trained as a sign-writer in the UK before immigrating to Rhodesia to seek his fortune. He'd wandered into Filabusi with nothing more than a small bag of clothes. As to why he chose Filabusi, well, no one quite knows. He found a job on a small gold mine but soon the ore ran out. The owner decided to sell so John made an offer and bought it for a few dollars. He spent his days sifting through the dumps trying to extract what gold he could. One day a mines inspector came visiting and decided to help John by sending a sample from the dump off for assaying. It turned it there was no gold but plenty of scheelite. John had never heard of the stuff but following the inspector's advice he began processing the dumps and, with demand for scheelite climbing rapidly, John had soon made his fortune. However, he recklessly spent his money on cars, booze and women, one of whom he married and who in no time took him to the cleaners. John lost everything and, as suddenly as he had arrived with a small bag of clothing, he left, never to be seen again.

I was called to a 'sudden death' that had occurred underground at Epoch Mine. As policemen we were not allowed to go underground; it was left to the miners to retrieve the body so we could take statements from everyone involved and put a docket together. In the mine, ore was collected and put in to a coco pan (an open-carriage bin that runs on tracks) which was then manhandled until positioned over a vertical shaft. A miner would then pull on a lever at the bottom of the coco pan, which would tilt the coco pan and empty the contents into the shaft below. The lever was spring-loaded and it was critical the operator released it as soon as he'd activated the mechanism. In this case, the miner forgot to let go of the lever and was catapulted into the shaft below, crushed to death by tons of ore.

While waiting for the body to be retrieved, I took a walk around the mine. At the workshops I saw a welder at work, so ambled over to see what he was doing. We struck up a conversation and, as I'd never welded before, he asked if I'd like to give it a go, an offer I enthusiastically accepted. It was fascinating work and after ten minutes or so of welding I felt I had the knack. The only thing—I wasn't wearing welding goggles.

The body was eventually brought to the surface, so I took the necessary statements and returned to Filabusi. Shortly after I'd arrived my eyes started stinging; it felt like someone had thrown sand into them. The pain was excruciating and before I knew it I was unable to see—I thought I'd gone blind. One of the P/Os took me to the local hospital where the doctor quickly diagnosed a case of 'arc eye'. He gave me some eye drops and painkillers, instructing me to lie on my bed in the dark until the pain subsided.

I should have gone back to the mine workshop and given that welder a fat *klap* (slap). Instead I bided my time and much later I arrested the mine captain (who disliked me and had set the whole welding thing up) and detained him overnight for a relatively minor charge that carried a small fine.

The war hadn't yet reached Filabusi so the only weapon I needed to carry was a 9mm pistol. I barely considered using this for any reason other than shooting a rabid or badly injured animal. Rabies was rife throughout the country. As a result, if an animal were even suspected of being rabid it was shot immediately, burned and buried on the spot. I had a very disturbing experience when I received a report to the effect that a rabid jackal had been bothering people in a nearby kraal. When I got to the kraal I went looking for the jackal and saw it coming out of some low scrub. Instead of running off it saw me and started walking towards me. This was unusual in that a wild animal will run off before you get anywhere near it, but this jackal kept coming towards me, completely unafraid. To my mind this made no sense at all so I hesitated and it kept coming at me as if in a trance. By the time I pulled the trigger and shot it, it was but two or three paces from me.

Chapter ten

The murder of the Viljoens

My favourite time of the day was dusk—that time of the day when everything started to quieten down. As I headed back to my camp I would see the cattle being herded into the cattle kraals and hear the dull *clunk clunk* of the cowbells. Chickens would disappear to roost, goats and sheep would amble off to their resting places and everyone would settle down for the night. As the sun settled below the horizon smoke fires would be seen flickering as locals prepared their evening meal.

It was a great life but then it all changed rapidly and dramatically one Sunday morning in late 1976 when the bush war finally came to Filabusi.

I was Duty Patrol Officer and was sitting reading my Sunday newspaper when the telephone in the single-quarters lounge rang. I answered it and the breathless caller, in a clearly distressed voice, blustered, "You must get to the farm; there is trouble at the farm." He was not making any sense. Much as I tried I was getting nowhere in trying to understand him.

"The Viljoens have been attacked!" he eventually blurted out.

The Viljoens were an Afrikaans husband-and-wife farming team, well into their fifties, who ran a successful cattle ranch about forty kilometres north of Filabusi. They were a friendly couple that the P/Os used to make a point of visiting whenever they were on a rural farming patrol. For a tired and thirsty policeman you were guaranteed a sumptuous lunch—as much as you could eat and drink—and friendly conversation. If you so wished there was always a room set aside for you for the night. In the wonderful way of the Afrikaner nothing was too much trouble. Regardless of how warm it was there would be a thick duvet on the bed, a ceramic wash bowl on the dresser with a towel, a fresh bar of soap, a jug of cold water and of course a Bible, placed next to the bedside lamp.

The Viljoens ran a prosperous farm. The homestead consisted of a large, whitewashed farmhouse with an immaculately kept lawn in front that rolled down to a barrage of riotous flowerbeds. At the back of the house were orchards of peach and plum trees that in spite of the shortage of rain always seemed to bear fruit. I never left the house without first being given a large plastic bag laden with ripe plums and peaches.

The Viljoens had generously allowed a prospector by the name of Tommy Thompson to run a goldmine across the road from their house. The mine, which had started life as nothing more than wishful thinking, now prospered and consisted of five buildings and a four-stamp mill discreetly hidden from view behind some large gum trees. Included among the buildings were a one-roomed, face-brick building that housed the copper trays and mercury used to extract the gold; a run-down galvanized-iron shack that was used as a magazine for the explosives; a small, windowless room with a wooden door that was effectively Tommy's house and, finally, a solid whitewashed-brick building that Tommy used as his office and security room. In it he stored the gold he had laboriously extracted. The door was made of sheet metal braised onto iron bars. The barred windows were set in concrete and covered with plastic sheeting to prevent nosy intruders looking in.

Tommy had a phone in his office. It was here where he spent most of his time—his own private little haven.

I had met Tommy a few times. From years of prospecting in the harsh Rhodesian sun he had developed a mottled-brown complexion. His skin looked like badly tanned leather, a typical 'Rhodesian tan', much admired by visitors from overseas and much vilified by local dermatologists. Tommy was a bachelor and a loner who jealously guarded his privacy. If he so chose to give you anything more than a cursory nod he would invite you into his office for a cup of tea and a chat, but you needed to be concise and to the point—idle chatter was neither wanted nor appreciated.

In his own way Tommy did try to be congenial but you had to respect his space and not overstay your welcome. I liked Tommy. In his own way he was a gentle soul with a heart of gold—he was a kind man who got on well with the Viljoens and that was good enough for me.

I hung up the phone and yelled to two other patrol officers, Keith and Paul, to call the member in charge, Reg. We drew our rifles, donned our webbing and sped off in two Land Rovers—Keith and me in one and Reg and Paul in the other.

The road to the farm wound its way through commercial farms and ranches. At any one of a hundred places we could have been ambushed or have hit a landmine but we were inexperienced in matters of war and such things did not even occur to us. (At least we were now well armed with FN rifles and plenty of spare ammunition.)

The final stretch of road led past Tommy's mine, situated to our left in thick bush among the gum trees. As we drew level with the mine the entrance to the homestead came into view.

It took a few seconds to register what I was looking at. Eighty or so metres in front of us the Viljoens were lying in front of their silver Mercedes Benz, clearly dead. Keith braked and as we came to a stop I heard a gunshot coming from the direction of Tommy's mine. I left the others and ran the short distance to the mine. As I sprinted through the gum trees I saw Tommy lying on the ground and, just beyond him, running away, were what I presumed to be three terrorists who soon disappeared into the thick bush.

I never fired a shot. I was a policeman, not a soldier and my only concern was for Tommy's safety so I ran over to him. He was lying on his left side, the soil beneath him the reddish-browny colour of dried blood. He had a look of surprise on his face as he stared up at me—much like he had just woken up from a deep sleep and was trying to gather his senses. Empty gin, brandy and beer bottles lay scattered around him. When he registered who I was he said, "The terrs are a useless bunch of *munts*." It was if I had just walked into his office and we were having one of our chats. He did not appear to be in any way distressed so I let him continue talking while I did a three-sixty-degree search of the immediate vicinity until I was satisfied the area was secure.

I was on my own with Tommy. I knelt down next to him and saw that the lower front of his shirt was torn with damp red blood on the edges of the tear. While he continued talking I lifted up his shirt and saw that he had been shot in the lower right side of his abdomen … with his intestines bulging out through the wound.

"Tommy you have been shot," I said to him, not knowing what else to say.

"Oh, have I?" He looked at me and as if somewhat surprised.

There was very little blood and no visible bleeding so I covered the wound with a field dressing to prevent further infection and to protect the exposed intestine. I saw an empty explosive box nearby, grabbed it, propped his back up against it and straightened his shirt.

I did not know it at the time but I was watching a man die.

For a short while our talk consisted of two or three phrases but very quickly the words started to flow. Tommy was telling me what had happened. As he spoke he began to slur and there were moments of silence when it seemed as if he were pausing to gather his thoughts.

Sure, he had a gunshot wound to his gut but I just knew that something else was not right. I had done a brief preliminary examination of Tommy and aside from the gunshot wound could not find any broken bones or sign of any other wound.

I did another, more thorough examination. This time, as I ran my hand beneath his shorts in the area of his upper right thigh, I felt a wet patch. When I removed my hand I noticed my fingers were bloodied. I pulled up the leg of the shorts and noticed a few drops of blood and a small, dark bullet hole. It looked so innocuous.

I managed to piece together what had happened.

Tommy had heard the sound of gunfire as the Viljoens were being attacked. He rushed to the edge of his property, saw what was happening and then fled into his office, locking the door and hiding under his desk. When the terrorists had done with murdering and butchering the Viljoens they sauntered across to the mine.

"Tommy, Tommy, where are you?" they called out as they approached the office.

Tommy, in an absolute blind panic, picked up the phone and rang exchange. They in turn got the message to us which was the call I had taken.

The phones of those days gave a short ring every time the handset was lifted or replaced. So when making the call, Tommy had inadvertently sealed his fate as the terrorists heard the ring and knew where he was hiding.

The terrorists started banging on the door demanding that Tommy open it. Unfortunately it was not as secure as he thought. With a quick burst of fire from an AK-47 they shot away the padlock, kicked down the flimsy door and dragged Tommy outside from under the desk. By now he was paralyzed with fear and incapable of running away or fighting it out.

One of the terrorists then shot the Tommy in the stomach ... deliberately so. They were in no hurry and knew we were at best forty minutes away. As Tommy lay writhing on the ground they took bottles of brandy, gin and beer from his quarters and, taunting him all the while, began their drinking spree. They then heard the sound of our vehicles approaching.

One of the terrorists then calmly walked over to Tommy, pulled up his trouser leg, drew his Tokarev pistol and, at point-blank range, shot him. The round entered his right leg at the hip, went up through his stomach and came to rest in his left kidney, destroying everything in its path.

The gunshot was intended to be painful and fatal. It proved to be both—a merciless act done clinically and in such a way that the wound would not be noticed at first glance.

I could do nothing for Tommy other than comfort and support him. I watched him die. The pauses between his sentences became longer. I responded as best I could with anything that came to mind. He vacillated between extreme anger and inconsolable sadness. He spoke of the futility of life and I empathized with him. He became angry again, vehemently cursing me. Such outbursts of energy seemed to be a positive sign so I encouraged him to keep going. He then quietened down, interspersed only with occasional bursts of a few words, nonsensical and meaningless.

I was absolutely transfixed.

His eyes began to open and close, again and again, and then he would stop breathing for up to half a minute or longer. Just when I thought he would breathe no more he would take another deep breath ... and so it went—his eyes opening and closing, opening and closing. I do not know for how long this continued.

In spite of all the trauma and pain he had endured he now appeared peaceful, so much at rest. Then, with a start, he opened his eyes and stared at me with a look of surprise on his face. Just as I thought he was about to say something he closed his eyes, inhaled deeply and then slowly exhaled—much as he had been doing for the last few minutes.

I waited expectantly for another breath but none came.

I sat there looking at Tommy, unable to fully comprehend what had just happened. I could not detect any breathing, neither chest movement nor body movement so I reached across and felt his wrist for a pulse. I couldn't feel one so tried for a pulse in his neck. Still nothing. It slowly dawned on me that Tommy had died. I was very much aware that I had been with him as his life force, his soul, had flowed from his body and entered the ether.

It was only when I stood up that Keith arrived. I do not believe this was a coincidence. I had been put with Tommy during his death for a reason. I have talked with doctors, nurses, policemen and hospice counsellors, all manner of people, who are associated with dying and death and they all agree that no matter how much pain and suffering a person is experiencing, the moment immediately before death is one of peace and tranquillity. The passing from life on Earth to the Afterlife is not traumatic. It is a peaceful, perhaps blissful, experience. I have seen it many times.

An air force helicopter arrived and troops from the Rhodesian African Rifles (RAR) disembarked, did a sweep of the area and commenced a follow-up operation (which was unsuccessful).

I left others to deal with Tommy's body and went back to the site of the Viljoen ambush.

The terrorists had set up the ambush at a cattle grid at the end of the Viljoen's driveway, and waited, hidden from view in waist-high bush. As the Viljoens approached the grid they slowed down and the terrorists opened fire on the unarmed, defenceless couple. Critically wounded, they were dragged from the car and bayoneted to death.

Such is the ideology and *modus operandi* of terrorism, then as now.

The bodies of Mr and Mrs Viljoen, grotesquely distorted, almost hideously obscene, were a macabre warning that the war had indeed come to Filabusi.

Chapter eleven

Ground Coverage, Fireforce and RLI *skelms*

The murder of the Viljoens was a clear indication that terrorists had been operating in the Filabusi area for some time. In spite of the fact that rural patrols were carried out on a regular basis neither we nor Special Branch had picked up that terrorists had infiltrated the area. To say it was cause for concern would be an understatement. The fact was something had to be done … and fast. The solution was to form an intelligence-gathering unit.

As things stood the primary sources of information-gathering were Internal Affairs (Intaf) and the BSAP. Internal Affairs was a government department which took care of all domestic affairs. Internal Affairs officers were in constant contact with locals and arranged everything from marriage licences to cattle-dipping. The District Commissioner who oversaw the whole operation in each area ran his own district court which dealt with minor civil cases. The information sought and gained was focused on domestic affairs, crime and general community awareness. If a criminal from an outlying area wandered into our area and we found out about it then we reckoned we had done our job as this was all that was asked of us.

Special Branch (SB), an autonomous branch of the BSAP, was the primary internal intelligence-gathering organization in the country, but specialized more in military and political matters. Ground Coverage (GC) was therefore formed to gather intelligence from the locals—on the ground in the rural areas so to speak. We referred to this as 'grass roots' intelligence. In each police area, where warranted, a Ground Coverage unit was established. The GC unit came under the logistical control of the member in charge of that particular area and the operational control of a Special Branch co-ordinator based either in the area, or at the nearest JOC (Joint Operational Command centre). The member in charge ensured that leave, pay and pension were taken care of, and that transport and standard equipment such as radios, rations, bedding and so on were supplied. The SB co-ordinator oversaw the operational functions of the unit. He briefed and debriefed the operators and assisted with the supply of operational requirements such as weaponry, support troops and Special Forces reconnaissance units. He was effectively the liaison man with the army and the air force.

Very soon after the Viljoen murders Reg decided to form a GC unit. The P/O who was initially appointed to run it only lasted a couple of weeks and much to my surprise Reg called me in to his office and told me that I had 'volunteered' to run it. My official title became 'Ground Coverage Co-ordinator Filabusi'.

Four new GC co-ordinators were appointed in Filabusi and the surrounding areas—Alpha, Bravo, Charlie and Delta. As each co-ordinator was known as a 'scouter' my call sign became 'Scouter Delta'. Every police station had a coded radio call sign. Filabusi was known as 307.

I couldn't have had a better mentor as, prior to his Filabusi appointment, Reg had been the GC co-ordinator for the Wankie area in the northwest of the country and had an excellent track record. I am not quite sure why I got the appointment. I have said that Reg saw something in me that others didn't so this might have had something to do with it. I suspect, though, it was more because I was the scruffiest Uniform Branch man he had ever encountered, that I was something of a loner and a complete non-conformist and that he had to find a place for me.

One of the first points I need to stress is that GC was not considered a Special Forces unit. The two primary Special Forces units in Rhodesia were C Squadron Special Air Service (SAS) and the Selous Scout Regiment, with the Rhodesian Light Infantry (RLI) being appointed the third in 1978. The role of the SAS was to conduct close-in reconnaissance in neighbouring Zambia, Mozambique and Botswana, and carry out attacks on external ZANLA and ZIPRA terrorist bases. The role of the Selous Scouts was a) to undertake pseudo-terrorism in order to infiltrate terrorists groups operating within the country and b) the manning of clandestine observation posts (OPs). Once a terrorist group was identified, the Scouts would call in 'Fireforce' (see explanation following) to contact and eliminate the terrorists. (Selous Scouts also fulfilled a similar role to that of the SAS in external operations.)

Although my brother and father-in-law were in the Rhodesian SAS I never had the fortune to work with this unit but as a GC operator I worked closely with the Scouts. There were other units that played prominent roles. Among those I worked with were the Rhodesian African Rifles and the Rhodesian Light Infantry, both specialist airborne units in the primary Fireforce role. Both had similar roles, the difference being that the RAR was made up of black soldiers (with white officers) and the RLI only white soldiers.

Rhodesia was divided into several operational areas, which are shown on the map in the front of the book. Filabusi fell under the Operation *Tangent* area, which covered the western portion of the country.

A Joint Operational Command (JOC) oversaw the movements of all troops in these areas and was commanded on a rotational basis by a senior army or air force officer, with a senior Special Branch liaison officer *in situ*. The objective was to have one Fireforce unit based at every JOC headquarters but in reality deployments were restricted as the Rhodesian Air Force (RhAF) had a limited number of aircraft. There were only so much to go around and as the war escalated the RhAF was hard-pressed to supply enough aircraft for Fireforce needs. 'Fireforce' was a term originally coined by RLI officers in the early 1970s during Operation *Hurricane* in the northeast of the country when it became apparent that traditional methods of closing with the enemy—e.g. tracking, ambushing, follow-ups etc.—were simply not working as they had in the earlier days of the bush war in the sparsely populated Zambezi valley; the guerrillas were now mixing with the *povo*, the local peasants, in the heavily populated TTLs. In essence, Fireforce was quite simply an airborne force comprising aircraft and troops, on twenty-four-hour standby to rapidly react to an enemy sighting. A typical Fireforce comprised ground troops (normally RLI or RAR) who were deployed by troop-carrying Alouette III (and latterly Bell 'Hueys') helicopters or by parachute from ageing DC-3 Dakotas. The troop-carrying helicopters, known as 'G-cars' (G for 'gunship'), carried a 'stick' of four troops and were crewed by a pilot and gunner-technician who manned twin Browning or MAG 7.62mm machine guns mounted on the left-hand side of the helicopter.

When Fireforce was called out the ground troops would emplane and take off. On the way to the 'scene' (the contact area) the Fireforce commander, normally an army major, would contact the call sign on the ground that had initiated the call-out, assess the situation and develop his plan of attack. The Fireforce commander travelled in an Alouette III helicopter called the 'K-car' (K for 'killer') armed with a 20mm Hispano cannon mounted on the left-hand side of the helicopter. The Fireforce commander sat next to the pilot, but facing backwards, to direct the G-cars and his ground troops.

On arrival at the contact area the K-car would go into a left-hand, or anticlockwise, orbit, and open up with the 20mm cannon, which generally signified the commencement of the action. G-cars would land and disgorge their sticks and take off, either to return to base to collect more troops, or remain in the area to offer air support as the commander saw fit. Once the heli-borne troops had been deployed the Dakota would commence its run-in to drop the paras, and as far as possible the terrorists would now be encircled, thus completing what the Fireforce commander hoped was a total envelopment of the enemy—vertical and horizontal.

In support, was a 'Lynx', a Rheims-Cessna 'push-pull' ground-attack aircraft armed with phosphorus rockets, pods of 'Frantan' (napalm) and machine guns, which was on call for air strikes against the enemy as directed by the Fireforce commander. In extreme cases, Hawker Hunter and Vampire fighter jets and Canberra bombers, out of Thornhill air base at Gwelo, were used to soften up any tiresome enemy resistance. As a GC operator I called in many air strikes and used Fireforce on numerous occasions. Every single time I knew that without fail I was getting the best of the best. These guys, air force and army, delivered the goods every time.

The RLI Fireforce soldiers, or 'troopies', were characterized by the fact that their combat gear consisted of green T-shirts, shorts and *veldskoene* (lit: bush shoes in Afrikaans) or Super-pros (black 'takkies' or sneakers). Like the RAR they were fearless fighters who worked hard and played hard. The average age of an RLI trooper was around eighteen or nineteen.

The records show that the RLI were great soldiers and much has been written about their exploits. But there was another side to them—their sense of humour and wild behaviour, which were no more apparent than when they went on R & R. Two of my favourite stories come to mind:

The troopies used to make a point of baiting the cops in Bulawayo and Salisbury and there was no better target than a cop in a patrol car. Typically, a couple of RLI *skelms* (rogues) would be cruising around Salisbury, see a patrol car, drive up to it and display a middle digit. The patrol-car driver would always take the bait, give chase and inevitably lose them.

On this particular occasion the car was an old blue Anglia Prefect—the model almost square in design but very popular with younger people as, like the Cortina and Datsun, it was affordable. The incident happened in the middle of Salisbury when the driver of the Anglia saw a patrol car stationary at a traffic intersection waiting for the lights to turn green. He pulled up next to the patrol car, gave the driver 'the finger' and before the lights turned green 'wheelied' away in a screech of burning rubber. The chase was now on, only in this case the patrol-car driver was determined that the Anglia should not escape.

The chase continued through the city streets, along main roads, up side roads and down alleyways. The cops began to consider that there may be more to this than a bit of fun-and-games so more patrol cars were summoned to try and intercept the Anglia. On a couple of occasions the car was nearly stopped but managed to escape through some amazing driving on the part of the RLI *skelm* at the wheel, who then decided that the only way he was going to get away was to head out of town.

The route he chose was the Gatooma road, past the Seven Mile Hotel. Salisbury Central control room correctly guessed this and quickly arranged a roadblock comprising two patrol cars parked nose to nose to block off the road. As the blue Anglia approached at full speed, the RLI driver spotted the B-cars and with the reflexes of a young leopard zipped around the side of the patrol cars and in a cloud of dust continued heading west towards Gatooma.

And so the chase continued—until the troopie got thirsty and turned into the Seven Mile Hotel. When the fleet of patrol cars arrived he was doing perfect three-sixty-degree hand-brake turns, with a frosty Castle beer in hand.

As the cops jumped out of their cars and pointed their weapons at the Anglia the driver stopped his games, got out the car, put the bottle of beer on the roof and dramatically raised his hands in a gesture of surrender, all the while laughing maniacally.

Rather than finding stolen goods, weapons or drugs (usual RLI accoutrements) the police found a traffic bollard in the back seat and another one in the boot. Stealing a bollard was hardly a major offence. The police were intrigued.

"Why on earth would you want to steal a bollard?" they asked.

"I was driving along very peacefully," the troopie answered, "when I noticed a bollard looking at me suspiciously so I decided to capture a couple of them and take them back to barracks for interrogation."

In all fairness the cops must have thought that this was a fair explanation as a bollard does look like a Dalek and with a stretch of the imagination could be considered as villainous—after all we were at war. As for 'capturing' two Daleks, the explanation was that the troopie "needed the second one to corroborate the first one's story".

The other story concerns a friend of mine, a well-known ex-RLI character by the name of Blondie Leatham.

Blondie had left the RLI and found a job as a game-ranger with National Parks and was posted to an area with a large lake. Like all of us he had learned the fine art of fishing with dynamite. Blondie and a buddy decided to sneak off one morning to do some 'fishing'. They climbed into a small wooden boat and rowed across to a narrow tributary which their combined bush instincts and appreciation of all things natural had led them to believe was very deep.

The plan was to lob a one-kilogram bunker bomb over the side and scoop up the fish that floated to the surface after it had detonated. Blondie pulled the pin, dropped the bunker bomb into the water and waited for the explosion. And it came ... but it transpired they were in a mere three feet of water and the boat disintegrated. Blondie and his buddy were left standing, deeply shaken, in knee-deep water wondering what had gone wrong.

Another ranger who was camping nearby heard the explosion and rushed to the scene. When he asked what had happened Blondie replied, "We were torpedoed."

Ground Coverage was a unique unit yet very little has been written about it. For me, some of the GC operators were among the true unsung heroes of the Rhodesian war, being as hopelessly undertrained as we were. Our training while in Police Depot consisted of normal police counter-insurgency (COIN) training—a ten-day course where you learned the very basics of soldiering such as ambush drills, map-reading and identifying the different types of Communist Bloc weapons. We also spent time on the range getting in shooting practice and zeroing our rifles— all very basic stuff. In no way were any one of us prepared for what lay ahead but none of us had even heard of GC, let alone expected to get into it. And, as mentioned earlier, 'rain stopped play' during my COIN-training exercise. We were hopelessly ill-prepared for the reality of bush warfare ... yet somehow we managed.

My first 'bush deployment' had been in 1975 when I was despatched for a few weeks to Operation *Hurricane*—to Mount Darwin in the northeast of the country—to gain 'live' experience of what it was like in a combat zone. Our job was to base ourselves deep in the operational area and carry out normal police investigations. We were told that we had to wear our standard summer uniforms i.e. grey shirts, socks and leather shoes. Wearing a grey shirt in the dense Rhodesian bush made you stand out like a sore thumb. As we had good-quality camouflage uniforms I decided to wear it instead of my grey shirt. My section leader turned a blind eye but one day the OC carried out a surprise visit at our base camp and noticed me wearing my camo gear. He called me over and gave me an enormous bollocking, demanding to know why I had "flaunted Police Standing Orders". When I told him it was because I didn't want to get shot he went white with rage and stormed off in a huff.

Not only were we up against the terrorists ...

As a GC operator it was my job to patrol the three thousand square kilometres that made up the Filabusi area. To do this effectively I had to personally get to know every chief, kraal head and 'Nationalist' (local politician) living in the area and needed an intimate knowledge of the geography of the Filabusi district and the surrounding areas. The means at my disposal were my Land Rover and a black sergeant—Sergeant 'M'. We operated alone or in a pair. We cultivated and debriefed contacts, informers and sources and attended and investigated the murders of 'sell-outs', but our main task was to find the terrorists and have them eliminated. When we were sure of the location of a terrorist gang we would call for Fireforce and, if unavailable (as was mostly the case), we would send in ground troops whom we would brief and deploy. The idea was not for us to engage the terrorists but to locate them and let the military do the rest.

In the way of things this seldom happened. When you were getting close to a terrorist gang it was likely that they would know your whereabouts before you knew theirs. These were people who had probably grown up in the area and who knew intimately the lie of the land and locals. Much like a wild animal they saw you before you saw them. Inevitably they would initiate a fire fight and you would have to fight your way out of it.

The consequences were often tragic.

GC as a unit took a lot of casualties and many good friends of mine were killed in this manner while on operations. This was simply because we were undertrained and hopelessly outnumbered. There was no selection procedure for GC—you were 'volunteered' albeit never forced. Some fellows adapted and developed their skills, while others didn't and paid the ultimately price. I'd like to believe I am of the former category—well, I am; I survived.

George Vernon was a GC operator in the Belingwe area, which bordered Filabusi. We used to meet every month or so to brief each other on the goings-on in our respective areas, and look for common ground and plan accordingly. One day George was driving up a steep hill. The loose gravel meant that he had to engage second gear and keep the revs static. If the revs changed his wheels would lose grip on the gravel and he'd lose control. Under normal circumstances this was no big deal. All he'd need to do was brake, engage first gear and gently move forward until, with a flick of the wrists and some dextrous driving, he could slip in to second. That was under 'normal' circumstances.

The road George and his constable were ascending was bordered on one side by a steep rock face and on the other by thick bush. As George was about two-thirds of the way up and thus committed to the ascent he was ambushed by terrorists hidden in the thick bush. As he accelerated instinctively the revs changed, the wheels lost traction and the vehicle started sliding backwards—right into the killing ground—and there was nothing he could do. To make matters worse the gravel at this point was so loose that the vehicle slid sideways into the rock face and came to a halt. Hundreds of rounds hit the vehicle and riddled George's body. The constable miraculously escaped and ran off into the bush.

As mentioned earlier, Africans are petrified of snakes. They don't bother me because as a kid I used to catch them and keep them as pets.

I was with two sticks of Rhodesian African Rifle soldiers, leading them into an attack on a guerrilla camp. I was particularly nervous—not only because of the terrorists but also because I had provided the intelligence for the attack on the suspected base camp and I was determined that it was not going to be a 'lemon' (a dud).

It was a dark, moonless night as we made our way in single file through the thick bush. A veteran RAR sergeant had picked up on my nerves before we'd left and took it upon himself to look after me. He positioned himself behind me with a trooper in front.

As we progressed I managed to stumble upon every rock and stone in my path which only served to increase my state of anxiety. We eventually broke through the thick bush, which opened up into a clearing of tall trees with vines hanging from them.

"Look out!" the sergeant shouted as he grabbed me by the shoulders and threw me aside.

As I lay on the ground, desperately trying to prevent myself from hyperventilating, I looked up at him and whispered (loudly), "What's happened?"

With quivering finger he pointed to the tree above and said, "Snake!"

I followed the direction of his finger, saw what he was looking at and said, "Ah! Not snake. Vine!"

As the sergeant helped me to my feet, to allay his fears I reached up and grabbed the vine and broke off a piece to show him. In doing so I managed to redeem myself and also found myself positioned behind the sergeant while he walked in front of me.

Gathering good intelligence takes a lot of time and a lot of hard work and is anything but a straightforward process. In the context of what I was doing people who provided information were classed as either a 'contact', an 'informant' or a 'source'. A contact was someone you had an informal relationship with who fed you the occasional piece of information. It might be a petrol-pump attendant at a business centre or a waiter in a hotel. An informant was someone who was briefed on a specific subject and who sought out such information on a semi-formal basis. They included tribesmen, dip attendants and shopkeepers. A source was someone who was given regular payments and tasked with gathering information on a full-time basis. These were usually highly placed people who lived and worked with terrorists. A source may have been a *mujiba*, a 'nationalist' or a kraal head. It took years to 'cultivate' a good informer. First you had to identify someone who was in a position to give you information, and then arrange to meet with this person, gain his confidence and establish a rapport. In time he would be asked to 'help'. You might be rejected; if so you moved on. If he was willing he would be asked to provide information on something you already knew about in order to test his reliability. And so the process continued from there.

An informant would let me know by some pre-arranged signal that he needed to talk with me. This was often an envelope addressed to a postal box, with only my address written on the envelope. As I knew the handwriting this was a pre-arranged signal for us to meet at a certain place on a certain date at a specific time—normally well away from his kraal. At times, GC operators had to walk many kilometres under cover of darkness through terrorist-infested bush get to the meeting point. We never knew if our informant had been compromised. If he had then there was every chance that terrorists would be waiting in ambush for us—often with tragic consequences. The only way to deal with this was to have troops on stand-by back at base to attempt to rescue you if trouble occurred.

The threat of informants being identified by terrorists and murdered was very real and happened all the time, yet they took huge risks for very little reward. When compromised they were brutally murdered with the vilest of methods.

Terrorists arrived one day at a communal beer-drink in a TTL where one of my most trusted informants was quietly getting drunk. Although they had no idea as to his real identity they randomly selected him from the crowd and accused him of being a sell-out. He was told to strip naked and the assembly was ordered to beat him to death with small sticks—a merciless act of pure sadism as one, twenty or even fifty blows would not kill a man. A few hundred blows later his entire body was covered in thick black welts; he went in to shock and died.

In order to work together an operator had to spend many hours talking with his new recruit, trying to understand the way he thought and behaved. In time a bond of trust developed and scraps of information, such as a minor theft, were passed to the operator. The information might then develop to "suspicious people" being observed in the area and ultimately you might get to the point where a high level of information, the location of a base camp or arms cache for example, was transmitted. Operators did everything they could to protect their informants. We came to know them like family and would go to extraordinary lengths to protect them.

Chapter twelve

Boneshaker McDonald's operational crossroads

Many GC operators died operating on their own in inaccessible areas. When contact broke there was little chance of getting help in time. Others were killed by landmines and still others in conventional fire fights. The most lethal combination and the one I feared the most was a landmine–ambush. It was bad enough hitting a landmine, which at best destroyed your vehicle and totally disorientated you. The terrorists would place a landmine in the road and lie in ambush. As the vehicle detonated it the ambush was initiated. Few people got out alive. Occasionally the terrorists would boost the eleven-kilogram landmine with around fifty kilograms of explosive. You stood no chance when this happened. Even with a conventional landmine you were not aware of the blast. One minute you'd be driving along, keeping a look out for likely ambush points and the next sitting on your backside covered in dirt, your ears ringing, clueless as to what had happened.

Some bright spark got the idea that if you travelled really, really fast your vehicle would detonate the mine and by the time the explosion reached the wheels you'd be miles away. One of the boffins looked at this and worked out that a Land Rover or troop-carrying vehicle would have to travel at something like four thousand kilometres an hour to get one metre past the blast.

The government had a bunch of experts who designed mine-proof vehicles. The basic concept was a V-shaped body loosely mounted on the chassis with the troops securely strapped inside with elaborate safety belts. The idea was that when a wheel detonated a landmine the blast would cause the body to detach itself from the chassis and come to rest without damaged to neither life nor limb. The other concept was to fill the wheels with water instead of air. We were told that when a wheel detonated a landmine the water would absorb eighty per cent of the blast. I don't know how much of this was true.

What I can say is that when I got to the scene of a landmine explosion the area often looked like a mudslide had taken place. Everyone was covered in mud, wandering around in a daze, looking at each other, saying things like, "*Jislaak boet!* Did you check that *moer se* blast, hey? I *sommer* scheme it was a tin." ("My dear brother, did you happen to observe that large blast? I rather suspect the cause was a landmine.") But they were stunned; what else would they say?

I often make reference to my Land Rover which was my main form of transport. For all GC operators our Land Rovers were as close to us as our rifles. They needed to get us from place to place and keep us safe in the event of an ambush or a landmine, and they often did. We paid special attention to the needs of our Land Rovers and kept them perfectly maintained and in excellent mechanical condition.

Our Land Rovers were open-backed with roll bars and with armour plating under and behind the cab. In 1978 they were modified to become gunships. AK-47s, with butts removed, were placed at various points of the vehicle—one mounted under the bonnet (to the left of the air filter) and two on the back facing outwards. At the commencement of a journey a forty-round magazine was placed in each AK, the weapons cocked and the safety catch set on 'Fire'. The triggers of all three AKs were connected to a solenoid that was activated by three firing buttons mounted above the rear-view mirror. Although I never actually fired the AKs in a contact they did give me much comfort knowing they were there.

The tactics used by the insurgents were based on the rule of terror, an ideology that can never be considered a legitimate strategy or tactic of warfare—they were nothing more than brutal criminals. That is not to say that all insurgents who operated in Rhodesia were wholly evil. Among these people were some honourable men who fought and behaved like real soldiers. Whether or not I believed in their tactics or agreed with their way of thinking was neither here nor there. The fact is that, in order to survive as a GC co-ordinator, you had to know and understand your enemy, his tactics and everything about him. I did so and believe that this is, in part, why I survived four and a half years on operations.

In an area such as Filabusi terrorists would operate in the following manner: Sections of about forty terrorists would operate in a designated area under the control of a sectoral commander. In each section was a political commissar (PC) who was in reality in charge. His task was to indoctrinate the locals with political propaganda and ensure that the 'cadres' (terrorist rank and file) were kept politically indoctrinated and motivated. Any deviations were either reported to the commanders in the external base camps, or more usually, disciplined *in situ*—often summary execution. The PCs were characterized by their absolute devotion to keeping a diary and scrupulously taking notes of everything—contacts, informers, 'sell-outs', rendezvous points, locations of base camps, nominal rolls of cadres etc. Such notes were invaluable to us. After a contact the first thing I looked for was the body of the PC. The notebook or diary was usually kept in canvas webbing strapped around the PC's shoulder.

In the three thousand square kilometres of Filabusi there were three loosely defined terrorist operational areas. What complicated intelligence matters were that the areas overlapped and groups often transited through one area to another. When they met they would often exchange weapons so that a particular rifle used in the east of the country would end up in the far west. Keeping track of who was who made things that much more difficult.

Each terrorist had a '*chimurenga*' name given to him or chosen by him (or her) as a *nom de guerre*. The name said something about the individual who had chosen it. In the 1970s James Bond was idolized and being the hero he was there were seven James Bonds operating in Rhodesia. The most notorious was killed by security forces in the south of the Filabusi area (though the RLI claimed to have killed the premier Bond in Op *Hurricane* in 1976, in the same contact when Comrade 'Mao Tse Tung' was despatched). Other names that come to mind are '*Shumba ye Mabhunu*' (Lion killer of Boers /white men), Comrade Bazooka and my favourite 'Boneshaker McDonald'! (Why??)

As the terrorists came to know the GC operators they gave us names too. Roy, because of his ability to speak Shona fluently was called '*Mzeruru*', chiShona for a man from the Mzezuru clan. I, apparently because I was always rushing from one place to another, was known as 'Babaleka'—an Ndebele compound of baba (father) and baleka (lit: run fast)—meaning holistically 'a man who is everywhere at one time'. We all denied it but secretly we were quite proud of our ZANLA- or ZIPRA-given handles—it meant we'd made some sort of impact.

Africans have a wonderful sense of humour. I still chuckle over P/O Bailey who was called 'Aspro' because he gave all the constables such a headache with his constant whining and Section Officer (S/O) Drake whom the constables called 'MaDucks'.

The African is a very much a tribal man and as such we were up against the Ndebele ZIPRA, who operated in the west and south of the country and the Shona ZANLA in the north, east and south. ZIPRA operated out of Zambia and was Soviet trained and supplied. ZANLA operated out of Mozambique and Tanzania and was trained and supplied by the Chinese. Various other Eastern Bloc warmongers managed to get in on the action—Cuban, East German, Ethiopian, for example. Both ZANLA and ZIPRA were enthusiastically supplied their food and medical requirements by such neutrals as the Scandinavian countries, the International Red Cross, Oxfam and UNHCR, to name but a few.

Filabusi was in a somewhat unique geographical position. The eastern border with the Belingwe area extended along a range of hills—the Doro Hills. This range also served as the ethnic and operational boundary between ZIPRA and ZANLA. Tribal differences run far deeper that any difference in colour ever would and although ZIPRA and ZANLA both fought for the 'liberation of Zimbabwe' and, on the face of it, on the same side, nothing could have been further from the truth. They despised each other.

The conflict played right into our hands. ZIPRA and ZANLA patrols would occasionally come across each other and instead of sitting down and exchanging notes, would do everything they could to kill each other. I would often be on patrol and hear the sounds of battle in an area I knew there to be no security forces. It was ZIPRA and ZANLA having another go at each other. The fact that they had compromised their position to us meant little to them. I would wait a few hours, maybe a day, and then investigate. Inevitably the bodies of a few dead terrorists would be found festering, stripped of their weapons. When their contacts took place at night it looked like a fireworks display with hundreds of tracer round and rockets flying across the sky accompanied by the dull *thucks* of grenades and mortars.

There were some reasonably good soldiers among the terrorists I fought against but in the main their soldiering abilities were poor—especially ZANLA, whose training was more about political indoctrination and subjugation by terror. In a typical contact their sole aim was to fire as many rounds as possible, make the biggest noise and then flee.

Apart from the SKS carbine the guerrilla weapon of choice was the ubiquitous AK-47 assault rifle. It had been designed in a rather clever way. On a conventional semi-automatic rifle (e.g. the FN or SLR) the change lever is on the left side just above and slightly behind the trigger. It is designed in this way so that with a small flick of the thumb (for a right-handed person) the lever can be moved in an arc from 'safe' in the top position to 'rapid fire' at mid position and 'automatic' at the bottom. You have to be very well trained to know how to effectively use an FN rifle on automatic fire. For starters, the rifle barrel will 'drift', moving away from the target due to the muzzle blast and secondly, a twenty-round magazine would be emptied in just over one second. The other disadvantage is that a poorly trained operator would instinctively switch to automatic fire. The AK, however, is designed in such a way that automatic is mid position and rapid fire the bottom, thus less ammo is wasted. The AK is an excellent weapon—small robust and can take any amount of dirt without sustaining stoppages—ideal for poorly trained guerrillas.

The outcome of any successful military encounter is determined, in a large part, by the accurate gathering of intelligence and dissemination of information. We had our methods and the terrorists had theirs which we referred to as the 'bush telegraph'. How they managed to transmit information from one end of the country to the other quicker than we could with our high-tech radios remains a mystery to me.

Top: Police recruits relax outside their barracks, Morris Depot, Salisbury.
Above: Police recruits' passing-out parade, May 1974.

Left: The BSAP band.
Below: The author as a young patrol officer next to his Land Rover, Mzilikazi police station, December 1974.

A police B-Car negotiates an alleyway at night. *Photo Allan Brent*

A woman patrol officer (WPO) looking like she means business on her Vespa scooter.

Above: Filabusi
police station.

Left: Sub-Inspector
Chingoka at his
desk. The veteran
black policemen
were the mainstay of
the BSAP.

Top: Rural patrol, Filabusi area.
Above: The fortified Avoca police base camp, Filabusi area. The vehicle in the centre is a 'Pookie' mine-detecting vehicle, a very effective Rhodesian invention. Note the modified Land Rover at right, with doors removed and roll bars added.

Ground Coverage operators take a break on a low-level bridge over the Insiza River, Matabeleland.

Patrol Officer Billy Glen, killed in action in 1979.

Left: BSAP patrol in the Filabusi rural area, before the war came to Matabeleland South.

Top: Gordon Nutt 'going bush', shooting all and sundry with his pellet gun in a Filabusi base camp. Note the anti-mortar sandbagging on the roof of the new building.
Above: A typical granite kopje in the Matabeleland South area.

Top: A typical white farmer's Matabeleland homestead.
Above: Two very relieved Ground Coverage operators smile sheepishly for the camera having just hit a landmine in their Land Rover. *Photo Neville Spurr*

Top: One of ZIPRA's and ZANLA's most effective—and indiscriminate—weapons was the landmine. Pictured here are the bodies of black civilian passengers after their bus detonated a landmine.
Above: A heartbreaking and all-too-common picture—a black toddler killed in a landmine blast.

Top: A mobile family-planning clinic utterly destroyed by a landmine blast.
Above: A government Water Department vehicle having hit a landmine.

Top: A rural bus after a landmine blast.
Above: A civilian truck …

Top: Two Ground Coverage operators pull over for a chat on a main road.
Above: The author (kneeling) prepares to test-fire a Rhodesian-manufactured 42Z rifle grenade. The author's brother Ian is on the left.

Top: An army corporal instructs a recruit in the intricacies of firing an antiquated British-manufactured 28R rifle grenade. Rifle grenades were hit-and-miss affairs with Rhodesian soldiers preferring the communist RPG-2 and RPG-7 rocket launchers. *Photo Tom Argyle*

Above: An Alouette III G-car with a stick of RLI Fireforce troops prepares for a call-out. The air force gunner-technician on the right checks over his guns. Note the flak jacket at his feet. The overhead wire netting in the aircraft revetment is for protection against mortar and rocket attacks. *Photo Tom Argyle*

A Craig Bone impression.

Top: A Lynx ground-attack Fireforce aircraft, armed with pods of napalm, white phosphorus rockets and machine guns—a crucial weapon in a Fireforce's armoury. *Photo Tom Argyle*

Above: An Alouette III K-car parked at a temporary Fireforce base in Matabeleland. Noticeable is the 20mm Hispano canon protruding on the right. The armoured personnel carrier at left is a mine-proofed 'Crocodile'—a Rhodesian-modified Nissan truck. *Photo Tom Argyle*

Above: A police Land Rover comes to grief after hitting a landmine. The weird-looking vehicle approaching through the trees is a mine-proofed 'Hyena' APC—another Rhodesian-designed contraption. *Photo Neville Spurr*

Left: Neville Spurr, with his two Ground Coverage operators, grits his teeth after his Land Rover is effectively cut in half by a landmine blast. *Photo Neville Spurr*

Top: GC operators interrogating the *povo*, the locals, in a kraal in the Rhodesian bush. The little girl ignores the handcuffed suspect sitting on the right while she chats to the policemen. *Photo Neville Spurr*

Above: The handcuffed suspect refuses to look at the camera while the little girl poses. *Photo Neville Spurr*

Top: Typical Domboshawa scenery, Salisbury North. *Photo Tom Argyle*
Above: A typical granite outcrop in the Domboshawa area. Such features abound in Mashonaland and provided ideal hideouts for ZANLA guerrillas.

The author prepares for a patrol.

The author briefs his GC operators prior to a patrol into the Chinamora TTL, Salisbury North.

This amazing sequence of photographs shows BSAP Ground Coverage and PATU operatives attacking terrorists taking refuge in a kraal. *Photos Neville Spurr*

A PRAW (Police Reserve Air Wing) aircraft, having crash-landed in a maize field, just south of the Chinamora TTL, Salisbury North. The aircraft had been involved in a contact with ZANLA guerrillas for several hours before the pilot noticed he was running on empty. Too embarrassed to permit the author to take a photo of him, he did, however, allow the author to pose!

Top: The Run 'em Inn
pub at Gatooma.
Left: The Run 'em Inn
after a hard night.

Top: The author's webbing and FN rifle, with a 30-round magazine.
Left: Mr Bojangles.

Top: An RhAF Bell 'Huey', used on Fireforce and external operations. Imported from Israel in a sanctions-busting deal in 1979, these helicopters were well past their sell-by date when they arrived in the country and gave the air force technicians endless headaches. *Photo Tom Argyle*
Above: Police sub-aqua divers recover a headless corpse from a pond.

The British Army monitoring force observer for the Chakari area, a colonel, poses by an RAF Puma helicopter.

Opposite page:
Top: The author poses with his group of TTs (turned terrorists) in the Chakari district.
Bottom: An RAF transport unloads provisions for British monitoring force troops, early 1980. *Photo Tom Argyle*

The author flanked by his brother Ian (at left) and his parents at the official disbandment of C Squadron SAS, Salisbury 1980.

Communist weaponry—a variety of AK-47s and an RPG rocket launcher.

Mujibas was one method. A *mujiba* was a young boy from eight to sixteen years of age who had not (yet) been trained as a terrorist, but essentially acted as the eyes and ears of the terrorists whom they idolized as role models.

Mujibas were in the main unarmed although some infrequently carried stick grenades. Their task was to cover the area ahead of the terrorists, keep a lookout for security forces and report their movements, assist laying landmines and act as messengers. They would 'innocently' roam the countryside, overtly herding cattle or fetching water, helping their mothers with the crops and or idling at a business centre, all the time gathering information.

I once watched two *mujibas* running through a maize field with a burning torch setting fire to the crop. At the time I was on the other side of a valley and could do nothing about it. To underestimate their effectiveness and the damage they could do and did was sheer folly. And what could we do? They were kids; to shoot them was against everything we stood for. They knew that too.

A 'sell-out' was a local male or female, young or old, who the terrorists believed had reported their movements to security forces (SF) or were SF informers. To be labelled a 'sell-out' meant certain death. It meant being slowly murdered using any number of unspeakably cruel and hideous methods.

This is what typically happened …

Terrorists walked into a kraal near Avoca Business Centre. The locals were summoned by the *mujibas* and told to gather together in the presence of the local political commissar while other terrorists stood positioned on the perimeter, weapons held casually by their sides, looking out not so much for security forces but to stop any locals leaving. The PC began his speech, posturing, waving his rifle above his head, talking about the "liberation of Zimbabwe" and how the "sons of the soil will free this troubled land and drive the Boers [the whites] from it". Then he stopped in mid-sentence and said softly: "One of you is a sell-out." The kraal folk's bowels turned to water. Men, woman and children had heard this before; they had seen it and knew what was coming.

There was a hush. Then, from skulking among the people, like a cur a *mujiba* rushed forward and pointing to a *madala*, a frail old man, shouted at him:

"Him! He is the one!"

No proof was needed. The terrorists were simply looking to make a point and assert their authority. All that was needed was for the *mujiba* to point a finger and 'close the deal'.

Again silence and then two terrorists moved into the crowd and grabbed the *madala* by his arms, supporting him because his knees had collapsed with fear. They dragged him to the front. As he stood there shaking and pleading for mercy the PC continued with his diatribe on the dangers of sell-outs, how they would not be tolerated and that they would be punished. The *madala* was now beyond fear; his cries for mercy had stopped. He was a broken man for he knew he was about to die. Knowing what always happened his only hope was that his demise would be swift and painless. His head hung forward with grief. He was still supported by the terrorists on either side of him who delighted in the fact that he had soiled his trousers, the smell of freshly evacuated faeces hanging pungent in the air.

He was then dragged a hundred metres into the open bush. His wife was told to dig a grave. She and her sons did so. The soil was hard and rocky which made progress difficult. They got down on their hands and knees and removed the soil and rocks by hand. Eventually the grave was eighteen inches deep. The *madala's* hands and feet were then bound together with barbed wire. He stood at the edge of his grave waiting to be shot but the terrorists had decided on a more painful death. The two terrorists holding him let him go. He fell to his knees and his torso dropped forward; he managed to support himself with his hands. In this position the political commissar then told the tribespeople to pick up stones for "he is a dog and dogs must be stoned". They hesitated, so he barked out another order and rifles were pointed threateningly at them. They hastily picked up a few stones and tossed them tentatively at the *madala*. More shouting, more threats from the PC and the lobs turned to throws which increased in ferocity until the *madala* collapsed.

As he lay there, the act of stoning to death was complete. The PC then instructed the locals to cover his body with the excavated stones and soil. After doing so they returned to their huts to quietly mourn his death. None would inform the security forces about the murder for fear of a similar retribution.

I found out about this murder while on patrol the next day. When I arrived at the kraal no one would say a thing and I was not about to try and make anyone speak. When something like this happened an experienced GC operator somehow knew. There was something in the air, a wall of silence that echoed their fear and grief. This murder was different in that there was no body clearly visual. Usually a sell-out was murdered in such a way that his body was left for all to see—a grim reminder of what would happen should you choose to talk to the Rhodesian security forces.

I had with me a PATU (Police Anti-Terrorist Unit) stick of five men plus Sergeant M. The ground was open, rising up to the lower slopes of a *kopje*. With my men in extended line we moved through the rocky outcrops looking for the body, every so often stopping to listen, constantly aware that we might be ambushed.

At one point in some open ground I stopped. I don't know why. I heard a low moan. I was trying to figure out where the moan was coming from when I realized that I was standing close to some disturbed soil, the shape of which indicated that it was a recently dug grave. I called two men over and we moved the loose rocks away and unearthed the body of the *madala*—he was still alive. He was taken back to Filabusi where he received treatment for his wounds and later asked to be returned to his kraal.

There are thousands of cases of sell-out murders that took place throughout Rhodesia. Many heinous methods were used to kill sell-outs. If the sell-out was not clubbed to death with rifle butts he would be bayoneted to death. The bayonet of an SKS rifle is a thirty-centimetre-long triangular stiletto, known as a 'pig-sticker'. A single thrust does very little damage. Most victims were bayoneted repeatedly until the terrorists had had enough. On one body I stopped counting when I got to two hundred bayonet wounds.

Or his wife might be forced to cut off her husband's lips, nose and tongue before being made to cook them and feed them to her children.

One local I found had been stabbed to death with a dentist's tooth extractors. They look like wire strippers little silver-type pliers with a 12mm 'blade'. They make maybe a three- or four-millimetre cut. This poor man was 'pinched' with these extractors until he went into shock and died.

The *povo* were in a terrible predicament. If they fed the terrorists and did not tell the SF we would arrest them as collaborators—a criminal offence. And if they told us the terrorists would torture and kill them. Rhodesian security forces realized the locals had no choice and as long as the locals did not actively fight against us we tended to leave them alone.

There was a base camp twenty-eight kilometres from mine in the Belingwe area called Humbane. This was where George Vernon had been based. It was infamous because of a tragic incident that occurred when terrorists laid a boosted landmine intended for SF. Instead of an SF vehicle a bus filled with locals hit it and eighteen of them died in the blast. The terrorist commander sent a letter of apology to the local kraal head promising that it would not happen again. The next time a landmine was planted another bus hit it, killing eleven. This time there was no apology.

Because of the increasing flood of terrorist incursions into the area we decided to call in the RLI. The plan was for them to sweep through designated areas and make contact with terrorist groups. While they were doing their planning a few of the logistics staff that were feeling left out asked to be sent on patrol. The troop commander, delighted with their enthusiasm but aware of their limitations, agreed to let them go and chose an area that was the last place he expected any terrorist presence.

The logistics men were deployed from Land Rovers and set off on what they thought would be a good bit of exercise in the sun. Instead they stumbled upon a high-powered regional meeting of terrorist commanders. A contact took place and as good fortune would have it a Dakota carrying a load of fully armed SAS troops on a training exercise was diverted to the contact area. The SAS parachuted in and killed fourteen terrorists.

The security forces had also taken casualties in the Humbane area and morale was low. I went to visit the troops at Humbane to 'fly the flag'. As I entered the shack that served as their canteen I saw a slogan on the wall. It was in the form of a crucifix made up of Castle and Lion Lager beer bottle labels. On either side of the crucifix were the names of the men who had been killed in the Belingwe area. At the bottom, instead of the SAS motto 'Who dares wins', was written 'Who cares who wins'.

Chapter thirteen

Ambush

Relay stations across the country, vitally important for maintaining decent 'comms' (communications), were manned by dedicated police reservists. They were absolute professionals to the core who provided an invaluable but unsung service. It was a lonely existence sitting on top of a mountain for weeks on end, directing the military airwaves.

There is one man I have always wanted to meet and thank for the service he provided to me. Derek Johns was the father of Vera, Miss Rhodesia 1974, and manned his own volunteer relay station from his farm. Unfortunately time has dulled my memory and I cannot recall the name of his relay station or the location of his farm.

There were times when I was on patrol in an isolated part of the country, afraid and aware of how alone I was and that communications had all but ceased because of atmospheric conditions. I knew there'd be terrorists in the area. For so many of us one of our biggest worries was that we might not be able to summon help should we need it. When it was just me or me and my sergeant, Rhodesia could be a very lonely place.

I would rig up my bulky, antiquated TR28 radio and call one station after another, anxiously trying to contact someone, anyone, to whom I could transmit my sitrep (situation report). Or to put it another way, to simply let someone know I was still 'out there'—another human being to talk to. So often Derek would pick up my transmission and in a manner that simply inspired comfort, ask if he could help. That was all it took. After a brief chat all my concerns would fade away and it would be back to business.

It was 1977. I was in the last vehicle of a small convoy consisting of an armoured personnel carrier in the front, a Land Rover carrying GC operators Phillip Dick and Oliver Griesl in the middle and my Land Rover bring up the rear. The Land Rovers had had the doors removed so that the driver and passenger could sit with their rifles pointing outwards and for an easy and quick exit. I was driving with P/O Gordon Nutt sitting next to me. (Gordon had recently been assigned to my patrols with his national-service PATU stick as support troops.) My rifle was conveniently positioned opposite my right knee, the butt on the floor and barrel resting in a grip on the doorframe.

As convoy commander I'd chosen the rear position. I preferred this because in the event of an ambush I believed I could shepherd everyone through it. The idea of travelling in convoy is mutual protection. There are two things to look out for—one is an ambush and the other a landmine. Keep well spaced out, about seventy-five metres apart and in the event of the vehicle in front of you hitting a landmine you will avoid the blast.

The roads were typical rural roads—dry sand with a prominent continuous mound of sand running along the middle of the road. We called this the middle *mannetjie* (Afrikaans for 'little man'). The middle *mannetjie* made steering difficult. If either wheel drifted onto it you could quite easily have the steering wheel ripped from your hands and lose control of the vehicle. On either side of the road was low scrub. Beyond the scrub on the left-hand side of the road was a four-strand, eight-gauge fence to prevent cattle from wandering onto the road.

We came to a stretch of road that I had travelled hundreds of times before— where coincidentally we'd been ambushed ten days before. As we came around a corner the road dipped into a dry riverbed and rose steeply up the other side. As I came out of the riverbed and over the crest I had to slow down to take a sharp turn and momentarily lost sight of the vehicle ahead of me.

A vehicle ambush, like any contact, is something you anticipate but which always takes you by surprise, if only momentarily. The first thing you hear is the sharp crack of gunfire—in this case a burst of machine-gun fire—coming from directly ahead. The personnel carrier had entered the killing ground taking the first few hits before the enemy fire was diverted to the vehicle in front of me—the Land Rover driven by Phillip with Oliver riding shotgun.

The armour on the personnel carrier served its purpose and they got through without any damage. Phillip and Oliver were not so lucky. Phillip was hit twice. One round went through his right leg just below his knee. That round saved his life because the impact jammed his leg against the accelerator which propelled the Land Rover through the killing ground before he collapsed. Another round went through his right cheek, smashing his jaw before continuing through his tongue and exiting via his left cheek. Oliver took a hit in the left leg with the bullet smashing his shin bone.

Seconds later I came up behind Phillip's vehicle which had come to rest more or less in the centre of the road. Phillip was hanging out from the vehicle head first with his back to us, his torso on the ground and his legs still in the cab. His right foot was wedged awkwardly between the accelerator and cab floor.

I stopped about eighty metres from Phillip's vehicle as Gordon and I jumped out and took cover in some scrub on the left of the road nearby. What I didn't know was that we had stopped right in middle of the killing ground and all that was between us and the eleven ZIPRA terrorists was a narrow road and knee-high scrub. The terrorists were no more than eight or ten metres from us.

The terrorists turned their attention on us. A fierce fire fight ensued. I had to radio for help or at least to let someone know what had happened. Realistically, I knew the contact would be finished long before anyone reached us. What I needed was for someone to help us with the casualties.

While Gordon kept up a rapid rate of fire I leopard-crawled to the Land Rover, reached in, grabbed the handset and called Hotel Alpha—the call sign for the relay station positioned high up on Belingwe Peak about forty kilometres away. When the operator answered I told him exactly where I was, that I had casualties and needed an urgent casevac (casualty evacuation). Normally you would give a six-figure grid reference taken from a 1:50,000 map, not only to pinpoint the exact position but also to make it more difficult for any unauthorized listeners to interpret. However, when a contact broke everyone knew what was going on anyway so there was no need to mask the location. The communication had to be short and succinct. This was no time for idle chatter. I knew that the radio operator would pass the information onto the Fireforce base at Gwanda, situated some twenty-five minutes' flying time away by Alouette helicopter and that I would, or might, have assistance within half an hour or so.

No sooner had I transmitted my message off and returned my position next to Gordon than the terrorists opened fire with everything they had. I told Gordon that we had to somehow reach Phillip and Oliver so as to help them. As it was, all we were doing was drawing a massive amount of fire which would continue until someone broke ground (gave his position away) and was shot or Fireforce arrived.

In any fire fight it takes a couple of seconds to pinpoint the enemy's position. These terrorists had positioned themselves in such a way that they were well hidden. Other than a flash of dark uniform against the brownish-yellow of the grass there was little to indicate their whereabouts. They, on the other hand, knew exactly where we were. If we stayed where we were we'd undoubtedly get hit; it was just a matter of time. The armoured personnel carrier was well out of danger but the troops were not experienced enough to mount a counter-attack so Gordon and I were left with no option but to sort things out on our own. We had to get out of the killing ground.

The fire directed at us was all small arms—AK rifles and RPD machine guns. When you are in an RPD's direct line of fire it has a distinct sound that takes a few seconds to make sense of. Instead of a series of loud cracks it sounds more like a series of clicks. Getting to the other side of the fence and using the scrub as cover was not an option as this would have meant further exposure. We had moved nearer to our Land Rover and were now using it as cover but the danger was RPGs—rocket-propelled grenades, the guerrillas' favourite weapon. If they decided to fire at the Land Rover, which they could not possibly miss, the chances of us being hit by secondary shrapnel from the blast were inevitable. I also knew that it was only a matter of time before the enemy assaulted our position—and we would be in deep shit.

Gordon had the presence of mind to grab the small two-way radio from the Land Rover. He clutched it to his chest and with a nod we jumped up together and ran like the devil, doubled over in the somewhat optimistic hope that we would present a smaller target. It worked. In spite of the intense fire neither of us got hit.

As we arrived breathlessly at Phillip's and Oliver's position the firing suddenly ceased. I have no idea why—possibly because the terrorists figured we might organize a counter-attack from the personnel carrier. Terrorist tactics are about hit and run. They had done the hit and now it was time to run.

Gordon tended to Oliver while I went to Phillip's aid. I released his feet from the pedals, turned him over, cleared his airways and tried to set up a drip. To do so I had to cut away a brand-new goose-down anorak that he had recently bought. Because he had lost a lot of blood and had gone into shock the veins in his forearm had collapsed. On our medic's course we had been told that if you couldn't get a drip into a vein the last resort was to ram the drip up the person's backside where the soft anal tissue would absorb the saline solution. As I mulled this over Gordon was making Oliver comfortable. At last, the needle found its mark in one of Phillip's veins and the drip took. I radioed the personnel carrier and instructed them to come to us and set up an all-round defence. Oliver's brother, Rupert, who had been travelling in the armoured personnel carrier, dashed over with alarm to be with his brother.

It was now well past the expected arrival time of the Fireforce so I raised Hotel Alpha on the radio again and asked them what was going on. The Fireforce K-car pilot heard my transmission, came on the air and told me he was three minutes' out. You can normally hear an Alouette when it is four or five minutes' away but in this case I heard nothing other than the rolling thunder of gunfire in the distance.

The Fireforce delay was due to another convoy being ambushed a few kilometres away on the other side of the hills—an RPG and been fired at a Land Rover and had exploded on the roll bar just above the driver's head, seriously injuring him. The Fireforce commander had reacted to this incident first before diverting a single helicopter to assist us. This made sense as I had extra troops with me and we were thus in a better position to defend ourselves. The other convoy was the priority—as always the Fireforces couldn't keep up with the volume of call-outs.

As it was, two Alouette G-cars arrived, both armed with mounted twin

Browning machine guns. The one went into a left-hand orbit while the other landed and took Phillip and Oliver on board. It then left for the nearest suitable hospital, which was in Bulawayo.

The next thing was to organize a follow-up.

I gathered all my men together and briefed them. The plan was to search for spoor and follow it until we caught up with the terrorists. As I was briefing my men three or four vehicles pulled up, filled with soldiers. They had come from Filabusi under the command of a fellow policeman, Section Officer James who, as it happened, outranked me. James made the mistake of interrupting my briefing and tried to take over control of the follow-up. I felt the hackles standing on my neck. Regardless of rank, by virtue of my operational experience and position in Ground Coverage, I was irrefutably and unquestionably in charge and very much in control. It doesn't matter who you are, you do not step in and try to take control of something you know nothing about. I had a follow-up to get on with and was in no mood for S/O James's shenanigans. In no uncertain terms was he told as much. Everyone present knew the way things worked so James had no option but to back down.

As it turned out, after several hours of diligent tracking we found that the terrorists had 'bomb-shelled' (split up into several directions singly or in pairs) and we could not pick up any meaningful spoor. It was futile so I abandoned the chase and we wearily made our way back to Filabusi.

I was told that the casevac chopper with Phillip and Oliver had landed at Filabusi to refuel. It had landed on the soccer field next to the police station just after the casevac chopper with the injured driver from the other convoy had taken off. A crowd of civilians had gathered to see who the casualties were— not out of any form of morbid curiosity but because there was every likelihood they might know the victims. The white Rhodesian community was very small and everyone seemed to know, or know of, everyone. The driver of the other vehicle had suffered severe head injuries and was permanently blinded. (He later studied hard and became a successful lawyer.) Oliver recovered from his injury and the last I heard of Phillip was that he'd completed an MBA and had risen through the ranks of the corporate world. He has a permanent speech defect as most of his tongue was destroyed.

I was later called to Reg's office for what I thought was a debriefing. Instead, as I entered the office, I saw S/O James standing next to Reg's desk, glaring at me and quivering with rage. He had laid a charge of insubordination against me and demanded that Reg take action. Reg asked me to explain my actions.

I had just come back from a patrol in which I had been ambushed and involved in a hairy fire fight in which two of my men had been injured—one seriously—and at that time I had no idea what condition they were in. I had spent nine hours under difficult conditions leading a follow-up which had led to nothing and here I was being confronted by a man who had tried to take over control of something he knew absolutely nothing about in order to satisfy his fragile ego.

I exploded and let rip with every swear word and profanity I knew and some that I made up as I went along. For that alone I could have been charged with gross insubordination. But Reg didn't charge me. He sat quietly, looking at me and allowed me to rant and rave. He was in effect letting me release all my pent-up frustrations and emotions.

"That's enough," he said softly when he felt I had blown off enough steam.

This registered. Somewhat startled I looked at him and calmed down. Reg looked at S/O James, informed him that he would deal with me and then dismissed him. With a smug look on his face James turned and left.

Reg told me to sit down and asked me to go over the day's events. He then told me that Phillip and Oliver would live and instructed me to go and have a shower, a change of clothes and meet him for a drink in the pub.

Not a word of the incident with James was ever mentioned. What he didn't say he'd left for me to think about in my own time which was a sobering experience. This is but one of the examples of his fine leadership and management skills that I have learned from and endeavour to practise all these years later.

Chapter fourteen

Brothers in arms

For people who have never experienced it, the real meaning of the expression 'brothers in arms' is quite incomprehensible. It's about a bond that develops when two or more people have been in combat or on operations together, have fought alongside one and other and, quite literally, have had to fight to the death to defend each other. Unless you have been in one of those situations you mightn't fully understand it.

Why is it that when fighting men come home for R & R (Rest & Recreation i.e. leave), having been away for weeks or months, they have no sooner greeted their wives than they are off to meet up with their comrades? For their immediate family it is difficult to understand. To some extent it is also difficult for the men themselves to understand and this inevitably leads to all sorts of difficulties, particularly with regards to relationships. By the same token when these men return to conventional jobs they have difficulty settling down and relating to co-workers. It's not just the way of life they have led; it's the bonds that have developed while on operations. They try and find it in Civvy Street and become increasingly frustrated because they never do.

I mention this because I have much empathy for ex-combatants who have fallen by the wayside. This is largely because of their inability to adapt and cope and because of the dearth of caring and understanding on the part of those people who have not 'been there'. Some would argue that it comes down to one thing—in Civvy Street there is no code of conduct. In the military there most definitely is, albeit unwritten, but as clear as day to all those who 'have served'.

I developed such a bond with a man. After the war he spent twelve years in a Zimbabwean prison and I grieved for him as if he were a brother. My wife and daughters felt but could not understand my grief and much as I tried to explain the bond by talking to them I was never able to put it across. Frustrated at my inability to do so, I sat down and wrote about it. This, in part, is what I wrote …

Gary came to Filabusi in 1977 to run a cattle ranch. He had been a regular soldier with Support Commando, the RLI. While with Support Commando he was acknowledged as one of their best trackers. When I met Gary I had been with GC for about four months. My entire combat training had consisted of a ten-day basic counter-insurgency course. The little I knew about the way terrorists operated I had learned during informal discussions with colleagues. In summary, I knew very little about guerrilla warfare and as keen as I was, I was hopelessly unprepared for the job that lay ahead.

Gary realized this and took it upon himself to come out on patrol with me whenever he could. From him I learned the skills I needed to survive what turned out to be four and a half years on continual operations. Gary had the gift of being able to teach—to share and impart information while making me feel part of the process, as if we were learning together. In the beginning Gary led and I followed. As I learned the necessary skills and the ability to make decisions under fire I was able to 'walk beside him' until finally I became his equal. We became a formidable team. In this partnership Gary was predominantly the 'soldier' and I was, for want of a better word, the 'brains'.

But let us not be deceived. No matter how much training a person gets, no matter how much you are taught you will never know, until it happens, how you will behave under fire. Everyone who joins the military thinks about this. "How am I going to react?" "Will I make a fool of myself?" We had all heard stories of how guys, full of bravado during training, suffered the ultimate humiliation during their first contact when they had literally shat themselves. "What could possibly be worse than this?" "If it happened to him, will it happen to me? After all, he played First XV Rugby at school!" You dared not reveal such thoughts to anyone because 'real men' didn't think like that.

That first contact is something you dread yet desperately invite. You want it to happen, to get it over with. It was a rite of passage that most young Rhodesian men felt they had to go through. My first contact was a vehicle ambush in the Mount Darwin area. I will never forget it. It was 22 February 1975, sitting on the back of an open-sided personnel carrier. When the ambush was initiated I heard the sharp cracks from the terrorists' small-arms weapons; we drove through the killing ground unscathed and called in Fireforce. That was it. Contact over. I thought I had behaved pretty darn well, body in once piece, everything hunky dory.

As far as thinking and decision-making under fire goes, in my first contact I had no idea what was going on. I pointed my rifle, somewhere, fired a few rounds into the bush and that was it. During the second, a camp attack, also in Mount Darwin, I had an idea what was going on and fired in the vague direction of the terrorists. It was only during my third contact, in Filabusi, that I began to get a clearer picture, located the terrorists' firing positions, returned fire accurately, followed up and thought on my feet. A few hours later, having safely returned to Filabusi, I knew I could make it.

Gary taught me how to track. I learned that the best times to track are when the sun is still low on the horizon, the shadow cast by highlighting every minute indentation making the tracks clearer and therefore easier to follow. I spent hours practising, starting off by looking back at my own spoor, learning the characteristics of spoor prints, then following my constables studying their tracks, learning to distinguish between individuals, who was dragging his feet, who was running. And when they moved over rocky ground how to cast for, and pick up the, spoor again … putting all the pieces together.

One day we were on follow-up after a disciplinary ZIPRA murder. During the contact that ensued Gary and I split up and because one of our radios broke we could not locate each other. I thought I knew where he was heading, picked up his team's spoor and set off after him. The spoor went from sandy paths into bush and over rocky outcrops but I managed to keep on it. I was quite pleased with myself but couldn't figure out why Gary's team was setting such a pace. We started to run on the spoor. We were running through thick bush when it abruptly ended and we found ourselves in the open on the edge of a newly ploughed mealie field about fifty metres across.

No Gary. Instead, on the other side were eight ZIPRA terrorists. As we opened fire on them they disappeared into the bush. For us to expose ourselves by moving across open ground while they waited under cover of thick bush would not have been the brightest thing to do. The contact ended as abruptly as it had started. Stalemate. They went their way and we ours.

It is a thrill to be able to track—animals or humans. More so humans. When you know that they are armed and very much the enemy then that thrill is heightened.

There are many stories about trackers during the Rhodesian war. I was fortunate enough to work with three of the best—Gary, Carl Douglas who will appear later in my narrative and Maplanka.

Maplanka was a wizened old Bushman who worked with the police in Matabeleland as a tracker. He was tiny, slightly over five feet. As he moved from one operational area to another he carried all his worldly possessions in a huge backpack that he would not let out of his sight, insisting that he carried it with him even on follow-ups. As tough and tiny as he was this changed his profile, making him a much bigger target. It took a while but we managed to persuade him to let us carry his extra kit, which we dispersed among ourselves. All he carried were his water bottles, dry rations and an old, brown, moth-eaten blanket that served as his bedroll. He would not carry a weapon. An FN rifle was simply too big so we gave him a .410 shotgun. He fired it once on the range and handed it back in disgust, preferring instead to carry an old stick about the length of a walking stick.

In typical arrowhead tracking formation, Maplanka would pick up the spoor and start following it with one or two soldiers positioned on either side of him. Their main job was to act as Maplanka's 'bodyguards', thus allowing him to focus all his attention on the spoor. The remaining troops would be in single file behind Maplanka thereby forming the shaft of the arrow. Maplanka started off slowly then as the spoor became clearer and a picture formed in his mind he would pick up the pace. Typically Maplanka would be hot on the spoor, going at a steady pace and then stop suddenly. All heads would turn towards him. Without saying a word he would point towards the bush in front of him with his stick and then lie down on his stomach with his face buried in the sand. Literally seconds later a fire fight would ensue. So when Maplanka stopped and pointed it meant we were right on top of the terrorists. He had done his job—now it was our turn.

Maplanka died in tragic circumstances. He and a stick of policemen were on patrol in the Kezi area. They were in open formation, spread out like the fingers of a hand, each covering one another. As the patrol moved through dense bush everyone in the stick knew that contact was imminent. A young P/O lost sight of the stick, panicked and, on seeing Maplanka come into view, thought he was a terrorist and opened fire and killed him.

Gary taught me to develop my thinking skills in a fire fight.

We had gone out looking for terrorists. I'd received information that terrorists were hiding up for the day in a base camp but I only had a general idea where it was. We decided to move in to the general area, try and pick up spoor, maybe interrogate a few locals and see what happened. It soon became apparent that the camp was at the base of a small *kopje* where a meeting with terrorists and locals was in progress. Our job was to attack the camp before the terrorists realized we were in the area.

My patrol was made up of Gary, a white police reservist and six black constables. As events unfolded it became clear that we were about to take on over thirty ZIPRA guerrillas. That's a lot of terrorists for anyone to take on. I had to summon air support before we attacked the camp but it was only a matter of time before news reached the terrorists that we were in the area and we were compromised. The most effective way to eliminate terrorists is to get them while they are all in one place and that place was the camp.

I radioed Filabusi, gave them our position, told them that we were about to attack the camp and that we needed air support as a matter of priority. Filabusi asked Gwanda (the District HQ where Fireforce was based) for assistance and was told that Fireforce was committed elsewhere. It just so happened that a Rhodesian Air Force G-car, piloted by an ex-Royal Marine pilot, Ian Terry, was in the air flying to Bulawayo from Gwanda. He heard my transmission and said he would provide air support but first needed to refuel. An Alouette has forty-five minutes' flying time with a full load of fuel. It's not much. Ian Terry landed at Filabusi, refuelled and took off in our direction.

I had by now located the terrorists and handed over to Gary to take care of the military side of things. The camp was about four hundred metres from our position. Gary put us in extended line with him and me on the extreme right flank and directed us in. We were following a river line; the going was tough and the sparse bush provided scant cover. Terry called and gave me his ETA (estimated time of arrival). We knew that when he was four minutes' out the terrorists would hear him and things would start to happen very quickly. Sure enough, they did. The terrorists heard the chopper and instead of making a break for it decided to fight it out.

They realized where we were coming from when we were within two hundred metres of the camp. As they opened fire on us, now completely compromised, we started running towards the camp. Thirty ZIPRA terrorists means a lot of firepower. They had recently been re-supplied and weren't short of ammunition. They opened up on us with everything they had and although their small-arms fire was intense it was, thankfully, ineffective. But when they began firing their RPG-7 rockets things started to get tense. An RPG-7 rocket will self-destruct if it cannot find a target. Although some exploded as they hit the ground in front of us most were fired high and exploded above our heads. Nevertheless it was still an unnerving experience.

The terrorists then decided to bomb-shell but the Alouette intercepted them before they could make good their escape. The air-gunner was keeping them pinned down to enable us on the ground to close with them. But then the guns jammed. The terrorists would soon take the gap, but Terry then performed a stunt I have never seen before or since. He had to make the terrorists believe that he still had the upper hand so he dived on them and when the helicopter was just above their heads, flared out, keeping them pinned down. He did this over and over again until his gunner-tech was able to clear his guns.

As we closed with the terrorists individual fire fights erupted all over the area. At the base of the *kopje* was a small rocky outcrop where some of the terrorists had sought cover and were shooting furiously at us. It happened to be on our right flank where Gary and I were positioned. The fire was so intense that we went to ground and took cover. When I looked up through the dust and smoke I spotted a terrorist lying behind a *mopane* tree. He was about thirty metres from me. I could see the terrorist's head, his rifle and part of his shoulder as he fired at us but because Gary was lying on my right side he could not see him.

In spite of all the fire coming our way and the intense drama going on around me everything became crystal clear and seemed to start to slow down. Totally focused and in control, I carefully aimed at the terrorist's head, a very small and unstable target and, as if I had all the time in the world, made sure he was clearly within my sights. I squeezed the trigger, twice in quick succession as we had been taught to do. The idea is that if you only nick him with the first round the second will kill him. It's called a 'double-tap', which was far more effective than wayward automatic AK fire. The terrorist's head vaporized in a cloud of blood and brain fluid, the impact spinning him round so that his side was exposed to Gary who opened fire and hit him again—this time in the kidneys.

When you are under heavy fire and pinned down, very often the best form of defence is attack—it's a standard ambush IA (immediate-action) tactic. I had read the books and knew the theory but it still sounded like crazy talk.

We were under very heavy fire, the terrorists were gaining the upper hand and Terry had left the area to refuel. Gary decided to take the initiative. He yelled to the others to follow him, stood up and with a scream charged the rocky outcrop. I found myself following Gary also yelling and firing, clearing the bush, looking for targets of opportunity. We ran past the terrorist we had just killed, into the outcrop, through it, up over the other side and hit the ground. None of the others had followed.

By assaulting the terrorists head-on we had caused those remaining to flee. The area was now cleared and secure. We had to regroup and commence follow-up. It was up to Ian Terry to provide top cover and lead us in the right direction. We got some of the men together to begin the follow-up, with others remaining behind to clear up. Before we set off I went back to the terrorist I had killed to recover his weapon and look for documents. He was carrying a canvas satchel slung around his neck that was filled with documents. I ripped it off, put it over my neck and linked up with Gary and the other troops. Terry was now back overhead directing the follow-up operation.

One fire fight followed another; short fleeting contacts that became one long, blurred, running battle. During it all I was becoming increasingly irritated by some wetness around my neck but with all the adrenaline and shooting couldn't figure out where it was coming from. It didn't feel like sweat. When I got the chance I took the satchel off over my head and wiped my neck. Brownish red muck that I did not recognize smeared my hands— the brains of the terrorist I had killed. I wiped away what I could, put the satchel back on over my neck and continued with the follow-up.

To this day I can still very distinctly recall that smell and feel of cold wet brains on my neck, rather like the smell of tripe that my mother used to cook. It's something that you never forget.

Two more terrorists were killed in the ensuing contacts. In the way of things the rest bomb-shelled and when we finally lost tracks regrouped and headed back to Filabusi. Back at base that evening drinks had been laid on for us. I didn't know it but at that stage Reg had been having some doubts about my soldiering abilities.

While everyone was patting each other on the back and complimenting each other for a job well done I stood in the background nursing a cold beer and keeping pretty much to myself. To my mind Gary was the one who deserved the praise. This was his moment and I wanted to let him savour it. Although lost in my thoughts I heard Gary accepting some compliments and then call for silence.

People stopped talking and turned their heads towards him. I don't recall his exact words but they went something like this:

"You all think you know Tony. But I want to tell you something about him. You all know that today we came under very heavy fire. That fire was directed at a section that included Tony and me. The only way out was to assault the hill feature which the terrorists were firing at us from. I stood up and charged the hill. As I did so I noticed Tony running beside me. Tony gave me the inspiration to continue. He led, I followed. This is a brave man and I want you all to know that."

People began to applaud and congratulate me. Reg approached me and told me that he always knew I had it in me and that he was just waiting for the moment when I would prove myself. Now, I had done so. He then shook my hand.

My friendship with Gary grew.

Chapter fifteen

Crossfire slaughter

Most of the locals had cattle. Not only did they provide meat and milk, they were a symbol of wealth. The more cattle you had, the wealthier you were. The government had built an extensive network of dip tanks throughout the country, and on a given day the locals from the area would come and dip their cattle. Staff from Internal Affairs (Intaf) supervised the whole operation.

The terrorists figured out that one of the best ways to destroy the Rhodesian economy was to round up the locals and force them to destroy their dip tank. The terrorists supervised the whole operation. It wasn't the government who suffered, it was the locals—the cattle got diseased and died.

The government took a stand and demanded that the locals rebuild their dip tanks and so commenced a vicious cycle that continued throughout the war. Dip tanks were built, the terrorists got the locals to destroy them, we got the locals to rebuild them and so it went … on and on.

The day on which a dip tank was to be rebuilt was common knowledge. What was not supposed to be common knowledge was our arrival. If the terrorists even suspected that we were coming they would try and ambush us.

On one occasion I let slip to Intaf that I would be coming to check out the rebuilding of a dip tank. Instead of keeping this to himself the Intaf man telephoned the local dip-tank supervisor on an open line and told him I was coming. On a party line everyone listens in. You simply do not discuss anything even remotely confidential unless you specifically want it to be heard. Needless to say within minutes the local terrorist sectoral leader knew we were on our way and set up an ambush.

Gary and I were on our own driving steadily along in his farm Land Rover. It was white, the old type with a split windscreen. I was his passenger. We came to a sharp right-hand bend, slowed down and entered it. As we came out the other side and accelerated, a terrorist brazenly stepped out into the middle the road, raised his RPD machine gun to his shoulder, took aim at us and opened fire. With my weapon pointing sideways out the cab I had no time to bring it to bear over the windscreen.

Simultaneously the terrorist ambush party opened fire from our flanks. Gary put his foot down and sped through the killing ground as the RPD gunner dived out the way. Later on I established that we had been ambushed by twenty-five guerrillas—this time ZANLA.

There was no point in starting a follow-up. As Gary and I were on our own it would have been foolish to even attempt it. After the ZIPRA guerrillas had withdrawn Gary and I stopped, alighted and began looking over his Land Rover for any damage.

"Hey, Tony! I think I've been hit," he blurted out suddenly.

He was feeling the top of his head so I snatched his hand away. As a general rule if you thought you had been hit in the head or another part of your body that you were unable to see you let someone else inspect the injury before you touched it. Head wounds particularly bleed profusely; even a nick produces a lot of blood. To the wounded person they always appear much worse than they really are. Then again, it's pretty difficult to be objective when you have just been shot.

There was a lot of blood on Gary's head, mostly at the back where the hair meets at that that strange-looking whorl. I probed around with my fingers but could not feel anything untoward so I poured water over the area and cleaned it up. With Gary reassured we went back to have another look at his Land Rover.

What had happened was quite extraordinary. We found two bullet holes side by side in the centre of the aluminium bar that split the windscreen and two bullet holes in the back of the cab directly opposite. As the terrorist with the RPD had opened up on us Gary and I had instinctively ducked our heads towards each other in the centre of the cab. In milliseconds the round had penetrated the vertical bar, fragmenting tiny shards of glass. The two rounds had passed between us and the atomized glass had hit Gary in the head, causing dozens of small pinprick-type wounds that collectively produced a lot of blood.

The terrorist's aim had been on target. With the rapid rate of fire of an RPD I cannot even begin to imagine where the other rounds went. They should have taken us both out. Once again, 'through God's Grace ...'

Ten days later I was again ambushed in the same spot by eight ZIPRA guerrillas. The difference was amazing. ZIPRA had planned their ambush well and continued fighting until they heard the sound of the incoming helicopters. Unlike ZIPRA, ZANLA had initiated contact and as soon as we returned fire they ran away. I had a lot of respect for ZIPRA and little if any for ZANLA whom I considered as little more than a bunch of ill-trained thugs. This made a big impact on me because I always knew that with ZANLA I had the upper hand.

I have thought long and hard about whether or not to write about the following incident and eventually decided that in order for my narrative to be complete it must be told. It was never going to be easy to write and even now it is very difficult for me to read—but here it is ...

Towards the close of 1977 I received information to the effect that approximately eighteen ZIPRA terrorists were based up in a temporary camp in the hills in the southern part of Filabusi. My informant told me that the camp was situated in a saddle between two hills and that locals visited it every day to feed the terrorists. That was all I was told.

I wanted to find the camp and then attack it. In order to do this I needed ground troops but there were none available in Matabeleland so I roped together a group of men comprised of Uniform Branch policemen and Internal Affairs officers from the Filabusi DC's camp.

Although I had a reasonable idea where the camp was I was unsure of its exact location. My plan was to infiltrate the area in the early hours of the morning under cover of darkness, snatch a local from a nearby kraal whose residents I knew were feeding the terrorists, get from him the location of the camp and attack it. Simple.

I left with twenty men, did our 'snatch' but gleaned nothing.

I knew that having moved into the general area it was a merely a matter of time before one of the locals tipped off the terrorists as to our presence. Time was not on my side and the element of surprise in danger of rapidly being lost. The best we could do was a sweep of the kraal, look for spoor and follow it. We were fortunate; as daylight broke we found spoor fairly quickly. It was of a large group of people heading in the direction of a nearby *kopje*.

We started following the spoor with Gary tracking. Billy Glen, a P/O, and I were on his flanks, with the rest of the men in single file behind Gary. The tracks led us towards a rocky outcrop which skirted the base of the *kopje*.

Daylight revealed that the bush had thinned. The ground around us was open, sandy vlei (low-lying marshy area) which meant we were completely exposed to anyone who might be hiding in the rocky outcrop.

As we approached I signalled my team to halt. I then indicated to them to fan out so we could sweep through the outcrop and up the *kopje* when one of the Intaf men began arguing with Gary, insisting that we continue around the *kopje* and not up it.

I was about to tell him to shut up when Gary, in a loud, urgent whisper said, "Look!" and pointed towards a large, grey rock. Initially I could not make out what he was pointing at but then I saw a wet stain where a man had recently urinated against the rock. The terrs were in the saddle!

Immediately Gary and I ran around the rock into an open area surrounded by large boulders. The ground rose away from us. At the top of the rise were more boulders and beyond that on either side dense *mopane* scrub. We had stumbled right into the enemy base camp. They of course had seen us coming and had made their own plans.

The terrorists were in the high ground in front of us and on either side of us, well hidden in the rocks, with dozens of locals—men and women—between them and us. Depending on where they had pre-positioned themselves they were anything from ten to fifteen metres from us when they opened fire.

We on the other hand were firing from low ground, with screaming locals running away from us, at us, in circles, in complete terror. We had been taken completely by surprise and were under heavy fire. It was very difficult to distinguish between friend and foe, more so because the terrorists were dressed as civilians. We tried to defend ourselves by firing back in the general direction of the incoming fire as we desperately tried to identify a target.

I picked out a terrorist. He was on the high ground firing over a rock. He knew what he was doing as he was aiming at me in a deliberate manner instead random bursts, which was their usual tactic. With locals rushing all around us and bumping into me I aimed at the terrorist. As I took a bead a woman, wearing a yellow and orange dress, ran in between the terrorist and me, right into my line of fire. I adjusted my aim to shoot over her head and sighted on the terrorist. Just as I was about to pull the trigger I clearly saw her head split open like an overripe water melon, the impact causing her blood and brains to splatter over my shirt and webbing. The terrorist had fired milliseconds before me, hitting her instead of me. In the second or so that it took for me to again find the terrorist, he had disappeared from view.

I continued picking out other targets and, where I couldn't find one, put down clearing fire into the rocky crevices where I thought the terrorists might be taking cover. I continued doing this until it dawned on me that we were not receiving any incoming fire. Only Gary and I were still shooting. I shouted to Gary to cease firing. He did so and as quickly as the fire fight had started it ended.

Looking about me I saw the dead and dying ... everywhere.

I instructed Gary and a couple of men to carry out a sweep of the area and do a body count while I radioed Gwanda to report the contact. Communications were difficult so we had to set up the old TR28 field radio and tune it.

My first priority was to my own men; there was still much to do to ensure their safety. These were ZIPRA terrorists and being ZIPRA there was every chance that they would regroup and counter-attack. I ordered some men into all-round defensive positions.

When I was sure that the immediate area was secure I instructed other men to collect the dead and dying and bring them to a central point. The other uninjured locals had long since disappeared.

It was a gruesome task as my men dragged the corpses into a pile in the open ground in front of me. The wounded were in a terrible state, all with major gunshot wounds. With our field medical kits there was little we could do to help them and, quite honestly, at that particular moment with the safety of my own men still a priority, they were the least of my concerns.

My radio operator had made contact with Gwanda. I told the radio operator in Gwanda that we had had a contact. I remember standing on a high point transmitting my report while the bodies were stacked up next to me. By the time they had all been collected there were seven dead and six mortally wounded. Not one of them was a terrorist. The OC must have been near the radio shack because he came onto the radio almost immediately and asked for details.

"We have seven confirmed kills, copied?" I replied dully.

"Confirm Charlie Tangos?" he queried. (Charlie Tango was radio-speak for CTs, Communist Terrorists.)

"Negative. All civilians. We also have six critically wounded, all locals."

There was a momentary silence from the other end of the radio, before the OC advised he was sending vehicles from Filabusi to collect us all—troops and corpses.

I stood there, silently, much like a king viewing his subjects, only mine were all either dead or dying.

I gathered my men together and instructed one of them, Gilly, to take three others and do another sweep through; I was still niggled about enemy presence. Gilly worked at Pangani Mine and was on a six-week call-up with Intaf. I had known him from my days as a town cop in Bulawayo where I had arrested him for drunkenness and causing a fight at a nightclub. But I didn't have a gripe with him —I gave him a job to do that I believed he was quite capable of doing.

With four men carrying out a sweep of the area and others on perimeter defence, Gary, Billy and I sat together, all still buzzing with adrenaline, lost in our own thoughts. We waited for the vehicles, but the bush was very thick so I knew it would take some time for them to arrive.

A gunshot rang out. I jumped to my feet, rifle at the ready, but I was not overly concerned as it was only one shot—definitely not an AK and therefore most likely an accidental discharge.

There was a commotion to my left as I saw Gilly emerging from the bush, dragging a young boy, probably a *mujiba,* who had been shot in the left arm.

The bullet had hit him just above the elbow, almost severing his arm. I watched Gilly. As he approached me he let go of the boy, who then wandered over, like a zombie, to the wounded locals moaning softly near the pile of corpses. Gilly informed me that during the sweep he had seen the boy and called to him; he thought the boy was carrying a weapon so he'd shot him.

If this were true I would have to go along with it but it wasn't. Gilly had seen the boy cowering in the bush, called him over and shot him with his Uzi—as confided to me later by one of the other soldiers.

The carnage we had inflicted was beginning to dawn on me as Gilly related his version of events and I suddenly felt very much alone. Perhaps this was the catalyst that led to my actions later that day. In any event I took Gilly aside and dealt with him in my own way— I took him for a short walk out of earshot and out of sight. I challenged him, but he argued so I found it necessary to dispense a few blows to his body with the butt of my rifle.

I heard the vehicles approaching and saw them emerging from the bush, crushing the bush under wheel. Reg had sent Sergeant-Major Dlamini with the two vehicles. He was an ex-Selous Scout who had been taken off operations when his identity became known to ZIPRA high command and he'd been put on their hit list. He was transferred to BSAP Filabusi—it was hoped—to disappear into anonymity. The sergeant-major was a big man—tall, powerful and very much in control. Like most big self-assured men he said very little but when he spoke, you listened.

I warmly shook hands with him as we greeted each other. He summed up the scene without comment and ordered his men to start loading the dead and wounded into the back of the vehicles.

I was standing next to the sergeant-major, perfectly calm and in control, discussing the day's events. In one hand I had a knobkerrie (a tribal fighting stick—I have no idea where I got it from) and in the other my rifle. One after another the dead and wounded were loaded into the vehicles.

Someone carelessly dumped a body on top of another and Dlamini reprimanded him. I added a few more words of censure, which developed into a few harsher words and then total verbal abuse. Without knowing what I was doing I found myself attacking the corpses with the knobkerrie. I was hammering away at them, beating and cursing them. I don't know how long this went on for.

Sergeant-Major Dlamini put his hand on my shoulder and squeezed it. "Tony, it's all right. It's over," he said softly.

I stopped, and with a stunned realization of what I was doing, let the knobkerrie slip to the ground. He looked at me with quiet reassurance and walked away to leave me alone with my thoughts.

After loading the bodies we boarded the vehicles and started the long trip back to Filabusi. I have no idea how many of the wounded lived or what happened to them afterwards. In view of their injuries, lack of medical attention and the four-hour journey back to Filabusi, I very much doubt if any of them lived.

Such is the way of war.

The anguish of war comes in different forms—one is to witness a friend 'cracking up' under the strain of it all. We were ambushing a kraal in which a terrorist was known to be sleeping in one of the huts. I did not know exactly which hut so I placed my men in an extended line on one side of the kraal from where we could observe all the huts. The plan was to wait for the terrorist to wake up and, as he came out the hut, shoot him. Gordon Nutt was on the right flank and I on the left. Without saying a word Gordon got up, walked to a hut with his rifle at the trail, opened the door and entered. I was so surprised that the thought of restraining him never entered my mind. Of all the huts to choose Gordon chose the one in which the terrorist was sleeping. Gordon never saw him, perhaps because he'd come from the light outside into the dark interior of the hut. But the terrorist saw Gordon, grabbed his AK and fired at him from less than two feet. God knows how, but the bullets somehow missed Gordon, went through the mud wall of the hut and hit a constable outside in the leg. In the confusion the terrorist escaped, leaving his AK behind.

(The constable was later awarded a medal for bravery, bizarrely. I don't know who recommended him for it or quite why he got it.)

It was clear Gordon had been on operations for too long and was suffering some form of post-traumatic stress or, more realistically, 'present' traumatic stress. After the incident Gary and I discussed the matter with Reg and persuaded him to take Gordon off operations while he recovered.

As for me, I was fine … wasn't I?

Chapter sixteen

The innocents

The year was 1978 and the conflict was escalating at an alarming rate. I had a temporary base camp right next to the Avoca Business Centre, fifty-two kilometres south of Filabusi. The camp was an Intaf rest camp which had been fortified with huge earthen walls that had been bulldozed into place. There was a 'no man's land' gap between the walls and a ten-foot-high fence—admittedly not much of a deterrent but it served some purpose. Less than a hundred metres from the camp was a small dam.

The local District Commissioner had nurtured and raised a small flock of rare geese which lived in the reeds on the dam. I was in need of fresh rations so I shot some geese one day thinking they were ordinary ducks—at least that's my excuse. The DC arrived at the camp for a surprise visit and went to check on his flock but they were nowhere to be seen. He asked me about it and I vehemently, quite convincingly I thought, denied all knowledge. While I was rattling on about how "I wouldn't dream of harming the poor creatures" and that "they had probably migrated south" he opened the door of my gas fridge to grab a cold beer. What he saw were six neatly dressed rare ducks roasted to perfection, all ready to be cut into portions to form the centre piece of a duck and mayonnaise dish I was preparing for supper that night. The DC went ballistic, stormed off and reported me to Reg who simply laughed it off. I still don't know what sort of geese they were or, for that matter, the difference between a duck and a goose.

I am absolutely petrified of frogs. The mere thought of these things sends shivers down my spine. Forget AKs; point at frog at me and I will tell you everything you want to know.

One day a group of territorial soldiers on call-up who'd stopped for the night at Avoca were sleeping in tents outside my bedroom. In the early hours of the morning my blissful sleep was shattered by the sound of a frog *ribbitting*, shattering the early morning silence. Were it the sound of gunfire, I'd have know exactly what to do. This was different and cause for much alarm. My immediate reaction was to call the camp to immediate stand-to but I held my tongue. Ever so slowly I got out of bed (in case the frog was waiting in ambush at my feet), I then shook my boots fiercely to make sure it was not hiding in them and went out to investigate. My senses heightened from fear I was able to zone in on the *ribbeting*. It was coming from beneath a monster of man— a boilermaker called Kooney who was sound asleep among the territorial soldiers.

I moved in on Kooney. I rationalized if the frog were underneath him it would have been crushed. I leaned over and decided the sound appeared to be emanating from inside his mouth. My God! Has he swallowed the frog? Images of a Pink Floyd record album with a picture of a frog in someone's mouth sprang to mind, so I knew this was a real possibility. The thought made me turn cold. I sat staring at Kooney, wandering what the hell I was going to do. His buddy Albert awoke and in a whisper asked me what was going on.

"I know this sounds crazy but I think Kooney has a frog in his mouth," I whispered back.

Albert, also a boilermaker (presumably there was now a dearth in the trade back in Civvy Street) raised an eyebrow, listened awhile and said, "Ag man! Don't worry, that's just Kooney grinding his teeth."

I didn't know people ground their teeth so, hugely relieved, I made out that I was concerned about Kooney's state of health and spent the rest of the night curiously watching him while he ground away. The reality is I was in a state of shock and couldn't sleep.

I also had a couple of cats that became my constant companions. Every night they would go off on their own patrol and catch lizards and bats which they swatted out of the air. When they had caught them, in the way of cats, they bought them to me to show me what good hunters they were. The cats would release the still-very-much-alive bat or lizard, swat it around to induce some movement and then pounce on it and recapture it—all done but a few inches from my head. Every time they recaptured the creature they would chew at it a bit more. The sound of high-pitched squeaks and bones being crushed became something that I got used to. What I didn't like was the regurgitated remains which I inevitably stepped in when I got up in the morning.

Billy Glen arrived at the station fresh from Depot. Billy's role in life was always going to be that of a 'peacemaker'. In terms of police experience he had none and joining the station fresh from Depot made him very much the 'rookie'. Like all new postings he had very little time to adjust. Arriving at a station that was in the midst of a war zone made things that much more difficult for Billy but he did adjust. With his irrepressible sense of humour and eternal optimism nothing was too much trouble for him. Living under such conditions tempers would often flare but no matter how angry or upset any of us became Billy was always there to calm things down.

Billy didn't mind being stationed in 'District'. In fact he had the makings of a fine policeman. What he did have a problem with was fighting a war. It wasn't that he was overly nervous or scared; he was just never able to settle down in an operational area. In such a frame of mind no one is able to think clearly and life becomes a misery. Billy stuck it out and did everything that was asked of him. His parents would often phone and no matter who answered they would talk to us as if they'd known us for years. They really were wonderful people. Whenever we went to Bulawayo we knew that their door was always open and could sit down, have a beer, sound off to Billy's father and have a good chat. His mother was always sending us goodie packs, with little luxuries, that kept us going for weeks.

One day Billy and his father went to visit Billy's brother Dave who was working on a ranch in southern Matabeleland. To get there they had to travel over sixty kilometres along dirt roads. They didn't have a mine-proofed vehicle so Dave, who did have one and had met them at the start of the dirt road, led the way—the idea being that if there were a landmine Dave's vehicle up front would hit it before their soft-skinned car.

Tragically that is not what happened.

I was on leave at my parents' house one night in Salisbury watching the news on TV when the announcer stated in the daily 'Security Forces communiqué' that Patrol Officer Billy Glen and his father had been killed in a landmine incident in the West Nicholson area. They had hit a landmine and had their legs blown off. As if that wasn't bad enough Billy's brother could not do anything to save them and had to watch them die.

Billy died doing something he should not have done. If you suspect that a road is mined you don't drive along it in a soft-skinned vehicle. War graves are filled with the bodies of people who died when they dropped their guard. We know for example that forty per cent of all Allied deaths in the Second World War were from 'friendly fire'. When you look at the Vietnam War Memorial in Washington know that sixty per cent of all those names were people killed by friendly forces. I don't know what the figure was in Rhodesia and don't want to. What I do know is that some of my closest friends died doing things they should not have been doing.

John Miller was another good friend of mine. We'd been at the same school and had kept in regular contact with each other. He used to travel the same route through an operational area five times a day. On that fateful day he found he needed to make a sixth trip—his vehicle was ambushed and his head was blown off by a rifle grenade that hit the roll bar of his Land Rover. I was told of his death by his father while I was watching my brother play rugby at school.

Dave Fry was advised not to travel along a particular road at night, as it was an infamous ambush route. He did. His vehicle was hit by an RPG-7 rocket and burst into flames. Dave was burnt to death.

Rob Delby used a live round instead of a ballistite cartridge when firing a rifle grenade. It blew up on the end of his rifle killing him instantly. The list goes on. More names to add to the Roll of Honour with cause of death invariably listed as 'Killed in Action'. These were all good men, who dropped their guard for an instant.

Every so often GC operators would be instructed to assist colleagues in other operational areas. ZIPRA terrorists had abducted four hundred schoolchildren from Manama Mission in the Tuli area which is on the border with Botswana. The kids were rounded up and marched off towards Botswana. For these children their schooldays were over. Once they got to Botswana they would be put in trucks and ultimately end up in a remote camp in some faraway place where they would be politically indoctrinated, trained as terrorists and the girls raped.

My team and I arrived in Tuli but it was too late —the children were already over the border. We remained behind to gather as much intelligence as we could about the terrorists' movements and helped supply the local GC co-ordinator with a solid intelligence base from which to work.

Tuli is an incredibly beautiful area. The police station is situated on a hill above the banks of the Shashi River with the Tuli Circle on the other side. There is very little in the way of human habitation but plenty in the way of wildlife. A normal day's patrol is like a day-trip through a game reserve. In those days the river always had water in it; the riverine vegetation was lush and green. On any evening you could go down to the river and watch many different types of wild animals drink. The three weeks I spent there were like a holiday safari.

When we got back from patrol in the evening we would have roast venison for dinner, mostly kudu or impala, washed down with ice-cold beers. The only downside was the bats. The light of the toilet, which was thirty metres from the sleeping quarters, was left on all night thus attracting insects on which the bats fed. On the way to and from the toilet the bats flicked past at a hell of a rate and sometimes flew into you with a loud *thwack*! The only way to deal with this was by carrying an old tennis racquet to swat them away.

Tuli was an isolated, very lonely, two-man station. The P/Os were stationed there for eighteen months at a time and in that period never saw a white woman. This is where Sue Roberts came in. Sue was a civilian who manned the radio in Filabusi during the day. Although in her early sixties and showing her age she had the voice of a sex goddess. When you heard her talk on the radio she conjured up visions of a ravishingly gorgeous woman. The men imagined her to be absolutely everything they wanted in a woman—more so when they were stationed in the middle of nowhere with only a constable and a few prowling hyenas at night for company.

Sue was happily married but having something of a maternal nature felt it her duty to encourage the P/Os in outlying areas by providing motherly advice, flattery and ego-boosting. To the lonely P/Os this was misconstrued as flirtation and more than one P/O fell in love with her from a distance. I didn't do anything to disillusion them.

Alan Smith had been stationed at Tuli for fourteen months and was coming to the end of his posting. He had become infatuated with Sue and never stopped enquiring of her. Whatever he said and whatever he fantasized about I not only confirmed but encouraged and embellished. I told him that Sue was a raving nymphomaniac and that he was guaranteed to 'get his end away' should he ever meet her.

I never gave it much thought until I heard that Alan was reported as missing from Tuli. In a moment of lust-filled passion he had decided that he could not allow Sue to wait for him any longer, climbed into his Land Rover and drove all the way to Filabusi. The way he figured it, from what I had told him, any punishment would be worth it once he'd met his true love and consummated their relationship.

I was not at Filabusi when Alan arrived. Without a word to anyone he stormed into the radio room, saw a woman sitting at the desk and asked to speak to Sue.

"Oh, hi! I'm Sue," said Sue.

Alan glanced at her, then took a longer look and with a dismissive gesture retorted, "No, you are not. Where is she?"

When Sue adamantly insisted that she was the very person he was looking for he adamantly insisted that she was not. It was only when Reg was called to the radio room that Alan realized he had been set up before being gently guided to Reg's office for some counselling.

Farm attacks continued without respite, but the farmers, like others in the rest of the country refused to give up. This in spite of the massive losses they were sustaining in terms of livestock destroyed, crops burnt and the deaths of family members and their workers. We were all one team, one people who refused to give up. Because of their resolve to carry on regardless crops were sown, harvested and sent to market. In spite of the war ravaging the country, the agricultural sector still managed to prosper. Some areas, in the northwest of the country, for example, like Mtoko and Mrewa, were totally cleaned out of white farmers, but somehow the farming community in general survived.

The terrorists turned their attention to even softer targets like road-works camps, isolated homesteads, Veterinary Department posts and lonely mines. There were hundreds of mines scattered throughout Rhodesia. The vast majority were small workings staffed by the mine owner who oversaw production and a very small labour force. Filabusi had many such mines. One was Teutonic Mine, a gold mine run by Stewart Allen. He, his wife and two small children lived on the mine in a house surrounded by a ten-foot-high security fence. About a hundred metres from the house was the mine and beyond that the workers' compound.

We had spent the afternoon training twenty or so police reservists in radio-procedure and were having a drink in the pub when I was called to the radio room. It was Stewart, frantically asking for help—his homestead was under attack. Because it was a training exercise we all had our weapons and combat kit at the ready so it only took a couple of minutes to jump into a 'Crocodile' (a Rhodesian armoured personnel carrier) and set off for the mine. There was only one route in and the odds were that if it weren't ambushed it would be mined. That night the odds were with us. We arrived at the entrance of the mine without incident only to be confronted with a pile of gum poles dumped in the middle of the road as a crude barricade.

Again, the odds were that the barricade would be booby-trapped, rigged to set off an explosive charge when we tried to dismantle it. I made a decision to crash through it, hoping the 'Crocodile' would protect us. It did. We smashed through the barricade at speed and hurried towards the homestead.

As we pulled up and our headlights lit up the area we saw the terrorists scrambling over the fence into the bush. As our only concern was for the Allens we fired at them to chase them away but did not pursue them. To do so would have meant following them into bush in the darkness and that would have been foolish.

Stewart and his wife were shaken but otherwise alright. The terrorists had arrived at the compound in the late afternoon, then took the foreman by force to the mine and as it got dark blew up the pump that kept the water level at bay thus flooding the mine.

Then they moved to the homestead and tried opening the main gate. It was securely locked so they started firing at the house. That was when Stewart sounded the alarm. The terrorists had fired hundreds and hundreds of rounds at the house with Stewart returning fire when he could. (This was a scenario that was being played out every day all over the country with a husband and wife moving from window to window and letting off a few shots, while older children reloaded the weapons and the smaller children took cover under beds or tables.)

Stewart was running out of ammunition when the terrorists scaled the fence. Had they accessed the house they would have butchered the entire family. Four of them managed to climb over the fence into the garden and only then did they think of cutting through the fence with their AKM bayonet wire-cutters to allow the others terrorists to crawl through. Had they done this earlier we would have arrived too late.

While Stewart and his wife were in the house with a few of my men I was in the garden looking for anything that the terrorists might have left behind. It wasn't unusual for them to leave behind a rifle, perhaps a magazine or some form of documentation. It was a very dark night and seemed unnaturally quiet after all the action—in fact almost serene—until I saw tracer rounds flying towards us from the bush and heard the distinct crack of AK rounds. It was a bit of a cheap shot but the terrorists had decided to have another go at us and were spraying rounds in our general direction. They got plenty back. As everyone ran outside we centred on what we thought were their firing positions and all twenty-two of us, Stewart and his wife included, returned fire—a total of four hundred and twenty rounds in a couple of seconds.

Before leaving I left two of my men at the house to protect the Allens and the mineworkers. Placing personnel on farms, mines and remote homesteads to protect the occupants was something that continued throughout the duration of the war even though it sorely depleted our manpower reserves.

There were the attacks on mission stations. Missions had been set up in the more remote areas in Rhodesia mainly by Americans and Jesuit priests. The missionaries provided medical attention for local tribespeople, schooling for their children and training courses and classes from literacy to pre-natal to sewing to cooking to agronomy for the adults. We knew that most of the missionaries assisted terrorists in some way or the other but tended to adopt a *laissez-faire* approach to it all. The missionaries were effectively in the same catch-22 position as the locals in terms of offering succour to the guerrillas. There were occasions, however, when pro-liberation missionaries did overstep the line by openly supporting terrorists. When this happened we took action—normally closing the mission and expelling the missionaries from the country.

In Filabusi we had two missions. Two German Jesuits, Father Thaddeus and Brother Erasmus, ran the Silalabuqhwa Mission. Twice a year, on Easter Sunday and Christmas Day, I was invited to a Sunday lunch of roast duck accompanied by Father Thad's special orange sauce. I always looked forward to these meals but was wary of the sort of reception I would get because Father Thad would notify the community beforehand that I was coming. Thus far I had not been ambushed on the way to any of his lunches so I was beginning to think that the terrorists weren't interested in the mission. This wishful thinking did not last long.

On Easter Sunday 1978, after a superb meal, Father Thad asked me to address the locals and give them a 'pep talk'. I really didn't know what to say. I stood on a raised platform before a couple of hundred of local people and spoke about how we were winning the war and how I looked forward to the years of peace that would surely come soon. Everyone applauded—including the nine terrorists, who, I later discovered, had joined in the festivities. I could just imagine them going back to their sectoral commanders and saying something like "We had a good time. *Babaleka* gave us a long speech telling everyone how he was winning the war. The man is mad. If everyone is like him we will win it within a couple of weeks."

Wanezi was the other mission. It was manned by Americans who provided a much-needed and invaluable service to the locals. They boasted excellent medical facilities with fully qualified doctors and nurses on call. On the night the mission was attacked the terrorists shot the place up, burned down the buildings, smashed up the medical facilities and attempted to murder the staff members. My most vivid memory is of the missionary in charge relating how a terrorist had tried to smash down the door of his house. The terrorist eventually managed to open the door an inch or so, stuck his rifle barrel through the gap and sprayed bullets everywhere, before the missionary, with astonishing courage, grappled with the barrel of the gun and turned it away, out of harm's way. Amazingly no one was hit.

After the attack, I and a few others stayed behind to guard the mission and see its inhabitants safely through the night. The duty I allocated myself was to escort the doctors and nurses to the clinic should they be called to attend to a patient. I was hoping for a decent night's sleep, not seriously believing that anyone would bother them—not the brightest decision on my part. At about ten o'clock a doctor summoned me and I accompanied him to the clinic. He had to attend to a woman who was about to give birth and told me to wait outside. My knowledge of childbirth amounted to what I had seen in the movies and as that never lasted more than a few minutes I figured I would be back in my bunk in no time.

Six hours later I was still waiting outside with no indication that I would get any sleep and wondering what on earth all the screaming was about. I assumed that maybe the lady giving birth had a fear of needles. To keep myself occupied I took a walk outside the clinic and found one of those cylinders of local anaesthetic left among the trashed medical supplies—the type where pure alcohol is sprayed on a wound which freezes it. I called one of the mongrels over and as it stood wagging its tail I sprayed some on its nose. It yelped and ran away. As soon as the anaesthetic wore off I called it again; it came back and we went through the whole process several times, much to my silly amusement.

Attacks on missions, like so many other attacks, made no sense. The terrorists were destroying facilities and killing people whose sole purpose in life was to provide for the welfare of the tribespeople. The worst such atrocity was the attack on Elim Mission near Inyanga in the east of the country. Who will ever forget—who *could* ever forget—those photographs, published in the world press, of butchered babies bayoneted to death.

Probably the most written-about missionary in Rhodesia was John Bradburne who ran the Mtemwa leper colony near Mtoko. John was born in 1921 in England. In 1940 he was commissioned into the 9th Ghurkhas Rifles and served in Malaya where he was awarded the Military Cross for gallantry. After World War II he became a Catholic and later made his way to Rhodesia, arriving in 1962. In 1969 he became the warden of Mtemwa leprosy settlement where he remained until his death.

During the war Mtoko was an extremely 'hot' area and John's life was always in danger. In spite of this he continued to work with the lepers—bathing, feeding and clothing them. In 1979, accused of being an informer for the Rhodesian security forces, he was abducted by *mujibas* and taken to the nearest terrorist sectoral commander. The sectoral commander, clearly a compassionate man, knew who John was and the work he did, and subsequently released him. However, as John was making his way home to Mtemwa, a ZANLA political commissar who viewed John as a security risk intercepted him. At gunpoint he ordered John "to kneel down and pray" before shooting him dead. John's body was later found by the side of the road where the terrorists had left him.

As a young boy I used to visit John at Mtemwa with my friend Frank, where we handed out rations and clothing that Frank's father had provided. It was apparent to me even then that there was something very special about John.

And then there were the two Viscount civilian airliners that were shot down near Kariba by ZIPRA in September 1978 and February 1979 respectively. One was blown out of the sky by a SAM-7 missile with no survivors. The other was also hit by a SAM-7 missile; however, through a remarkable piece of flying the pilot managed to crash-land the aircraft in a ploughed field. The survivors, though, were rounded up, the women raped and all cruelly butchered by ZIPRA 'freedom fighters'. Five of the survivors, who'd been on a scouting party, however, did manage to escape.

The following day Hawker Hunter jet fighters circled Salisbury in an act of morale-boosting defiance before attacking terrorist camps in Zambia with devastating effect. Our pilots and technicians achieved miracles with the aircraft and resources that our small air force had at their disposal. We were very proud of them.

From the mid-1970s to 1980 the entire country was at war. If you were capable of walking you were given some form of military duty. Everyone took part, whether it was on the front line, patrolling your own suburb, manning roadblocks, doing paperwork at police stations or packing parachutes. Many of our womenfolk established 'Forces' Canteens', set up in every town, village, hamlet and military base. For next to nothing you could buy a hamburger, a steak and egg roll or a variety of sandwiches. With it came tea, coffee and the warmth and affection of the women. I wonder if these good people ever realized how grateful we were for the invaluable service they provided.

These are the types of people that make Rhodesians what they are and I am proud to count myself of that number.

Chapter seventeen

Gone bush

We started using some Communist Bloc weapons that suited our needs. For covert operations AKs or AKMs were popular as they were lighter and more manageable than our issue FNs. For the larger, more conventional operations RPG-2s and RPG-7s were useful as they were far superior to our locally manufactured rifle grenades.

Both these shoulder-held, self-propelled rocket launchers have a very strong back-blast. Before firing you have to make sure that there is no one behind you. On one occasion in the middle of a contact an RAR sergeant zeroed in on his target, looked behind to make sure all was clear, focused on his target again and pulled the trigger. In between making sure everything was clear and pulling the trigger a trooper had run behind him and took the full back-blast in his groin. He died a few days later—yet another casualty of friendly fire.

My own stick nearly came to grief in the confusion of the same contact which was spread over a large area. A K-car pilot saw us, thought we were terrorists and dived towards us.

When I realized what has happening I screamed into the handset: "Yellow One, Yellow One. Abort, abort! Friendly forces!" and he pulled out of the attack at the last second. Although this brief encounter with a K-car was terrifying, it made me feel good to know these fellows were on our side!

On the subject of friendly fire, Selous Scouts would come into an area and 'freeze' it. No security forces were allowed into the area in case the Scouts, in their pseudo role, were mistaken for real terrorists and shot at. Conversely, if they saw us first, in order not to compromise themselves with the locals they had no option but to initiate a contact with us. Security forces could pass through by road but were not allowed to stop and certainly not permitted to linger without express prior permission.

There were rare occasions when we had to enter a frozen area. Scouts would be told beforehand exactly where we intended to go and what we wanted to do—and we'd hopefully leave each other alone, although I'm sure I had more than one contact when what I took for terrorists were actually Scouts.

One day, while sweeping through fairly sparse bush towards a *kopje* which I suspected of being a terrorist base camp a *mujiba* was suddenly seen running away from us to our front. To my mind this confirmed there was a base camp nearby. We chased the *mujiba* up a rise and into some open ground surrounded by rocks. As we got into the clearing we heard the distinct popping sound of mortars being fired and seconds later they landed among us, exploding with terrifying blasts. This was really like something out of a movie. We had been perfectly set up. Hats off to the terrorists—it was done to perfection. They had worked out our intentions, moved to higher ground, sighted their mortars and then got the *mujiba* to run from cover so that we would chase him and run right into their trap.

The only escape was to get out of the open and into the surrounding rocks. In the seconds it took us to do this I was knocked over by the blast from a mortar. It barely registered as I scrambled desperately from the killing ground. When I found cover among the rocks I groggily searched for target—almost impossible as I knew the terrorists would be gone as soon as the last mortar bomb had left the tube.

I was scanning the hills around us when I saw, of all things, a terrorist wearing a white shirt firing in our direction. He was taking cover behind a rock. He would move from cover, fire a few rounds and then take cover again.

"Hang on," I thought, "terrorists don't wear white shirts and they certainly don't have FN rifles." I suddenly recognized the man as my Special Branch co-ordinator (whom I despised at the best of times). He must have been patrolling the area (without having warned me), heard the commotion and had come to join in the action. He probably had less of an idea where the terrorists were than I. I just hoped to hell he knew where we were positioned. I tried calling him on the radio but he either didn't want to answer or he didn't have a set with him.

"Okay," I thought, "he doesn't know where I am and he probably thinks

I don't know where he is. He will have no idea where any incoming fire is coming from."

The contact was all but over with only a few desultory rounds being harmlessly let off, so I devoted my attention to my colleague. I waited until he ducked for cover and then slowly and methodically emptied my magazine into the rock. I knew I wouldn't hit him and never intended to but made the most of having a go at him.

When it was all over and we linked up he made a meal out of telling everyone how a terrorist had "zoned in on me and let me have it until he ran out of ammo". With the appropriate 'oohs' and 'aahs' my colleague undoubtedly earned himself a few free beers in the pub that night.

My life was all about my work and I relished it. In six months I'd only had five days R & R. Reg, noticing signs of 'bush fatigue', tried to force me to take some leave. Signs like leaving for patrol in the morning then, fifty metres from camp, realizing I had forgotten my rifle and thinking "Ag, what the heck! I have grenades. They'll do."

People started to appreciate that I needed a break when I made a point of looking for baboons and Guinea fowl as we drove through the bush in convoy. When I spotted the baboons or Guinea fowl I would hit the brakes, come to an abrupt stop, leap out, run, dive for cover and open up on them. My reasoning was that the Guinea fowl were for the pot and as for the baboons, well, I just didn't like them. Thousands of rounds were fired at these poor creatures. No baboons were killed and only a handful of Guinea fowl shot.

My favourite baboon story is a wonderful tale about a long-serving P/O who was carrying out a rural patrol. He received a message instructing him to get to go and see a local farmer—as a matter of urgency.

The farmer was very distressed and when asked what was wrong told the P/O that a troop of baboons had been raiding his crops and had virtually wiped out an entire maize field. The farmer had laid traps, shot the baboons but nothing had had any effect—they just kept coming back. The P/O thought about this and advised the farmer that he could sort out the problem. The P/O then climbed into his Land Rover and went to the maize field, with the farmer following at a discreet distance. What the farmer saw was this:

The P/O walked across to the hill where the troop roosted and as he stood in open ground at the foot of the *kopje* the baboons began filtering out from the bush until they had gathered in front of the policeman, barely metres away from him.

Then the baboons suddenly burst out laughing, rolling on the ground, holding their stomachs and pawing each other in delight. Then, as suddenly as they'd started, they stopped, looked at the P/O in horror. The next thing the baboons were sobbing their eyes out, wailing and moaning, wandering around in circles with their hands on their foreheads trying to come to terms with their apparent grief.

Again, they suddenly stopped, and looked intently at the policeman. And then, a few seconds later, the baboons took to their heels, fleeing into the hills on all fours, babies desperately clinging to their mothers' bellies.

The P/O got back into his vehicle and the baboons were never seen again.

A few weeks later the bemused farmer met up with the P/O and asked him what he'd done to drive away the baboons.

The P/O responded: "When I got to the base of the *kopje* the lookout saw that I was a man in uniform and alerted the others. The baboons, being curious animals, all came down to see who I was. When I told them I was a patrol officer in the British South Africa Police they burst out laughing. When I then told them our conditions of service they started crying. When I told them I was on a recruiting drive they fled into the hills to spread the word and alert other troops."

So the story goes ….

I once chased an old female *nganga* (witchdoctor or traditional healer) who lived in the bush just outside Avoca base camp. Every day she would wait for me as I drove up the road. As I neared she would step into the road and hurl all sorts of abuse at me, cursing me royally before jumping out of the way as I slowed down and gunned the motor.

My sergeant was terrified. There is no understating it. To him, to black folk with their ingrained tribal beliefs, she was a powerful spiritual force that you didn't mess with.

Eventually I decided I'd had enough and would put a stop to this morning ritual of hers. My solution was to leave without my sergeant. As she ran into the road I stopped my Land Rover, engaged four-wheel drive and ominously inched towards her as if I were going to run her over. Her solution was to head off in to the bush. Wherever she went my trusty old Land Rover was able to follow. She hobbled along, all the while looking back over her shoulder, waving her stick and directing hideous invective my way. Through ditches and dry riverbeds the old crone went, and then up towards a fence thinking that I'd have to stop and she could escape. Not a chance. I followed her everywhere until she simply stopped, turned and faced me, challenging me to run her down. The game, which had taken up most of the morning, was now over. I had no idea where anyone else was and returned to base.

No one said a word when I got back.

Gordon Nutt was beyond being bushed; he was simply fed up. He wanted to go home. During one of his trips back home on R & R he dug out his old pellet gun (air rifle) and brought it back with him. It was one of those sunny warm days. We'd returned early from patrol and I had a couple of beers. I was dozing on my mat while others were outside sunbathing. A constable woke me.

"Sir, please try and talk with NSPO [National Service Patrol Officer] Gordon because sir, he is *bichana penga* [slightly mad]."

I got up and went to see what the commotion was all about. Through blurry eyes I saw Ian, a huge troopie, saying to Gordon, "Gordon, fuck off! Put that bloody thing down or I'll *bliksem* [punch] you, you bastard." And then as he was hit with a pellet, "*Eina!* [ouch] Man, I'm telling you put the damn thing down or I will hammer you, *Eina!*"

Dear old Gordon; he was bored and had decided to go hunting for 'terrorists'—in the base camp—with his pellet gun! Anyone in camo kit (all of us) was a legitimate target. He'd edge along the blockhouse, back to wall with his rifle at the ready. As he came to a corner he'd take a quick peek around the corner, identify his target, duck back in, bring his rifle to the shoulder and in combat style leap out, fire one round and duck back into cover. The pellets didn't penetrate the skin but they hurt like hell.

Gordon and I had an understanding. A quiet word in his ear and he gently put the pellet gun down, had a few beers and fell then asleep. No (major) harm done.

I know Gordon doesn't believe this story but I have the pictures to prove it—as seen in the picture sections of this book.

A final word on Gordon. He was bushed and desperately needed a break. There was no arguing that and I really did try to help him along with all the compassion and understanding that was his due. But I am only human and one day I could not resist playing a prank on him.

Gordon was nearing the end of his bush trip and was wound up as tight as a spring. We were driving back to Filabusi after having spent a few days at the District Commissioner's Intaf camp at Silalabuchwa Dam. Just the two of us in my Land Rover. We had been involved in a several contacts and knew there was a chance, as always, of being ambushed which only added to our anxiety levels.

I had an idea. As we were driving along I started playing with the accelerator pedal, depressing it and releasing it, causing the Land Rover to shudder and jerk—a clear indication, so I told Gordon, that there was problem with the fuel feed. This was a common problem with Land Rovers but all it took to fix it was stop, detach the fuel line, drain it, re-attach it and continue.

I chose a section of the road where there was lot of clearance on either side thus reducing the chances of an ambush and told Gordon that I would stand guard while he sorted out the problem.

Very nervously Gordon opened the bonnet, climbed on the front bumper and reached into the back of the engine to detach the fuel line, the bonnet an inch above his head. He kept calling to me, saying, "Hey, Tony! Are you there?

Is everything okay?" and I would reassure him accordingly.

Other than the rustle of the wind and the occasional *clunk* of a cow bell there was not a sound. While Gordon assumed I was on guard—which I technically was; I simply changed my position—and absorbed in his task, I quietly walked over the driver's side of the cab and pressed the horn. Gordon got such a fright that jerked his head upwards, whacking it on the bonnet.

I felt awful as I'd only expected Gordon to get a bit of a fright. I apologised profusely, saying that I had accidentally "bumped the hooter".

Gordon could not have cared less as he was by now mildly concussed and the drive back to Filabusi did not bother him in the least.

For all that I have said about Gordon he was an excellent soldier and companion. For months he provided me with the protection I needed and was an integral part of our team.

Some of the Filabusi folk have had a lasting effect on me.

Mr Marais was a retired miner who had worked all his life in the South African coal mines. After contracting pneumoconiosis he had bought a plot of land in Colleen Bawn, a farming area on the southern extremity of my patrol area. When in the neighbourhood, I always made of point of crossing the Umzingwane River to check up on him and see that he and his wife were okay. Every so often he gave me a lamb, which I took back to Avoca. It would quickly fatten up, feeding off the lush grass growing on the earthen walls of the base perimeter. After six weeks or so it was slaughtered, dressed and before we left on an early-morning patrol, put on a spit and slowly roasted for a good eight hours.

When we got back from patrol in the evening we would sit down next to the spit with our beers, or in my case brandy and Coke, and slice off strips of the well-seasoned meat. These were some of the best meals I have ever had.

Dougal MacDougal was a Rhodes Scholar who'd boxed for Oxford and qualified as a geologist just before the Second World War. He joined the Parachute Regiment and saw action at Arnhem. As he was descending in his parachute he somehow lost his rifle, landed among the Germans, but managed to fight his way out without a weapon. He was severely traumatized and sent home back to Rhodesia where, unable to settle down, he moved into the very remote Filabusi area and took up the life of a hermit.

The government, respecting his right to privacy, gazetted a statute granting a patch of land to him, effectively preventing anyone from building any sort of habitation near his small-holding. He had lived this way for thirty years and other than an annual supply drop from some relatives in Bulawayo he was completely self-sufficient.

I knew of his existence. From a distance, so as not to intrude, I would keep an eye out for him. Like others I respected his privacy but had never actually spoken to him let alone seen him in the flesh close up. I am sure that by now he has long since passed away and I don't think anyone would object to my telling this story.

Because of the mystique surrounding him the locals believed Dougal had some sort of spiritual powers and stayed well away from him. Terrorists had attacked a farm in the Essexvale area on our northern boundary. Although security forces had lost tracks they were pretty sure that the terrorists were headed in the general direction of Dougal's 'home'.

I told the SF stick on follow-up that I would rendezvous with them and under certain conditions, which Reg insisted upon, that I would speak with Dougal. Dougal's mood and character apparently changed all the time so one never knew how he would react. He did not want company and bitterly resented any intrusions on his privacy. I had been told that if I were seen with my rifle as I approached he would not speak to me.

With this in mind we travelled to within two kilometres of his abode and walked the rest of the way in. When we were within sight of his residence I handed my rifle to a member of the follow-up stick.

His 'house' consisted of two thatched pole and *dagga* (wattle and daub) huts next to each other, surrounded by sparsely populated, but neatly kept, flowerbeds edged with light-coloured sandstones. Dougal had seen us long before we saw him. As I approached he came from behind a hut and stood stock still, waiting for me to come to him. If you can imagine a typical caricature of Robinson Crusoe, well, that's what Dougal looked like. He was wearing an old cotton shirt and trousers made of hessian cut from old maize sacks. His long, blond hair and thick beard contrasted with his dark tanned skin.

I introduced myself, half-expecting him to start ranting and raving. Instead, in a perfectly calm and rational voice he asked me what my business was. There ensued a general discussion about terrorist movements in the area; he also told me that the very terrorists we were following had tried to rob him earlier and he'd chased them away. I sensed that forcing a conversation would only anger him so having found out what I needed, brought our meeting to a close and bid him farewell.

As far as I know he was never again disturbed by terrorists.

As 1978 drew to a close, so my time in Filabusi was coming to an end. I think it is fair to say that I was becomingly increasingly 'bushed'. Much as I had enjoyed my three and a half years in Filabusi I found myself craving for civilization. I therefore applied for a GC posting in the Salisbury area. Gordon had long since left. On completion of his national service he went to university and became a lawyer. I missed him.

Instead of Salisbury I was posted to Bulawayo where Reg and I met with the Officer Commanding. For some reason the OC thought I wanted to return to Uniform Branch. I don't think he knew what to do with me and was about to persuade me to stay in GC when Reg gave him a glowing report of the GC work I had done in Filabusi. I was therefore posted to GC in Western Commonage— a township police station similar to Mzilikazi.

I had been living in comfortable single quarters for three years and did not want to go back into a hostel. As it turned out I moved into single quarters reserved for senior patrol officers. This was pure luxury. Instead of a single room in the police hostel I was given my own vehicle and a small two-roomed apartment in the police camp with access to all its facilities. I stayed there for a month. From an operational point of view nothing much happened in that month—in view of the short time I was there I would not have expected it.

I have never been told officially but I am sure that I was posted to Bulawayo to 'settle down'.

A month later whoever was watching over me decided that I had calmed down enough and I was informed that I had been posted to Ground Coverage, Salisbury North.

Whoever was in charge of pulling the strings, I would like to warmly thank you. That month of 'time out' was exactly what I needed.

I was ready to return to the fray.

Chapter eighteen

Salisbury North

Salisbury, the capital city, was really a city under siege, but you would never have thought so—not superficially anyway. The genteel northern suburbs were still beautiful with their rolling lawns and beautiful gardens. The southern and western townships of Highfields and Harare were still abuzz, throbbing to the beat of an African city and the southern industrial sites still churned out the production necessary to keep the economy, and the war, afloat.

In November 1978 when I was transferred to GC Salisbury North the number of terrorist incursions into the country from Zambia and Mozambique had increased dramatically. It was becoming a deluge. The SAS, Selous Scouts and RLI were launching massive external raids against ZANLA and ZIPRA terrorist training and holding camps in these countries and killing thousands, but still they came. Those who had made their way into Rhodesia were headed towards the ultimate prize, Salisbury. To reach the capital from Mozambique they infiltrated mainly through the Chinamora, Msana and Masembura TTLs, all northeast of Salisbury adjacent to the Enterprise, Bindura and Shamva commercial farming areas.

Although operations in Salisbury North were monitored from Salisbury itself, intelligence-gathering in the form of Ground Coverage and troop deployments were controlled from a small base next to Borrowdale police station, a small suburban station twenty-four kilometres northeast of the city centre.

The station personnel were responsible for policing Chinamora and the farms to the north of Salisbury. Marlborough police station was a similar station eleven kilometres from the centre of Salisbury and was responsible for policing the farms to the west and northwest. Highlands police station, eighteen kilometres out, was responsible for the eastern districts of the city.

My first duty was to gather intelligence relating to terrorist movements on the farms covered by Marlborough police station. To do this my team and I moved into a house in the outlying suburb of Christon Bank. Christon Bank was unique in that it was situated twenty-one kilometres from Salisbury among the Mazoe Hills. At that time this effectively put its residents way out in the bush, away from any other suburbs. An odd assortment of folk, mostly people who wanted to be away from mainstream suburbia, lived in Christon Bank.

It quickly became apparent that not only did I have to monitor and combat terrorist movements in Christon Bank but also its inhabitants with all their idiosyncrasies. One of my first dealings was with a high-ranking civil servant who insisted that my predecessor (Tiny) give him a security force radio so that in the event of Christon Bank being attacked he could act as a link between us and locals in the centre of Christon Bank. It made good sense. He was given a radio but after tinkering with it the novelty wore off so he gave it to his gardener, without telling me. His gardener put the radio to full use by conscientiously monitoring security force communications and passing them on to his terrorist masters.

Another of the residents, Derek, contacted me and told me that he had received reliable information to the effect that terrorists were moving through Christon Bank into the Chinamora TTL and that their route took them through the bottom of his small-holding. He wanted to know "what was I going to do about it". I was somewhat doubtful but not only was he adamant he was also convinced that he heard the terrorists talking every night at the bottom of his garden. His wife confirmed this information.

Because the information was at best vague and Derek was wildly eccentric I said I would do nothing until I received confirmation from one of my informants. Derek was not at all happy so he went direct to Police General Headquarters and managed to convince a high-ranking officer there that the information he had was genuine. I then received an order telling me to react to Derek's information.

My best option available was to clandestinely put two sensitive listening devices at the bottom of his plot in the area that the alleged meetings were being held and place the receiver in Derek's house. This done I waited and of course nothing happened for the next four nights. On the fifth night my phone rang.

"The terrorists are meeting now," Derek said in an urgent whisper. "I can hear them talking. I am going to be attacked, Heeelp!"

Again still somewhat doubtful and with no other option I gathered three of my team together and we executed a long, circuitous walk to his house and managed to get in without being seen. Derek was hunched over the receiver with his wife and kids listening to every word the 'terrorists' were saying.

"Listen, listen," he waved me over.

I can speak a bit of Shona, quite a lot of Ndebele and of course English. The language the 'terrorists' were speaking was not one of these. It was a language I had never heard before. With Bantu languages there is some overlap in the diction and you can usually pick up one or two words even when listening to a language you have never heard before. Much as I tried I could not recognize a single word and nor could my constables.

The 'terrorists' were yakking away like a bunch of old hens. From the level of discussion and in keeping with terrorist tactics I assumed they were ensconced for the night and would only move out at dawn. But I still wasn't convinced. Nevertheless I was confident that if they were terrorists we could creep up on them and attack them. The four of us left the house and leopard-crawled for what seemed half a kilometre to the bottom of the plot. We lay there listening, rifles ready for immediate action. And then suddenly one of the terrorists let out a loud "*hee haw, hee haw*". The terrorists turned out to be two donkeys that had wandered from their pens and were having an illicit late-night snack among some lush green grass. They had been completely compromised.

You would think that this would have put any resident of Christon Bank off ever reporting anything to me. All it seemed to do was make them more determined to find the terrorists themselves. Our phone never stopped ringing. Fortunately I had a Field Reservist Chris Prinsloo on call-up with me who was a marketing director in Civvy Street. As public relations was his strong point and definitely not mine I let him deal with all the calls, none of which ever amounted to anything.

Chris epitomized the word 'yuppy'. He had completed his national service and was doing a marketing degree part-time. He had managed to work a deal in which he was sent to Christon Bank where he could do his call-ups and attend evening classes. Chris would probably describe himself as "a lover and not a fighter". He had a string of female admirers and a well-defined image to maintain which centred around wearing the latest designer clothing , keeping up to date with all the latest buzz words such as 'stunning', 'paradigm' and 'absolutely', and, most important of all keeping his blond hair immaculately groomed in the style of Face from *The A Team*. No matter what was going on, as long as Chris had all his hair in place he felt he could deal with pretty much anything.

That is until I told him to put on camouflage cream.

The idea of wearing camo cream is to break down the reflective outline of your skin and enable you to, in some way, conceal yourself without being seen. Contrary to popular belief, it is not designed to make you disappear altogether. It shouldn't be smeared on but rather 'streaked' on. On clandestine operations all of us, including the black soldiers, applied camo cream so that it covered every bit of any exposed skin, including arms, neck and face.

I had called my men together and briefed them on a clandestine operation we would be doing that night. The men all went away to clean their weapons and prepare their gear before a final briefing. While were waiting around, covered in camo cream, weapons and webbing secure, packed and ready to go Chris arrived looking like something out *The Black and White Minstrel Show*. We all looked at him curiously.

"And this; what's going on?" I asked him.

He looked at me somewhat sheepishly but did not respond. Chris was no wimp but try as he might he could not convince himself of the need to cover *all* of his exposed skin with camo cream. He had carefully dabbed it on his face until there was an inch-wide shiny white gap between hairline and camo paint. He was sent off with orders not to come back until every bit of his exposed skin was covered.

The house we used as a base was next door to a house owned by a mad Pole called Stanislaw. He also owned the land behind our house. We had to traverse thirty or so metres of his land to get to a dirt road that accessed the farming area. Using this short cut instead of the usual route saved a good five to ten minutes of driving time. It doesn't sound like much but when you are responding to a farm attack and can knock five minutes off the reaction time and possibly save someone's life, it is a long time.

Stanislaw was determined not to let us cut across his land. Police General Headquarters had formally asked him to allow us to do so and in spite of their requests and visits from the Member in Charge Marlborough trying to persuade him otherwise he adamantly refused. Sure, legally he had every right to stop us but weighed up against what we were faced with and his stubbornness, I ignored him.

It came to a head one day when I was with a new Uniform Branch P/O from Marlborough who asked to come on patrol with me so that he could familiarize himself with the area. As I drove through Stanislaw's land I had to stop because a half dozen forty-four-gallon drums had been put in the way to block me. I was about to get out of the Land Rover and remove the drums when Stanislaw who had sneaked up on the vehicle stuck the barrel of a shotgun in my face. This got me really angry. I had enough on my hands facing armed terrorists every day and now this fool. Much to my own surprise, instead of grovelling which would have been an understandable reaction, I grabbed the barrel of the shotgun, arrested him, handcuffed him and dragged him off to Marlborough station prison cells where he was charged with something we conjured up.

But that was not the end of it. Although he did not try and prevent us driving through his land he regularly stood at the fence bordering our properties and would hurl abuse at my men, all in Polish, which made a response somewhat difficult.

Things would inevitably come to a head and one day they did when he tried to shoot his common-law wife. I had just returned from patrol and was having a beer when I heard the gunshot. I called to my two sergeants and we ran over to his house to see what was going on. I saw Stanislaw standing in the garden outside his kitchen, his wife collapsed on the ground in a hysterical heap. He was walking towards me almost in a trance waving a low-calibre revolver and threatening to shoot me. Sergeant Nyama took the initiative and quickly snatched the revolver from him while Stanislaw stood glaring at me for a few seconds before continuing towards me.

I had an FN rifle in my hand, he was unarmed and you just don't argue with someone who has an FN. But he kept walking towards me like a rabid jackal, completely fearless. Before he got too close I handed my rifle to Nyama, took a step forward and hit him. My punch didn't have much effect and we got in to a tangle, both of us falling to the ground with me lying on top of him trying to pin him down. Eventually he said "enough" and became completely subdued. I lay there, still on top of him, trying to catch my breath when Nyama shouted "Look-out!" Stanislaw's wife had recovered from her hysteria and placed a carving knife in his right hand which he immediately brought over his head and tried to stab me with. Fortunately I managed to grip his wrist and wrestle it away from him.

Then I lost my temper and subdued him properly, pummelling him into oblivion. I arrested him, cuffed him, dumped him in the back of a Kudu (a mine-proof vehicle) and took him to Salisbury Central where he was put in the cells.

He was charged with all sorts of offences. During his trial I was called to give evidence as the arresting officer. I was on friendly terms with the public prosecutor who called me aside in the interval before I was due to take the stand and give my evidence. He told me that he might have to be "hard on me" and that "I shouldn't take it personally". I had no idea what he was talking about. But either way it didn't help my confidence.

The PP started by asking me if I had used excessive force to subdue Stanislaw. Aware that I had used a touch more than necessary I had beforehand studied the Police Standing Orders and quoting from it, said: "Your worship, I used the minimum amount of force necessary to subdue the accused and in doing so delivered a single blow to him upon or about his face."

The magistrate looked at me, grinned and held up a piece of paper: "Patrol Officer Trethowan, have you seen this?"

"No, your worship."

He then handed it to the public prosecutor and said: "Perhaps Patrol Officer Trethowan would like to have a look at this?"

The PP handed it to me. When I had finished reading it my first reaction was to mutter "Oh shit!" under my breath.

I didn't know that when Stanislaw had been detained he had asked to see a doctor and the piece of paper I had been given was the doctor's medical report, the details of which clearly indicated that I had done a tad more than "administer the minimum amount of force". Somehow I managed to talk my way out of it and was excused. I had so much going on at the time and never bothered to find out what the end result of the court case was.

Ozzie Bristow was a well-known conservationist who had bought some land forty-two kilometres west of Salisbury where he'd set up an animal sanctuary—a sort of mini game park. As the sanctuary was in my patrol area I used to visit him even though there was no danger from terrorists. I just liked his company and it gave me an opportunity to sit down and chat with him.

Ozzie had a giant Galapagos tortoise that was reputedly over a hundred years old. It was about the size of a coffee table, a friendly old creature that didn't seem to mind small children sitting on his back going for a ride. The tortoise had an endearing habit of wandering into the car park and, when it wanted its back scratched, would work its way under the front section a car and then, like a huge jack, flex its legs and stand up. The wheels of the car would be lifted two feet off the ground and would stay like that until the tortoise felt he'd had enough, with the owner of the car helpless until the tortoise wandered off.

Ozzie's main tourist attraction was a group of bush pigs that lived in the sanctuary. He also had a troop of baboons that he kept in a huge enclosure, fenced off on all sides and above to prevent them from escaping. Within the round enclosure Ozzie had built a small racetrack, a circle within a circle as it were. The railings surrounding the inner and outer track were made of sections of gum poles. Every so often Ozzie would round up the bush pigs and herd them onto the race track where they would start to run round and round in circles looking for a way out. When the baboons saw the pigs being shepherded to the track they would gather in the inner circle or squat on the railings, intently studying each pig as it ran by until they spotted a steed of their choice. They would then leap onto a pig's back, clinging onto the pig's mane for support. The bush pig would grunt in disgust and try to shake the baboon off by running away. The only way to go was round—and round and round they would go. Every so often a baboon would leap off to be replaced immediately by another baboon, or it might become dizzy and tumble off. It was great entertainment and as it only lasted a few minutes no harm was done to the animals.

There was a resident troop of wild baboons that lived in the hills near the animal sanctuary. Being territorial animals the troop looked upon the baboons in the enclosure as intruders—or sell-outs. They spent hours and hours barking at each other trying to pick a fight but, frustratedly, were unable to get to each at other because of the fencing. That was until one of the 'resident' baboons managed to dig under the fence and the whole lot escaped, went into the hills and attacked the 'wild' troop. There were many casualties on both sides and for Ozzie a lesson learnt. From that point on he no longer kept baboons. It was just too problematic.

Ozzie's sanctuary was not far away from a spot where locals would pray to the ancestors for rain in times of drought. We were aware of this and sent soldiers into the area on reconnaissance to gather intelligence on the terrorists' movements—for wherever locals gathered, so too the terrorists. Many times we could have ambushed the terrorists as they mingled with the locals, but it would have inevitably caused civilian casualties—which, because of the sacredness of the site, would have led to an irreconcilable polarization between us and the locals.

After six months at Christon Bank I moved the short distance across to Borrowdale and took over the role of GC Co-ordinator Chinamora which included the adjacent Borrowdale and Highlands farming areas. Chinamora is a relatively small TTL, about three hundred square kilometres in area, but is densely populated. On the northern border is the Masembura TTL; to the west the Marlborough commercial farming area; the Borrowdale and Highlands farming areas to the south and Masana TTL to the east.

There were literally hundreds of terrorists operating in the Chinamora. To deal with them we had my team as the intelligence-gathering team, and an assortment of field reservists as our back-up. Some were based at a camp inside the TTL to 'show a presence'. I was fortunate in that being so close to Salisbury I could call on whomever I wanted for military support and normally received rapid satisfaction.

High Command and PGHQ had permitted, in fact encouraged, a group of civilian pilots to form the Police Reserve Air Wing (PRAW) to complement the tiny Rhodesian Air Force (RhAF). These intrepid men flew their own single-engine civilian aeroplanes, most of which had had the passenger door removed and a single machine gun placed mounted at the entrance, manned by an observer, or 'spotter'. By 1979 most RhAF aircraft were fully committed either on incessant Fireforce duties or on external 'pre-emptive' strikes against external ZANLA and ZIPRA bases. It was indeed a rarity to call for RhAF air support and actually get it—in the form of a Lynx air strike or an Alouette gunship at best. So we came to rely more and more upon the ageing PRAW airmen, some of whom were extremely innovative, always scheming new methods of delivering ground-attack bombs onto the enemy.

In my GC role I had worked with PRAW in Matabeleland and had established a successful rapport with the pilots. We had worked out our air-to-ground tactics and built up a good working relationship based on solid communications. The same was to happen in Chinamora. I cannot understate how thoroughly professional these pilots were. During the initial stages of the PRAW formation we were all on a learning curve. Not so much in the technical aspects of flying and intelligence-gathering but more so related to ground-to-pilot radio communication, learning how to interact with each other and developing our skills relating to the spotting of terrorist base camps from the air. This was a primary role of PRAW.

I had done a lot of work with PRAW but had never actually flown with them. In fact I had never been in a light aircraft and had only done two of three short flights in an Alouette.

So I organized a flight with our local PRAW pilot Bill Nightingale and his observer. Chris Prinsloo came along for the ride and we sat in the back seats. Our objective was to fly over a group of hills to try and spot a terrorist base camp that I was sure had been established in among some hills in the Chinamora. My objective was to see if it was 'live' and then, if necessary, call in Fireforce.

We took off and climbed to five thousand feet as Bill levelled out and started flying in ever-widening circles, each one overlapping the other. Terrorists clearly knew that an aircraft circling above was likely to be looking for their camps, so by flying in increasingly wider circles the pilot gradually moved to a point where he overflew the intended point on the ground but hopefully without revealing his true intentions.

With the left wing dipped at a forty-five-degree bank we gradually moved towards the suspected base camp. I had been on operations long enough to feel when something ominous was about to happen, like a sixth sense. However, in this case I put it down to the fact that I was unsettled in the aircraft and it was really just a case of nerves. That is until I heard what sounded like a typewriter clicking away just outside the aircraft. It was a completely foreign sound to me. No sooner had I heard it than Bill put the aircraft nose down and dived earthwards. The terrorists had seen us and opened fire on the aircraft—that was the clicking sound I heard. Bill's immediate-action (IA) drill was to dive directly towards the ground fire to present a smaller target and then evacuate the immediate area while pulling out of the dive.

He managed to do this successfully, going from five thousand feet to less than a thousand in a matter of seconds. As you would expect there was no time for him to discuss tactics until we were well away from the ground fire. With the camp now confirmed as 'live' he called in Fireforce on standby at Salisbury's New Sarum air force base. He orbited the camp until the Fireforce arrived and then guided them in, his job now done. The end result was a successful contact.

For my part I got the fright of my life. I had no idea what was going on and I think the only thing that held body and soul together was that I knew that I was flying with Bill, an experienced PRAW pilot in whom I had absolute confidence.

It was always a bugbear of mine—over four years on operations and probably a total of fifteen minutes' flying time in an Alouette helicopter. Somehow I always managed to be the one doing the walking while others ended up airborne. (I made up for it a bit at the end of the war when I went to New Sarum and brazenly asked Squadron Leader Ian Harvey if I could have a ride in one his helicopters. He agreed and said that one of his pilots was due on a training flight and I could tag along. I enjoyed an exhilarating forty-minute low-level flight in the Lake McIlwaine area just west of Salisbury.)

Gerry Cleveland was another exceptionally good PRAW pilot with whom I worked. On many occasions he would fly overhead and direct me and my team towards terrorists. PRAW pilots were our eyes; with them flying above they were our scouts—they were able to advise us of the lie of the land and any likely ambush points, escape routes, short cuts and the like.

At the start of any follow-up I always plotted my position and got my bearings on a 1:50,000 map before setting off. However, if I had PRAW support I soon put it away and in doing so did away with the need for continuous map-reading; thus able to concentrate all my efforts on tracking, managing my troops, in fact all the things necessary to ensure a successful follow-up. At any time I could ask the PRAW pilot to give me my position and then quickly locate it on the map. By not having to continually stop and map-read I was able to save much time and keep focused.

However … no matter how much planning and preparation went into an operation, no matter how many brilliant PRAW pilots one might have overhead, things did not always work out exactly as envisaged.

Information I had suggested that terrorists were moving in to the Mazoe farming area, north of Salisbury through a valley in the Pote area of Chinamora. A *kopje* overlooking the valley was designated as a good OP (observation post) position so a PATU stick was briefed and deployed. (OPs were a major tool of the security forces in all operational areas. To be effective and to remain clandestine a stick was deployed anything up to fifteen kilometres from their objective with the stick walking onto the OP position under cover of darkness.)

The PATU stick managed to get to the OP without being observed by locals or *mujibas* and two days later came on air to report that terrorists had been sighted moving towards the OP *kopje*. An hour later the OP reported that the terrorists were getting closer and a short while later reported that the terrorists had in fact based up metres away from the OP position. This was all good news. The fact that the terrorists were resting up, oblivious to their mountain neighbours, meant that we had plenty of time to formulate our plan of attack.

The first thing to do was confirm the PATU stick's exact location. They gave us a six-figure grid reference which put them exactly where we wanted them to be, or where they should be. A call was sent out to Army Headquarters and six truckloads of soldiers were rounded up and transported to Borrowdale police station from where we would deploy. This was one of those rare occasions when, after confirming that I could call on air support, I was able to brief the pilot who, in this case, drove out in his vehicle to the station where we put our plan together. We had managed to access an air force Lynx, a ground-attack aircraft—the Lynx is a high-winged monoplane with one engine in front of the cockpit and one behind. It has bombs mounted under the wings and two light machine guns mounted on top of the cockpit. The pilot starts firing his machine guns immediately prior to releasing his bombs. The pilot's name was John. The plan was to get as close as we could to the *kopje* by vehicle, deploy the troops to surround the *kopje* and then have John come in and bomb the terrorists' position. The PATU stick on site would leave it until the last minute before they withdrew from the area—hopefully without being seen.

Everything was going according to plan. The troops surrounded the *kopje*. Jonathan flew overhead, turned and commenced his run-in. John was well into his dive when the terrorists opened up on his aircraft with everything they had, causing him to abort the strike.

The grid reference the PATU stick had given us was wrong. Instead of being the grid reference of the OP *kopje* they had given us the grid reference of the next-door *kopje* in error. Everything was falling apart. We had surrounded the wrong hill feature. With the wrong grid reference John had commenced his attack and, anticipating ground fire from immediately below him, had unwittingly presented a larger target and was fired upon from a totally unexpected direction. The small-arms fire severed the hydraulic lines of his aircraft, causing him to declare an emergency and pull out of the strike immediately.

The terrorists bomb-shelled in all directions. Fortunately for us some ran into our troops and were killed. John managed to nurse his aircraft back to New Sarum where he successfully crash-landed it. For his efforts in getting the aircraft back safely the air force awarded him a medal.

In peacetime, Chinamora is a lovely place to visit, have a picnic, go for a walk or view the renowned Bushman paintings at Domboshawa, a vast area of granite domes. A small business centre had been established at Domboshawa to cater for tourists visiting the Bushman rock art. A petrol station and a kiosk, a small convenience store, did a roaring trade. The petrol station had three resident fuel bowsers each containing forty thousand litres of diesel, petrol and paraffin respectively.

It was common for terrorists to vandalize, plunder and torch business centres. Essentially it was the locals who suffered as a result.

On this particular occasion the petrol, diesel and paraffin pumps provided an ideal opportunity to do some real damage. The terrorists broke the locks securing the pumps and drained the contents onto the ground. The fuel accumulated and flowed towards the kiosk. By the time the bowsers were empty a total of one hundred and twenty thousand litres of highly flammable liquid had saturated the earth over the entire area of the business centre.

One of the terrorists was ordered to walk into the kiosk, strike a match and drop it on the floor. The terrorist struck the match, covering it with one other hand out of force of habit to make sure a breeze did not blow it out. He then knelt down and carefully placed the burning match on the wet floor. The result was instantaneous—one hundred and twenty thousand litres of fuel ignited in a massive ball of fire.

I received the call minutes later, gathered my men together and went to Domboshawa, arriving as dawn was breaking. The entire business centre was destroyed. No trace of any body or bodies was seen. Tracks however were found heading off into the TTL. Confident of catching the terrorists I called for air cover and we set off on follow-up.

We followed the spoor through thick bush, through kraals, down into a dry riverbed, around several *kopjes* and on up towards Masembura. Two or three kilometres after setting off several items of burnt clothing were found carelessly discarded, hastily hidden in a bush beside a path. This could only mean that one of the terrorists was injured. What surprised me was that although the others were carrying him it did not seem to hamper their progress. They were moving at a rate of knots.

The PRAW pilot kept on notifying me of my exact locstat but the increasingly thick bush prevented him from seeing any sign of the terrorists. He then had to return to base to refuel. Eventually the bush opened up and it became apparent that a base camp was most likely ahead of us so we fanned out into extended line, cautiously advancing. Two shots were fired from someone on my left and then nothing. Tins of food and other signs of life were found which confirmed the site was in fact a base camp, but otherwise it was deserted.

On the approach one of my men stumbled upon a sight that probably still gives him nightmares to this day. A human being lay propped up against a rock, looking as if someone had painted him a ghastly white with faint streaks of green and yellow. This was the terrorist who had struck the match. He had suffered third degree burns over his entire body— except for his groin which was protected by numerous pairs of underpants (which terrorists wore in the belief that they offered some sort of protection from bullet) and his feet which were covered by his boots. It surely was an amazing feat of human endurance— that he and his comrades had managed to travel a total distance of thirty-two kilometres through the bush without us being able to catch them; his comrades alternating between carrying and dragging him. The pain the terrorist would have endured must have been unbearable and yet he still managed to survive. His comrades, knowing that a contact was imminent and that they could not do much more for him lay him against the rock before continuing their flight.

As we swept through a soldier spotted the apparition and instinctively fired two rounds into his head, killing him instantly.

Before departing the area, we booby-trapped the body by placing two hand grenades with pins removed underneath it. I despatched one stick into an OP position to observe the camp and await further developments. It didn't take long for the grenades to be detonated—not by other terrorists but by kraal dogs that had come skulking into the camp, attracted by the stench of charred flesh. Several were killed instantly.

The endurance of another terrorist was amply demonstrated just after a contact in the Chinamora. A base camp had been attacked and when it was all over one terrorist lay among the dead, wounded but still alive. We were desperate for a capture who could supply us with up-to-date intelligence so everything was done to keep this terrorist alive. He had sustained fourteen major gunshot and shrapnel wounds. Other than cover his wounds and get a drip in him there was not much more I could do. No helicopters were available so I put him in the back of my Land Rover, covered him with a blanket and drove to the Selous Scout fort at Bindura where I handed him over to an army doctor. The journey was at night and took over three hours. In spite of his horrific injuries he survived.

I was living in the Chinamora base camp when the oil storage depot in the Salisbury industrial sites was attacked by terrorists in December 1978. As the crow flies my camp was thirty-six kilometres from the depot and even from that distance at two o'clock in the morning I was able to see the sky lighting up on the horizon as the tanks exploded. It looked like a distant thunderstorm. The terrorists were tracked down and killed over the next few days in the Chinamora and Msana TTLs; nevertheless it was a major propaganda coup for ZANLA. Even today people who were living in and around Salisbury at the time have no idea how close the guerrillas came to bringing terrorism onto the streets of the city.

Chapter nineteen

"My bones will rise again"

We referred to the staunch members of ZAPU and ZANU as 'nationalists' (ZAPU and ZANU were the political wings of ZIPRA and ZANLA respectively.) The nationalists who lived in the rural areas regularly fed the terrorists and provided them with information about security-force movements. Part of my job entailed visiting their kraals and interviewing them, perhaps over a cup of tea or a bowl of *sadza*. We never underestimated the cunning of these people. An interview with a nationalist was like a game of chess in that they knew we were after information and we knew that they would use the opportunity to extract information from us. It was a battle of minds from start to finish and always exhilarating because most of them were very intelligent men who knew the game. The trick was to make them believe that you knew more than they did.

The strange thing about it all was that within minutes of arriving at a kraal the resident terrorists would have been informed that I was with the nationalist— equally I would know that the terrorists were watching me, probably from a nearby *kopje*. The terrorists could easily have ambushed me but they never did. I could easily have arrested the nationalist and taken him away for questioning but I never did. I think it was something of an unsaid truce, perhaps because either party was potentially more valuable to the other alive rather than dead or incapacitated.

Ngangas (traditional healers or witchdoctors, roughly pronounced 'nunga') play an important role in the lives of Africans—not only because they are healers but more so because they are the medium through which to communicate with the ancestors, the traditional spirits who are revered ... and feared. Two of the most renowned spirit mediums in the Shona culture were Mbuya Nehanda and her husband spirit Sekuru Kagubi (sometimes Kaguvi. *Mbuya* is Shona for 'grandmother' and *sekuru* means 'old man', or 'grandfather' similar to the Swahili *mzee*).

Nehanda and Kagubi lived in the hills between Goromonzi and Mazoe from the 1860s and were recognized as the most powerful spirit mediums in the country. They were instrumental in organizing maShona resistance to Rhodes' British occupiers during the Mashonaland Rebellion (known as the 'First *Chimurenga*' by the maShona) of 1896–1897. In 1898 they were arrested, tried for treason and hanged. Legend has it that Mbuya Nehanda's last words were "My bones will rise again".

Eighty years later her influence in Mashonaland, through the words she 'spoke', was still massive. I was once told that African huts are round to prevent evil spirits from hiding in the corners. This may or may not be true but it makes sense. The relevance of this to our intelligence community was that it was crucial we knew where the spirit mediums lived and ideally what the traditional spirits were 'saying'. When we had pinpointed the location of a spirit medium and knowing that terrorists would unfailingly visit him or her to obtain counsel, we could closely monitor enemy activities. Sometimes we'd specifically set up OPs to observe a particular spirit medium; they were an invaluable intelligence conduit.

It is important remember that the spiritual beliefs of all Africans are as real to them as any form of religion, perhaps more so. The *ngangas* were treated with the greatest respect—by the locals—and us. To have arrested a *nganga* would have been foolish in the extreme.

Nyaminyami is another well-known traditional spirit and is said to have lived on the banks of the Zambezi River, in the region of what is now Kariba Dam. Nyaminyami was the water god or river god of the Zambezi. He had the head of a fish and the body of a snake and was said to bring good fortune to all those who believed in him. One day he left his home to visit upriver while his wife was visiting relatives downstream. While he was away white men came and built a massive dam at the gorge in the mid-1950s, damming up the Zambezi

River into what is now Kariba Dam. Nyaminyami became incensed that the mighty dam had now separated him from his wife and he disappeared, never to be seen again. The unseasonal floods that occurred during the building of the dam, the subsequent deaths of dozens of workmen and the damage inflicted are all attributed to a vengeful Nyaminyami.

Years later my brother Ian was involved in an incident that illustrates the depth of tribal beliefs. He and a friend Paul were members of the army sub-aqua diving team based at Kariba. They had selected a point underwater at a depth of about sixty feet where they built an underwater obstacle course to train divers. Try as they might they simply could not recruit any black soldiers to the unit for fear of Nyaminyami's retribution. Eventually they did persuade one black recruit to give it a shot—John, an elite soldier with a fine combat record who had been decorated for bravery.

The plan was to do a slow descent to the obstacle course with Ian and Paul holding onto John. As they descended it was hoped that John, not seeing Nyaminyami, would realize that the water god did not exist and would thus overcome his fear. John could then tell all the other recruits that there was nothing to fear and it would be ... problem over.

But it didn't work out that way.

The descent was fine and they reached the obstacle course without incident. John was breathing steadily and gaining confidence every second—until a six-foot eel swam by. John saw it immediately, was understandably convinced that it was Nyaminyami and shot to the surface with Ian and Paul desperately trying to control his ascent to prevent him from getting an embolism. Nothing whatsoever would calm him down. Within minutes the word was out and from that point on no black diver would ever dive in Kariba.

I was a member of the police sub-aqua team at one stage and much of our job consisted of recovering dead bodies— mostly people who had drowned or had been murdered. We had a huge problem trying to get African policemen to dive for a body because of their beliefs. They believe that when a person drowns his spirit remains behind in the form of what is called an *mjusva* (roughly pronounced 'um-joos-wa'). An *mjusva* looks like a mermaid, half human and half fish and anyone going into the water would simply never return. (When all the white sub-aqua policemen left the force the police were obliged to use grappling hooks to recover bodies as blacks refused.)

Chapter twenty

'Unsure of his position'

Rivalry within the intelligence-gathering community, although rare, did lead to some awkward moments. It only ever happened to me once when a colleague, Hank Stander, who was operating in an area adjacent to mine, overheard me discussing with my men the location of a possible terrorist base camp situated on a hill close to Domboshawa. Our plan was to monitor movement in the area and if something developed to put a reaction plan together.

In fact there were many occasions when we knew the exact location of a terrorist camp and would put OPs up in the area; the troops would watch the terrorists until we had an accurate picture of their movements. If it looked like they were going to move camp we would attack immediately. If not we would wait until enough troops were available and the terrorists appeared settled before launching our attack.

When I left early that mid-1979 afternoon in to attend a meeting at Salisbury North Headquarters Stander went to the OC Salisbury North and told him he was in receipt of accurate information that terrorists were in that particular camp. The OC, also hoping to score a few points, hit the panic button and called out every available troop in the Salisbury area. The soldiers began assembling on a football field opposite Borrowdale police station early the following morning.

When they were all in place the army commander who was to co-ordinate the camp attack asked to be briefed. This was not the ways things were usually done. No one would think of calling out troops until the information had been presented to an army liaison officer and it was agreed that an operation might succeed.

I received a call very early that morning telling me to get to Borrowdale base as quickly as I could. When I arrived I saw all the troops kitted up, prepared and ready to deploy. It looked like something really big was going down. I was keen to learn all the details and in eager anticipation walked into the briefing room.

The army commander and his platoon leaders sat glaring at Hank and the OC who looked like they had been told their careers were over. They probably were. On further questioning by the army commander it turned out that Hank had very little information and eventually confessed that he "had overheard Trethowan talking".

I was informed what had happened and asked what I knew about the camp. I said it was at best a vague possibility but then at that time there were so many terrorists in Chinamora that if you threw a dart at a map the odds of finding a terrorist where it hit were better than even. That didn't cheer anyone up and it was not meant to. I was furious with Hank, determined to make him squirm before I let him off the hook. Hank was summarily dismissed and the OC, the army commander and I formulated a joint plan of attack. It entailed Butch, a PRAW pilot, doing a close reconnaissance over the target area to call us in should he spot anything unduly suspicious. The idea was to entice, or frighten, the terrorists into making a beak for it—into our stop groups pre-positioned along obvious escape routes.

Butch took off, flew over the *kopje* and said he had spotted "hundreds of terrs bomb-shelling in all directions". But none appeared in the gun sights of any of the stop-groups. Troops were ferried in by helicopter and swept through the area. They didn't find a thing and within hours were back in their base camps, empty handed. The truth of the matter is Butch didn't see anything but as a few reputations were at stake he had to conjure up something to save a few heads from rolling. To ease consciences we put it down to a training exercise.

Chinamora is a very hilly area with dense bush which makes it easy to hide. Aside from being a major infiltration route into Salisbury the verdant cover was one of the main reasons why there were so many terrorists operating there.

Being a very hilly area, with plenty of map features, map-reading should have been simple. Unlike the flat, featureless Lowveld areas, you just didn't get lost—no one ever did—except Dennis.

Dennis Buck was a Uniform Branch P/O stationed at Borrowdale police station. He was always champing at the bit to go on operations but none of his bosses had ever considered him "quite ready to do so". This might have had something to do with the fact that he was hyperactive and capable of conducting more than three conversations with three different people all at the same time. The problem was that none of the people he was conversing with had the vaguest idea what he was talking about.

In order to keep Dennis happy and out of the member in charge's hair he was sent to our bush base camp in Chinamora where he undertook general administrative duties. He started whining one a day as I was planning an operation, but I ignored him and he disappeared. Helicopters were on immediate stand-by at Borrowdale to fly in when the contacts were initiated and troops were in position, ready to close in. It was all looking good. That was until I got a call from the camp commander asking me if I had seen Dennis. It was a rhetorical question. Dennis had heard about the operation and had scurried along to the camp commander, pleading to be involved. The camp commander had succumbed to the constant whining and, without clearing it with me, instructed Dennis that he could take three constables and walk from the camp to a prominent hill feature where he should await uplift or further instructions by radio.

The hill that Dennis had been told to walk to was the biggest mountain in Chinamora, Ngomakarira, which was a) miles away from the area of my operation and b) the largest feature in the area and therefore simple to find— even without a map. But Dennis had other ideas and decided that he would take a map. Before setting a single foot outside the camp he took reciprocal bearings on the hills around him and plotted his exact position. He could of course have looked at map in the Ops Room which had a big yellow pin in it on top of an arrow with bold lettering stating 'YOU ARE HERE'. Somehow Dennis felt that by doing it his way he would get a more accurate locstat.

And so with his men fully armed he set off, stopping every few metres or so to check his position. Maybe Dennis spent too much time looking at his map and not looking where he was going because he somehow managed to veer off the Ngomakarira course and instead of heading north was heading southeast, away from Ngomakarira—and directly into the operational area.

Eventually he realized two things—firstly that he was lost and secondly that he was in deep shit. Rather than make a total fool of himself by radioing in and reporting his predicament he decided to keep walking until he came across any locals from whom he would ask directions. When it became apparent to even him that this was unlikely to happen, tribal folk not being the best at taking reciprocal bearings with a prismatic compass he got on the radio and said that he "was unsure of his position". (We were told in training that policemen never get lost they only ever become "unsure of their positions".)

That was when I got a call from the camp commander asking me if I or any of my men has seen Dennis. As I said a purely rhetorical question as he knew damn well that Dennis was lost and was heading for serious trouble. The only people Dennis was likely to encounter if he stayed in the area any longer to "ask for directions" were a bunch of angry terrorists determined to escape from a bunch of equally determined soldiers.

Because PRAW flights were a regular occurrence over Chinamora and therefore unlikely to arouse the terrorists' suspicions, I asked PRAW Headquarters at Mount Hampden (the airfield where they were stationed) for their assistance. In no time at all the pilot, Geoff, overflew the area, located Dennis and directed him to safety.

As good as PRAW were they also had their fair share of bad luck. Geoff was a PRAW pilot of long standing who provided air cover for us during the contact where we killed six terrorists (while Dennis was unsure of his position). He landed back at Mount Hampden and early the next morning took off again to come and help us out. I heard over the air that he had crash-landed in the Borrowdale farming area and being close by I was the first to get to him. He had forgotten to fill up with avgas, ran out of fuel and fortunately, before he reached the terrorist-infested Chinamora, crash-landed in a recently harvested mealie field. Other than a bruised ego there was not much damage to him, his gunner or the aircraft.

I earlier discussed the invidious position of coloured folk—or 'goffles' as they were derogatorily known—but they also 'did their bit' for the country, admittedly under sufferance. Serving with what were known as the 'Protection Units' or the Rhodesian Defence Unit (RDU, later RDR, Rhodesian Defence Regiment) their duties were essentially guarding installations and road crews, convoy escorts and manning radio relay stations. For weeks on end they would live in a base camp, go out on site in the morning to guard their charges and return in the evening. In the main they did not serve for the love of the country or for any career advancement. They did it because it meant 'easy bucks'—and because they'd been conscripted. Their duties were tedious in the extreme and although monotonous they were in the operational areas, very often in lonely, vulnerable outposts, so vigilance was needed. However, with little officer supervision, the opposite in fact occurred and it was not unusual to bump into a troop of coloured soldiers guarding a remote bridge for example, stoned out of their heads on the freely available local *mbanje*, or marijuana (a commodity which they sometimes traded with the guerrillas! Interestingly, neither ZANLA nor ZIPRA were averse to recruiting coloureds—some of their best guerrillas were of mixed blood).

They were kept out of harm's way as far as possible and did a reasonable job under what must have been demotivating circumstances. With their inimitable sense of humour they had developed a sub-culture and a language of their own, very similar to the RLI's *taal*—an incomprehensible pidgin mix of Cockney English, Afrikaans, local dialects and street slang. One of my favourite stories is about a couple of coloureds who had bought a six-pack of beers. While carrying it back to his room the man carrying it dropped it. He paused, looked at his buddy who was waiting for an explanation and said: "*Snaaied* by gravity, *ek sê*" (fooled by gravity, I say). Or the two coloureds who had a flat tyre and were going to be late getting back from R & R—they phoned in and said they had "no sky in their rounds".

The RLI were possibly one of the few white units which could converse freely with the coloureds and the two-way banter was understandably hilarious. A favourite 'chirp' the coloureds would throw at the white troopies was: "Hey, you honkies! 'Bout time you *naaied* some more nannies. Us goffles are a dying breed, *ek sê*." (Hey, you white boys! It's about time you fucked some more black women. We coloureds are a dying breed, I say.)

A couple of coloureds at Chinamora base camp decided they had had enough, pinched a radio and started walking home (as opposed to stealing the ammo truck and driving home—quite common). No one 'walked home' from Chinamora base camp. It was situated in the middle of one of the busiest operational areas in the country. They were reported missing the next morning and a patrol sent out to look for them but with no luck. Sometime about mid-morning our radio operator heard a voice coming up on the air saying repeatedly "hello, hello, hello". The radio operator managed to identify callers as the two who had gone AWOL (absent without leave). They had no idea where they were so a helicopter, call sign Yellow 4, was sent in to overfly the area and search for them. Their call sign was Romeo Bravo and the conversation went something like this:

"Romeo Bravo, this is Yellow Four. Come in."

"Hello."

"Romeo Bravo, this is Yellow Four. Do you read me?"

"Hello."

"Romeo Bravo, this is Yellow Four. I want you to depress your transmit switch, hold it down and I will home in on your position."

There was much clicking of the transmit button from call sign Romeo Bravo but not much else happened. By continuing to depress his transmit button Romeo Bravo cut out any chance of conversation and blocked the airways. The pilot was starting to lose his sense of humour.

"Romeo Bravo, this is Yellow Four. I want you to depress your transmit button, hold it down and I will HOME IN ON YOU. I say again HOME IN ON YOU. DO YOU UNDERSTAND?"

Silence.

Then, "HOOOOOOOOME … HOOOOOOOME."

That was good enough as the pilot was able to pinpoint their position, land in a half-decent LZ (landing zone), pick them up and take them back to base for the inevitable charges of going AWOL.

The humour and the culture of Rhodesia's coloured troops were legendary and did much to keep a smile on our faces.

Chapter twenty-one

Chinamora hotbed

When carrying out operations in Chinamora we operated from an old farmhouse situated near Hatcliff Estate about twenty kilometres from the centre of Salisbury and six kilometres from Borrowdale police station. The farmhouse was just off the main road to Chinamora and was surrounded by large gum trees.

At any time the base was occupied by members of Ground Coverage, Special Branch and other units that were clandestinely deployed from the base. Very few people, including high-ranking police officers, knew that we were there.

Some police officers from Police General Headquarters had been tasked with setting up roadblocks on the Domboshawa road leading northeast out of Salisbury. The spot the team chose was just opposite our camp. They chose a night when the base happened to be fully occupied. We knew the roadblock team were in position but they had no idea about us.

In any unit anyone who is desk-bound is considered fair game and this roadblock team was no exception. As the beer flowed late into the night someone suggested that we give the roadblock team a fright. There were many different ways we could have done this, the most obvious being to fire a few tracer rounds over their heads. But we had a truly gifted explosives expert with us who had devised a way of removing the incendiary compound from an Icarus flare and replacing it with a small block of pentolite with a detonator attached to it. When the flare was fired the pentolite charge would shoot upwards, slowly descend by parachute and then explode. At night as we discovered the effect was spectacular.

Four charges were made up and the flares given to four individuals who simultaneously fired their flares. They shot up into the sky and all four charges ignited within milliseconds of each other. The effect was that the roadblock team, believing they were under attack, jumped into their truck and fled back to Salisbury. We heard it over the radio and realizing we had overstepped the mark contacted Salisbury Operations (Salops) and told them that we had not been aware that the roadblock was in place and were testing a top-secret weapon and as such there was no cause for alarm. The next day I had to make a quick trip into Salisbury to plead our case before we got into serious trouble.

Terrorists operating in Chinamora would cache their weapons and come into Salisbury and surrounding areas for their own R & R, during which time they would visit the townships and beer halls and sometimes the nearby farm compounds. They were after beer and women and got it in plentiful supply in such places.

From intelligence obtained Chris Prinsloo and I knew that a group of terrs were going to go to a beer-drink in a farm compound on the outskirts of Borrowdale suburb. As these were 'open invitation' affairs I sent two constables in civvy clothes to the compound to see what they could find out. They had a two-way radio concealed in one of their jackets so if they saw anything untoward they could report it to me. Chris and I positioned ourselves, fully armed, underneath a bush at the bottom of someone's unfenced garden and waited. It was a big garden and being well away from the house we did not expect to be detected by the owner. I have to say we were not as cautious as we might have been in concealing ourselves. The owner must have heard something and came to inspect. As he approached he called out, "Hey you! Hey you! Come out, whoever you are!" We did and came face to face with an old schoolmaster of mine. I don't know who was more surprised. I muttered a garbled explanation which seemed to satisfy him and we continued our listening watch.

On another occasion we ascertained one night that a terrorist was shacked up with his girlfriend in a *kia* (outhouse or servant's quarters) in Borrowdale. We went in early the next morning with a stick of PATU armed with an RPG-7 and called for the terrorist to come out. When he did not an RPG rocket grenade was fired through the front door into the *kia*. The result was one very dead terrorist complete with AK and, from the rocket's back-blast, dozens of broken windows in the houses in the immediate vicinity—and dozens of complaints received at Borrowdale from people complaining about the noise we had made. We had to apologize because we could not let on about the terrorist; it would have caused panic.

As the war continued more and more business centres and clinics were destroyed by the terrorists until there were very few still operating. This worked against them. Venereal disease was rife amongst terrorists. The more clinics they attacked and shut down the fewer medical supplies became available to them. The staff on the more isolated clinics that hadn't been destroyed were closing them down and moving to the hospitals in Salisbury. Knowing that the terrorists would sooner or later go to the deserted clinics to rob them of penicillin it became a simple matter of identifying those clinics and ambushing them—with great success.

Terrorists also gave away their locations by holding large propaganda meetings, or *pungwes*. The locals would be summoned to attend the meeting and gather round the local political commissar who stood on a raised platform of sorts to address 'the masses'. They were told to chant and applaud as the PC extolled the virtues of ZANU and ZANLA. The noise they made attracted patrols in the area who would be listening out for just such a thing. The patrol would close in on the *pungwe* and with the aid of surrounding light or latterly with a night scope quietly take out the PC. Alternatively, the patrol would follow the terrorists back to their base and call in Fireforce at dawn.

Part of the process of gathering intelligence was to spend time talking with the locals. In rural areas one of the best ways to do this was to visit a beer garden. This was nothing more than a cleared space in the bush where the locals sat in a large circle and passed a five-gallon mug of beer from one person to another.

It was one of the weird things about the bush war that whenever I arrived at a beer garden and joined in a beer-drink, I was never once attacked or even felt threatened. Sure, I had troops scattered around the outskirts keeping guard, but even then we were at risk. I suppose it was one of those sacrosanct, unwritten rules in that you never disturbed a beer-drink.

The beer was referred to as 'seven-day brew' and was fermented from maize in forty-four gallon drums. It had the consistency of porridge, looked like vomit and tasted vile. The fact that the mug was being passed from mouth to mouth was probably not the most hygienic way of doing things, but no one seemed to mind. I got round to accepting it.

The locals always seemed pleased to see me. I never asked a direct question as that would have been an amateurish giveaway. My objective was to monitor the mood of the people. With some experience I knew that if they were nervous or frightened the terrorists were probably nearby, or if they were filled with the joys of spring the chances were the terrorists were not.

Conversations were about anything and everything. The Africans with their huge smiles, gleaming white teeth and wonderful sense of humour would laugh their heads off as we joked with each other. But I was always careful not to overstay my welcome and left when I considered it appropriate to do so.

I also found that the Africans are great mimics, especially if they have a few beers in them. Acting seems an innate quality in them—their tribal dances are full of drama, much acting takes place and the mood can change from raucous laughter to desperate despair in minutes.

One of my constables was a born showman. With very little prompting he would ask someone to name any bird or animal and he would mimic its sound and mannerisms to perfection. As we laughed and applauded he would take it further and slide into his 'hunting' act—he became the hunter, hunting down a wounded antelope that he had shot with a bow and arrow. (I am sure that his act was borrowed from films we'd seen of the Bushmen doing the same thing, but take nothing away from the constable—he was amazing.)

My brother Brian was also a policeman and tells a wonderful story about a constable he worked with while stationed in Que Que. Constable Ncube's favourite companion was the Oxford Dictionary. Every day or so he would, impressively, learn a new word and then try and nonchalantly insert it into a conversation to show off.

On one particular day he went from office to office in the station greeting each occupant with a "Good morning P/O Brown, how are you?" The response as P/O Brown looked up was "Fine thank you, Constable Ncube." And so it went on from one office to the next—asking the same question and getting the same response.

He came to Brian's office, knocked on the door and said, "Ah, good morning P/O 'T'. [Trethowan was always a bit of a mouthful] How are you?"

"I am fine, how are you?" Brian looked up and replied.

Ncube took a deep breath, chest puffed out, as a smile lit up his face. "Ah yes! I am salubrious and how are you?"

(When Brian told me this story I had a good laugh before quietly sneaking off to find out what 'salubrious' meant.)

One day on patrol we captured a *mujiba*. His name was Lovemore. He was a cocky little fellow, very self-assured and very clever. When captured he vehemently denied any involvement with the terrorists and as I thought him pretty harmless, I decided to leave him for a while and pick up our 'conversation' at a later stage. Eventually he became 'part of the furniture' and simply stayed with us on the base—a sort of unpaying, permanent guest.

I was sitting one day, practising stripping and cleaning an AK rifle. Lovemore came and watched me, every so often muttering something under his breath with a look of utter frustration on his face. I ignored him for a while and began to strip and assemble the AK again once again. I had just removed the dust cover that covered the firing mechanism when Lovemore let out a hiss of exasperation and indicated that he wanted to handle the AK. The weapon was not loaded so I gave him the weapon. He sat down and within seconds had stripped and assembled it and handed it back to me.

"I thought you knew nothing about this?" I said as I took it from him.

He looked at me with a blank expression, then a look of resignation and began talking about what had been happening in his area. It all came pouring out. He proved to be an invaluable source of information and worked with us for many months.

It was difficult to accurately establish how many terrorists had been killed in a contact. When troops were debriefed they would swear that they had shot and killed a terrorist and describe exactly what happened. You had to also take into account that a terrorist was often shot by more than one trooper. Although it could be confusing, with experience we were soon able to work out exactly what had transpired.

What used to confound us was that there were occasions when troopers were adamant that they had killed a terrorist and yet no body was found and therefore the kill could not be confirmed. This had a much bigger impact than one would imagine as all Rhodesians would eagerly listen to the eight o'clock evening news on TV to hear the latest security forces' communiqué. The news reader would start off by saying: "Security Force Headquarters announced today that X (number of) terrorists were killed in the operational areas by security forces." That figure was what everyone waited for. It had a huge impact on morale, particularly the civilians. (It had indeed become a war of attrition, confirmed by our fixation with body counts, not unlike Vietnam.)

Why then could we not find those bodies? Contacts seldom took place in one spot. They would start with a fire fight which became a series of individual contacts in different areas as the terrorists bomb-shelled and tried to escape from the security forces. It was only when the contact was over that Ground Coverage or Special Branch were called in to identify bodies, which might take hours or even until the following day. Years later I discovered that in the time between the terrorists being killed and us returning to the area the locals would come and either drag the bodies off for disposal or bury them on the spot, usually in an anthill. I know for a fact that after the war ZANU (PF) sent army trucks into Chinamora to old contact sites and retrieved some of these bodies.

Much as we had success we also had our fair share of tragedy. Pete Smith was doing a foot patrol in the farming area one night when his radio broke down. He decided to go to a farmhouse and phone the police station. He should have realized that it was a dangerous thing to do. As he approached the fenced-off farmhouse the farmer who had heard movements outside his fence shot Pete thinking he was a terrorist. Pete took a bad gunshot wound to the leg which left him with a severe limp. He was lucky.

Matambu was a regular policeman whose home kraal was in Chinamora. Because he was a policeman he couldn't go home for fear of being murdered by terrorists so he got transferred to GC and was attached to us. He was an excellent soldier who was involved in many successful contacts.

Electricity at our camp in Chinamora was supplied by a generator. It was one of those petrol-powered generators. To start it you attached a starting handle to the crank shaft, cranked like mad until it got going and then swiftly pulled the handle away from the shaft. I was doing this one evening when the handle slipped off the shaft and whacked me in the head, concussing me and leaving me with a three-inch cut in my forehead. We didn't have the facilities to stitch it up and could not go through to Salisbury General Hospital as driving on the roads in Chinamora at night was asking for trouble. Unfortunately the wound would not stop bleeding and Chris insisted that we make the journey. I was in no condition to disagree.

With Matambu driving and me riding shotgun we drove to the hospital and I was attended to in Outpatients. If it were dangerous driving into Salisbury it was even more so returning because there was every chance the terrorists would be waiting for us. Not wanting to risk this I told Matambu to take me back to my parents' house in the suburbs where we could stay overnight and travel through to Chinamora the next morning.

I then took a couple of painkillers and climbed groggily into the Land Rover. Two hours later I woke up in Chinamora camp. Matambu had taken a circuitous route through Salisbury waiting until I fell asleep from the painkillers and then drove through to Chinamora— because we had an important source debrief the next morning and he did not want to risk us being late for it. His actions were foolhardy but I prefer to think that it was indicative of his dedication to duty.

You can't keep a good man away from his family and Matambu was no exception. One day without letting any of us know he went back to his kraal while on R & R to check up on his family and satisfy himself that they were all safe. Sure enough, within minutes of his arrival, the terrorists discovered his presence and brutally murdered him. He was buried at Warren Hills cemetery. It was a funeral I remember well. All of us, black and white, soldiers and policemen of all ranks, stood at his graveside as the eulogy was read out. When the coffin had been lowered into the grave, one by one we took a handful of soil from a tray offered us and scattered the soil over his coffin. Without doubt Matambu was one of the finest men I ever worked with.

Constable Mike Manyika had been awarded the police force's highest medal for gallantry. He was operating with GC in another area when he and his co-coordinator were ambushed, both of them getting very badly shot. His co-ordinator was so badly wounded that he couldn't move. Mike fought off the terrorists single-handedly and although seriously wounded managed to walk to a nearby kraal to seek help, but the locals refused to help. Mike was in no mood for any this and threatened the villagers in an uncompromising manner. Only then did they scuttle off to alert any security forces in the area. The GC co-coordinator's life was thus saved, thanks to a very brave constable.

The thing that characterized Mike was his smile. We had taken a break for a day to attend the national parachuting championships at Mount Hampden. I parked the Land Rover and we climbed onto the bonnet where we sat with our backs against the front windscreen watching the displays. An aircraft high in the sky came into view, commenced its run-in as the parachutists jumped out, trailing smoke from canisters attached to their ankles so the spectators could keep track of them. Mike watched this for a while, became agitated and then shouted, "Sir, sir, they need help. They are on fire!" He jumped off the bonnet and grabbed the small fire extinguisher from the cab. Holding it at the ready like a Western gunslinger he anxiously awaited the skydivers as they gently descended under their open canopies. It took a while to calm him down. He was only convinced that the skydivers were alright when I took him over to inspect them and they showed him their smoke canisters on their ankles. Mike, what a truly wonderful man.

Christmas of 1979 came and went, and with it a supposed ceasefire. The politicians and the generals had done with their talking—the result a triumphant 'peace agreement', bull-dozed through by Lord Carrington at Lancaster House and signed by Prime Minister Bishop Abel Muzorewa, Ian Smith, Joshua Nkomo of ZAPU and Robert Mugabe of ZANU (PF), plus sundry other nationalist politicians and chiefs such as Reverend Ndabaningi Sithole and Senator Chief Jeremiah Chirau. The country had in fact changed its name and political dispensation during mid-1979, with Smith 'surrendering' power to Bishop Muzorewa of the UANC, the United African National Council, the largest 'internal' black nationalist party (i.e. not banned) in 'majority-rule' elections, naturally boycotted by ZANU (PF) and ZAPU. Without the latter's involvement the world took no notice of the self-declared Zimbabwe–Rhodesia and so the war had raged on, with Muzorewa stepping up the tempo, ably abetted by his white generals.

The Lancaster House agreement was a godsend for ZANLA and ZIPRA, with both guerrilla armies mere weeks away from total disintegration as a result of the relentless raids against their Mozambican and Zambian bases. In terms of the ceasefire, various assembly points (APs) were established throughout the country, under supervision of a British monitoring force, to house all the guerrillas who were supposed to 'come in from the bush'. Of course, still wary of security force attacks, both ZANLA and ZIPRA flooded the APs with recruits and untrained cadres, leaving their experienced guerrillas in the field—a dangerous thing to do, as in terms of Lancaster House any guerrilla still armed and not in an assembly point after 20 December 1979, unless under a flag of truce, was deemed 'hostile' and as such could be eliminated by security forces, who strangely enough, still had carte blanche to execute the war against such 'dissidents'.

All this politicking and jostling made little difference to us on the ground. As far as we were concerned it was 'business as usual'.

When I joined the police my ultimate ambition was to be a patrol-car driver. I soon got past this and dearly wanted to join Special Branch. There was no other unit I wanted to be part of and after having spent nearly four years with Ground Coverage on operations, I reckoned that I had done enough to be deemed suitable.

During my time in Chinamora I had applied to join Special Branch and while waiting for a response I wrote my promotion exams. Fortunately I passed and was promoted directly from Uniform Branch to the rank of Detective Section Officer (D/S/O) in Special Branch. And luckily the powers that be had decided I could waive the standard probationary period of twelve months with CID— normally a prerequisite to joining SB. The position was perfect for me. As a D/S/O I had a lot more authority than a D/P/O yet could still avoid the desk-bound work of the higher ranks.

With the promotion I was posted to Gatooma in the Midlands Province, west of Salisbury. In spite of the ceasefire, some bloody fighting still lay ahead … and more deaths.

Chapter twenty-two

Gatooma dockets

The name Gatooma is said to be derived from a hill near Golden Valley, called Kaduma, which is an isiNdebele phrase meaning 'which does not thunder or make a noise'. The name is also possibly derived from a chiZezuru (a Shona dialect) word '*kudoma*' meaning 'a word which must not be spoken because it refers to a holy place inhabited by spirits'. It is likely that the hill concerned was venerated as some early shrine but now it is silent for no tribal spirits speak from its depths. Today the town is known as Kadoma.

The town is situated roughly in the middle of Rhodesia, about a hundred and twenty kilometres southwest of Salisbury on the Bulawayo road.

When I arrived in Gatooma I was allocated a room in the Uniform Branch patrol officers' single quarters until I could find a flat of my own. As I was away on operations most of the time this took a bit longer to sort out than I would have liked. The single P/Os were a likeable bunch of lads who spent most of their off-duty hours in the police pub known as 'Run 'em Inn'. The pub was much larger than other police pubs mostly because the local civilian police reservists had helped build it. It had a full-time bartender and was more of a social club than the typical police pub.

One of the P/Os had a pet duck that used to follow him to the pub every evening. It would make its way to the top of the counter and take sips from everyone's drinks until it passed out. The poor thing, barely out of ducklinghood, died of cirrhosis of the liver.

One of life's wonderfully eccentric characters was a patrol officer named Paddy who'd joined the BSAP from Ireland. Paddy was about five foot ten, as thin as a rake with bright red hair and enamel-white skin. He had a deep Southern Irish accent that was pleasant on the ear but difficult to understand. Paddy also had a fondness for beer. He loved the stuff and would sit for hours gently sipping away in the Run 'em Inn while he regaled us with his Irish tales. The trouble was Paddy could not handle his beer—more than two and he got a little bit silly.

Paddy had a brand-new Citroën Club. The garage in which it should have been parked consisted of a corrugated-iron roof set on top of four poles. Parking should have been a simple matter of driving between the poles and stopping. This was too much to ask of Paddy. Every evening Paddy would have a few drinks and return at 10.30 p.m. You could almost time his arrival by the thud as his car hit one of the poles while he tried to park. Quite simply he was unable to negotiate the space between the poles. Although the dents were minor they had accumulated to the point where the car looked like someone had attacked it with a two-pound hammer.

He eventually wrote the car off. One evening I received a call from one of the P/Os telling me that Paddy had been involved in a vehicle accident. He had been on his way back from a nearby village when he rolled the car and had been taken to hospital where, totally uninjured, he'd been put in a side ward. The nurses suspected alcohol and had called for the OC to determine whether or not he had been drinking. The P/O, to his somewhat misguided credit, knew that Paddy was in deep trouble and was trying to stall the OC hoping that we could come up with a plan to protect Paddy.

When I arrived at the ward the P/O was waiting for me, while Paddy, with a look of post-traumatic desperation, pleaded with me to help him. After much discussion we all agreed that the only solution was for Paddy to tell the OC that the effects of "the two beers I consumed had been exacerbated by the effects of physical exertion sustained when I had gone for a long run in the afternoon". Well, straight off that argument had two flaws—1) Paddy would never be able to pronounce 'exacerbated' without sounding like he was stoned, and 2) the last time Paddy had done any running was when he was a recruit. In Paddy's opinion people only ever exercised because they were too bored to drink. We altered the story slightly and had just finished rehearsing it when the OC entered.

"Okay, Paddy. What is your explanation?"

Fully expecting Paddy to rattle off the well-rehearsed speech Paddy paused.

"You see, sir, it is like this … I was having a wee drink with my mates and being careful not to go above the limit I thought it best to return to the single quarters. As I was driving along the road I saw a huge flock of chickens approaching me from the bush on the right side of the road. When they saw my car approaching they all started running towards the road and before I knew it millions of the little buggers were in front of me. I took evasive action by swinging my car over to the left but the wheel locked and I rolled the car."

We held our breath—was the look on the OC's face one of bemusement, disbelief or incredulity?

"Paddy, if this is your story, then where are all these millions of chickens now?"

Paddy was waiting for this. "Och, sir, they are all roosting in their nests high up in the trees."

Practical jokes were common place and I had developed something of a rather annoying reputation for playing pranks of people. One P/O called Ian decided to get his own back on me. I had been involved in a relationship and had broken it off. In the way of things it got pretty tense and my ex-girlfriend and I did everything we could to avoid each other. Unbeknown to me Ian had told her that I was distraught, wanted to get back together and had asked her to attend a party being held at the Run 'em Inn for somone's farewell. When I arrived at the party Ian called for silence, stood on the bar counter and announced that my ex and I were now officially engaged. She came running up to me to say she knew it had all been a terrible mistake; and her parents came rushing over to congratulate me. I was last seen jumping through a window after Ian who had escaped through it into the night.

I got my own back on Ian when I heard that he had sneaked into Gatooma to see his girlfriend when he was supposed to be on patrol. I organized one of the P/Os to tell him that the OC knew about his indiscretion and wanted to see him on his return.

I forgot it about it and went on patrol. Ian didn't forget. He sweated it out for a few days and rather than wait for his patrol to finish came in early and went straight to the OC's office.

"The OC wants to see me," he blurted out to the OC's secretary.

"No, he doesn't," she countered.

"Yes he does," and walked straight past her into the OC's office.

Without a word from the OC everything came tumbling out—he confessed what he'd done and promised never to misbehave again.

"Thanks for telling me," the OC said when Ian was done. "This is the first I've heard about it. Consider yourself confined to your quarters for two weeks."

If Gatooma was known for anything it was probably its vintage fire engine—a bright red fire engine lovingly maintained by a voluntary crew from Gatooma who also doubled as the firemen. The fire engine was kept in a wooden garage (also grandly known as the fire station) and every weekend the crew would arrive and carefully polish its bright red body, brass fittings, tyres and leather seats.

In the event of a fire the crew would be notified by the police, rush to the fire station, jump into the fire engine and proceed to said fire.

And so it came to pass ...

The fire crew was phoned one night and told that there was a fire. No one actually asked where the fire was. Instead they all rushed to the fire station expecting to don their firemen's clothing, jump into their shiny fire engine and with bells ringing and sirens wailing rush to the scene of the fire. When they arrived at the fire station they saw to their absolute horror that it had caught fire—the station and the fire engine were totally destroyed. A combination of wooden walls, wooden ceiling and solvent-based cleaning fluids had contributed to the inferno. The poor crew were broken-hearted and failed to see the irony, or funny side, of it, which there wasn't, really.

I was in bed one night when I was woken and asked to come and assist the duty patrol officer who had been called to a case of arson and was unsure how to deal with it. We got to a kraal and saw that one of the pole and *dagga* huts had been burned to the ground, the result of a domestic dispute. After a fight with her daughter a grandmother had taken her daughter's two children into her hut and secured the door from within, refusing to allow the others to come in. The rest of the kraal folk thought that, given time, she would get over her tantrum and went to bed.

When everyone else was asleep the old woman set fire to the thatched roof. In seconds it was ablaze and the wooden poles that supported the roof collapsed on her and the sleeping children.

When we arrived it looked like a straightforward case of arson, but not murder. The hut had been completely destroyed. Looking at it, it appeared to be simply a mass of burnt charcoal. It took a few seconds to realize that among the charcoal were three bodies. In their final seconds they had woken up and attempted to crawl to the door with their grandmother dragging them back into the inferno. Their bodies were in the typically grotesque, almost obscene, position of someone who has been burned to death. On all fours, legs slightly splayed, hands clenched from scorched muscles contracting. It was gruesome and tragic.

This was the first sudden death that the young P/O had attended. It was a distressing enough sight for anyone and the P/O struggled to cope. I took over the investigation and made him stay with me while we took statements and arranged for the bodies to be taken away for further medical examination.

Attending sudden deaths was an everyday occurrence for most Uniform Branch patrol officers. A 'sudden death' was anything but a murder, a death that occurred when the cause of death was not suspicious. This included suicides, drowning, someone dying in their sleep from natural causes, cot deaths, anything along the lines of asphyxiation due to swallowing something and choking, heart attacks and so on. The role of the policeman was to attend the scene and if there was anything suspicious call in CID. If not, then make arrangement for the body to be removed.

Again, Friday nights featured when people got drunk and, while walking home, fell asleep by the side of the road, vomited and choked on their own vomit.

In the cold months Africans who lived in the urban areas in *kias* or shacks would line the gap between the bottom of the door and the floor with clothing or material, shut all the windows and light their little paraffin stoves. The burning fuel would use up the oxygen in the room and the end result would be death through suffocation. The telltale sign was the deceased's gums and nails ... which were blue.

Cot deaths were sadly an all-too-common occurrence but not necessarily from what is now know as Sudden Infant Death Syndrome, which is the sudden, unexpected death of an apparently well baby aged from birth to two years. I attended about half a dozen deaths in which the baby had fallen asleep in its cot, had got itself tangled in a blanket or a toy string wound round its neck and had died from asphyxiation.

Suicides such as hanging and poisoning did not bother me overly. A gunshot suicide was, however, a different story and inevitably the goriest. It is unnecessarily distressing to relate specifics but suffice to say that the effects of a suicide caused by putting a double-barrelled shotgun in the mouth and pulling the trigger is as unpretty a sight as one could ever imagine.

We tended to become somewhat indifferent, or callous, about this sort of thing. As a junior patrol officer I once attended an attempted suicide in Bulawayo. A young woman was standing outside her second-floor flat window, threatening to jump but she was talked out of it and coaxed back inside. She was taken to hospital for a check-up. When I arrived at the hospital the nursing staff told me that the woman was diabetic and that they urgently needed her insulin which was back in her flat. I don't know why but far from being empathetic I was angry and said something along the lines of "She wants to die, so why bother." What a crass thing to say. Quite rightly I was reprimanded and went to her flat where I retrieved the insulin in the nick of time. It must have had an effect on me because years later I became a counsellor with Lifeline in South Africa.

Drownings happened all the time. I did not attend any when I was in the BSAP but after I left the force I became a volunteer member of the police sub-aqua section and according to my log book retrieved the bodies of eleven people who had drowned. The most surprising thing about drowning is how quickly people actually drown.

A man would get drunk at a beer-drink after which he would find a prostitute and take her to the side of a river. After they had finished their business he would go for a wash in the river, momentarily forgetting he could not swim, and drown. Simple as that. There would be no cries for help, no indication that he was in distress—a straightforward and very quick drowning.

Before a thunderstorm dark clouds gather, the air chills and the rain falls in the form of short, very intense cloudbursts. Within minutes of the rain stopping the sun comes out and the only evidence of the storm is very wet, steamy earth.

After the rains one day three tribesmen who had been taking shelter in a kraal decided to go for a walk. The man in the middle was carrying a small suitcase with his two friends walking on either side of him. They heard a crack of lightning and instinctively ducked before continuing on their way. Within a few paces they realized that the man in the middle was no longer with them. They turned round and saw him lying on the ground, stone dead. One of them went to a nearby business centre and phoned the police. I left with a constable and drove to the scene. What amazed me was that the deceased was lying on his back, his fingers still clasped around the handle of the suitcase. Other than what looked like a burn mark in the shape of a clothing iron on his stomach, there were no injuries. Neither of the deceased's friends had so much as felt a jolt. It was incomprehensible, almost bizarre.

When I attended the post mortem the doctor showed me a small hole in the deceased's heel where the lightning bolt had exited; he also showed me the deceased's heart which apparently was larger than it should have been.

Attending a sudden death was bad enough for the next of kin and they needed to be given their space to mourn. One thing I could not stand was the wailing that occurred after the death. It was mostly the woman (and sometimes the men but more quietly) who would wail and cry and throw themselves about in grief as they appealed to their ancestral spirits. And then there would be silence, until another relative arrived, in which case it will begin all over again. The sound to me was like dragging a finger nail down a chalk board but with a megaphone attached to amplify the sound. But it was their custom and my job was to respect it and bite my tongue.

When one of our African operators died he was given a traditional burial which we all attended, after which we'd gather together to give him a wake. The wake was held at Blackfordby Tobacco Training Institute just outside of Salisbury. After the wake, which was really one huge piss-up, I and another fellow called Jerry were left with no transport home. We found a Vesper scooter with the keys still in and decided it would do. I am six foot and Jerry was around six foot four. He drove and I sat behind him. I don't remember any of that part. What I do remember is waking up, shivering with cold in the pouring rain in a drainage ditch by the side of the road. I could not wake Jerry and, as he looked comfortable enough, hitched a ride and made my way back home.

I accompanied the Gatooma SWAT team on a raid one night. They were after a known drug dealer who had been on the run for some time and was believed to be staying with his girlfriend in a house in one of the townships. We drove there in two Land Rovers, parked just outside the house which was at the bottom of a hill, secured the back and front entrances and called to him to come out. As we waited for a response I heard this yodelling coming from behind us; I turned round and saw a local reveller coming full tilt down the hill towards us on his bicycle. He didn't have a care in the world and because he was drunk and blinded from the pleasures of the night never saw us or the vehicles. I watched him and as he saw me took his hand off the handlebar to wave and then crashed in spectacular manner into the side of a Land Rover.

I always think of him as Mr Bojangles. He wore a multi-coloured beret, white shirt with blue sports tie, a patchwork jacket and blue trousers. When I picked him up to dust him off he was still laughing and wanted to dance with me. Much as I liked the chap this wasn't the time and place for that so I put my arm around his shoulder and got him to sit in the back of the Land Rover until the raid was over.

We never lost our sense of humour. My opposite number, a D/S/O whom I shall call Donald, and I did not get on well. Not that we had much to do with each other. His job was to focus on the counter-intelligence aspect of our work while I was solely SB operations. In other words he worked in an office and I worked in the field. The other difference was that he prided himself on his appearance and saw me as something of a slob. 'Slob' was perhaps too harsh a word but then again I have never been known for being neat and tidy.

Every day he would arrive at work with his just-short-of-shoulder-length fair hair immaculately 'done'—I suspect he used a hair dryer. He always wore a light blue or light green short-sleeved safari suit with long trousers. He was a walking Rhodesian cliché. He did tend to look down his nose at me whereas I looked on him as a typical 'desk jockey'.

And so the scene was set.

As I have said I was something of a practical joker and when I was back to Gatooma from operations Donald became my prime target. In those days telephones were made out of dark black Bakelite. Fingerprint ink was a gooey, black substance that was almost impossible to wash off. As luck would have it, it was the same colour as the telephone so one day when Donald was out of his office I sneaked in and carefully smeared ink on the earpiece of the handset. It blended in perfectly and no way was Donald going to see it—if I'd planned it right.

Donald had been looking for some way to get me into trouble so I gave it to him. As he walked into his office I got a Uniform Branch P/O to phone him. He picked up the handset and held it to his ear.

"D/S/O Trethowan has had a car accident and he has been arrested for drunk driving," the P/O stated over the phone.

Donald, totally 'hooked', held the handset even closer to his ear. "Give me all the details," he said in anticipation.

With that the P/O hung up. Donald felt the black goo on his ear and not knowing what it was wiped his ear with his shirt sleeve. The end result was his immaculately coiffed hair, his perfectly tailored safari suit and his large ear were covered in thick black ink. I honestly thought he would see the joke (well, not really) but he did not. He stormed off and did not come back to work for two days. When he did I got the silent treatment.

So I upped the pace. Donald's office was like a small fortress—thick walls, blacked-out windows with strong bars to prevent anyone breaking in, concrete floors and a solid metal-plated door. Sound was amplified to the point that if you dropped a pin it sounded like an empty tin can *clanking* as it hit the floor.

One of the D/P/Os and I thought we knew a bit about explosives (I stress the word 'thought') so we decided to set a trap. We removed the detonator from a hand grenade, wedged it beneath his desk and attached one end of a piece of strong twine to the pin and the other to the door. The idea was that when Donald opened the door of his office, the pin would be extracted from the firing mechanism which would release the plunger and a few seconds later the detonator would go off.

We had banked on Donald, what with his super-sleuth ability, figuring out instantly what was about to happen and either block his ears or get out. That was the theory. In practice it was slightly different. The trap worked perfectly but Donald did not suss it out. When the detonator exploded even the D/P/O and I got a fright. God knows what it must have sounded like to Donald. He came scampering out of his office, dashed to his car and drove off in a cloud of dust and screeching tyres.

When we cautiously peered inside the office the acrid smell of cordite was overpowering and there was a small indentation in the concrete floor. I should have been hauled over the coals for this but oddly enough my boss did little except give me a dressing-down.

But the best prank I played on Donald was yet to come. In the way of all good Special Branch operators I decided to monitor the movements of my potential target before making my next strike. I watched him closely, even engaging him in idle conversation so that I could gain a feel for his habits and mannerisms. As immaculately dressed and coiffed as Donald was, he also, naturally, kept his office perfectly neat and tidy in a classic anal-retentive manner. Nothing was ever out of place. He also had a tendency to smoke a pipe when he was feeling particularly at ease with the world. I suppose it went with the image. When he smoked his pipe he slowly put it in his mouth, inhaled deeply and ever so slowly exhaled as he watched the smoke slowly waft away with a look of utter contentment on his face. When I saw him doing this he looked so relaxed that I was convinced he was a heartbeat away from passing out.

Again … the scene was set.

I knew where Donald kept his spare set of office keys. Actually it was not that difficult. The fact is I had discussed my plan with my boss, Neville Spurr, because I knew I had been pushing things a bit far and needed his 'buy-in'. He'd given me the keys and also, truth be told, a couple of ideas to help me refine my plan.

One night I crept into Donald's office and opened the top right-hand drawer of his desk. I made a mental note of exactly where everything was placed and removed his pouch of tobacco. I had specially prepared a few 'twists' of *dagga* (marijuana) which an anonymous accomplice (Neville) had given me. The twists had been ground to a fine powder which I mixed with the tobacco. Never having smoked the stuff and having no idea of its potency I mixed in one twist, then another until seven twists were mixed in with the tobacco. Then I put everything back in its correct position, closed the drawer, locked the office and left.

I spent the whole of the next day being especially nice to Donald. So much so that he left that evening in an exceptionally good mood—with his tobacco. When Donald got home he greeted his wife, had a glass of whisky, sat down in his comfy chair, prepared his pipe and lit up. Donald had never smoked dagga and although he must have been aware that the taste of the tobacco was slightly different, the sweetness of it appealed to him. So he smoked some more, and then some more.

Neville got a call at two o'clock in the morning from Donald's wife. She told him that Donald had been behaving "strangely" (I think she meant 'amorous') and would Neville please come and speak with him. When Neville got to the house he found Donald as high as a kite. Neville knew what had happened so he put up with Donald's matey nonsense, got him to calm down and managed to get him to bed.

I have no doubt that he had happy dreams.

When Neville eventually left the force, he was replaced by Dick Gregan—a totally different kettle of fish who did his best to make life difficult for me—and I for him.

Dick's office had two doors, one facing onto the veranda outside and the other linking through to his secretary's office. His desk was positioned in front of two large windows that he kept open so as to allow the cooler air in. I knew that if Dick got a big enough fright he would head for the door and get out as quick as he could.

One morning, when Dick left his office to go for a pee—the toilet was accessed via the secretary's office—I sneaked in, locked his front door and removed the key. When he returned he instructed his secretary, as he commonly did: "I want some privacy. Close the door, will you? "

She did and locked it.

With a slight breeze blowing into Dick's office through the open window I positioned myself below the window sill. I had two tear-gas grenades with me. I pulled out the pins, gently placed the grenades below the window and left. The grenades exploded releasing a huge cloud of tear gas which blew straight in to Dick's office. As expected he panicked, ran for the door, could not open it and then frantically tried the other door which he also failed to open. In blind panic, eyes streaming, sobbing for breath, the poor man somehow squeezed unceremoniously, and miraculously, through the burglar-proofed window.

Dick knew I was the culprit but could not prove it. He knew it and I knew it. Rather than a truce we ignored each other, the upside being that he left me completely alone. Objective achieved.

All the African policeman spoke English but no matter how good they were they always seemed to have trouble saying the words 'cardboard box'. It always came out as 'cardbox'. If they did not know the name of something it was referred to as a 'whatcall' which I would guess was an abbreviation of "What would you call this item?", although no response was expected. Thus a constable intending to say "Do you have a cardboard box for the Icarus flares?" came out as "Do you have a cardbox for the whatcalls?" Once an object had been called a 'whatcall' it remained forever as such. All very well if there was only one item but when there were four or five 'whatcalls' it became very confusing.

The Africans did have a wonderfully quaint way of winding me up without me being aware of it and I am sure that referring to everything as a 'whatcall' was one of them.

Chapter twenty-three

Special Branch—*Pamberi ne hondo!*

'*Pamberi ne hondo!*' was a ZANLA slogan used during indoctrination and politicization exercises. It means 'Forward with the war', and in spite of the December 1979 ceasefire agreement, ZANLA had no intention of abiding by it, determined not to let Lord Carrington's heaven-sent let-off go to waste. In Maoist rhetoric Mugabe had declared 1979 as the '*Gore reGukurahundi*' or 'The year of the people's storm'. 1980 was to be 'The year of the people's power' and the thousands of ZANLA cadres on the ground were mobilized for the final push, all the while easily deceiving the British monitors that they were adhering to the terms of the ceasefire agreement. We Rhodesian foot soldiers were not quite so easily deceived.

As a D/S/O in Special Branch I reported to a Detective Inspector Neville Spurr. As mentioned in the previous chapter there were two D/S/Os who shared SB duties—Donald and me. Neville was a great boss. A hard taskmaster who demanded a lot from us, he had pretty much seen and done everything. I have never pretended to be an ideal subordinate but in Neville's case I realized I could learn an awful lot from him if he saw I was willing to put in the work. I did, and came to respect him enormously in the process.

My area of responsibility was huge, covering two TTLs, two middle-sized towns—Gatooma and Hartley—and lots of smaller ones including townships such as Chakari and Selous, two large gold mines and the commercial arming areas. From an operational point of view not much was happening. Terrorists had moved into the Chakari area and because of the dearth of SF presence were able to move about without fear of being attacked. From base camps within the TTL they were able to carry out attacks on farms and the surrounding civilian population.

To counter this Neville had managed to acquire six recently 'turned terrorists' despatched to Gatooma to work with me. A 'tame terr' (TT) was a terrorist who had been captured by security forces while operating in Rhodesia—a result of being wounded or surrendering during a contact. There is nothing terribly dramatic about 'turning' a terrorist. They all believed, as will be illustrated quite vividly shortly, that SF never took prisoners. In actual fact when terrorists were wounded in a contact they were generally casevaced to a military hospital and given the best medical care available. (Although strictly against Standing Orders, some ground troops in the field did execute captured guerrillas out of hand.) In the earlier days of terrorist incursions those captured were tried and if found guilty sentenced to death and hanged. As the war progressed, with the massive volume of terrorists captured, it was found that better use could be made of them by turning them—and in any case the judicial system simply couldn't cope. There was no heavy-handed stuff or mind-boggling psychology involved in the process of turning them.

After capture and having recovered from any injuries, the TT was interrogated. This process sometimes took weeks, with long sessions carefully going over everything—from the time of recruitment while perhaps working as a gardener or a waiter in Salisbury, routes taken to flee the country, training, infiltration routes back into the country, contacts he had been involved in and to his eventual capture. All this information was put down in written form and sent to SB headquarters where it was collated and analyzed. The information gleaned led to many external base camps being attacked and neutralized.

During the interrogation process the interrogation team could make a reasonable assessment whether the terrorist could be turned or not. If it was felt he could, he'd be despatched to the unit they felt would benefit the most from his services—generally the Selous Scouts or Special Branch.

I had six assistant TTs in my group. Edwin was my right-hand man. He was a black field reservist who had beaten up a colleague in a fight in a beer hall while working with Neville in another operational area. Neville managed to get him transferred out to avoid prosecution, which would have meant a certain prison term. Edwin was tall, slim and well built. He was a natural leader.

The rest were all TTs.

Daniel was probably the best from a soldiering aspect. His sectoral commander had disciplined him for insubordination; the punishment was having the middle finger of his left hand chopped off with a bayonet. Daniel was always on the lookout for a quick buck. As loyal as the day is long he had this habit of winding me up by asking me "How much?" every time I asked him to do something. The thing that characterized Daniel was that he was the scruffiest-looking person I had ever met. Not that sartorial elegance was a necessary attribute—it was just that no matter how dirty, battered and worn out we were returning from a patrol, Daniel always stood out as the scruffiest of all.

Christopher was the brightest of the group and a good soldier. He had the face of a child and was only just over five feet tall. I had to constantly remind myself that he was not a *mujiba*.

Andrew had only been operating in the country, as had Patrick, for a short while before capture. Andrew was a nervous little man who never stopped talking which made him the ideal person to carry the radio, which he did quite willingly. I had turned Patrick. He was very quiet and very afraid. Not that I had to do it often, but if I was ever forced to yell at my TTs I always went to Patrick afterwards to make sure he was okay; he was extremely sensitive.

The sixth member was Tom—tall, regal and very serious about life.

This was not a group of hardened ex-war criminals which most people imagined them to be. They were all good men who had decided that fighting for the Rhodesian security forces was a better option than fighting for ZANLA. None of them was forced by being threatened with death or bodily harm. You could never force someone to come over to your side—if you did, there was always the danger that they would turn again, this time on you. In the confusion of battle this is not difficult. I never took their loyalty for granted and I always took the necessary precautions to watch my back. Trust was essential and our first operation together would reveal just how effective it was, but still, it was no gilt-edged guarantee.

It was three or four weeks before our first deployment together. During that time we went for runs, did PT together, sat chatting and drinking Cokes, did weapons training and generally got to know each other.

We did not operate in a pseudo role—that was the job of the Selous Scouts.

The weapons we carried were weapons of choice. My TTs preferred the Communist Bloc weapons they had been trained on and my preference was my FN for short patrols and a Communist PPK for the longer ones—the FN because a short patrol inevitably meant a contact soon after deployment and I wanted all the hitting power I could get—and the PPK for longer patrols, which meant lying up in ambush for hours or days on end and I liked the bipod which kept me sighted on the general area without constantly having to reposition myself every time my arms got tired.

Our first deployment was a two-day patrol where we based up during the day and covertly watched a kraal line for suspicious movement at night. On the second night we shot and killed a stock thief. This caused much elation among the team, as stock thieves had become a real problem. Cattle were being stolen from farms and taken into the TTLs where they were distributed among the locals as a source of fresh meat for the terrorists and locals alike. The dramatic reduction of the national herd through rustling was having an adverse affect on meat production.

The Chakari district had by now been totally overrun by terrorists and it's fair to say the Rhodesians had effectively lost all control in the area. To classify it as 'hostile' would be an understatement—our patrols into the area would generally be engaged by an aggressive enemy and basically driven out.

I decided to take the terrorists on by going into the area on foot in broad daylight—to confront them head-on. On the day we deployed it had been raining and the locals were sheltering in their huts. We made our way to a kraal line and very quickly I became aware that there were terrorists in the area. I didn't have to speak to anyone to confirm this. You knew because the locals avoided looking at you directly and would scurry back into their huts when they saw you. You knew because there was no one working in the maize fields, or tending the cattle. You knew because it was very quiet, too quiet. And you knew because alarm bells were ringing in your head. It was all through experience.

We approached a kraal that boasted a brick building among the pole and *dagga* huts. It was of a simple design—whitewashed bricks, one door, one window and a thatched roof. Something was going on here. Either there were terrorists still in the kraal or they had recently departed. If they had just left we could expect to be attacked at any second. If not, then in which building were they holed up? Much as I studied the kraal my eyes always seemed to focus on the brick hut. The windows and door were facing us. As I looked around, out of the corner of my eye I saw a man who had just exited the hut walk away with his head bowed, looking away from me, before he broke into a run. As he ran his arms started waving, exposing the rifle he had been trying to conceal. No one else had been looking in that direction or had seen him. As he started to run he must have realized that he was compromised and half-turned to fire a few shots. By now my rifle was sighted on him. I fired three rounds at him and he dropped.

Things now started happening very quickly. As the terrorist I had shot dropped, I turned my attention back to the hut and saw another terrorist come out and, rifle in hand, flee in the opposite direction. My TTs opened fire on him and he also dropped.

A third terrorist was in the hut, firing at us through the window. When we returned fire he ducked below the window. I really wanted to capture him as killing him would not have achieved very much. There was no way he was going to get out alive if he did not surrender and no way that I was going to risk my men by going in after him. Daniel called to him in Shona, urging him to surrender. The response was another volley of AK fire from the window.

That left one other option. I removed the magazine from my FN, cleared the chamber, pulled out a rifle grenade from my webbing and fitted it on the end of my rifle. I took out a ballistite cartridge, inserted it into the chamber, removed the safety pin from the grenade, changed the gas setting on the rifle, aimed and fired at the window. Good shot—the luckiest shot I ever made; normally I couldn't hit the side of a *kopje* from fifty metres with a rifle grenade, the damned things were so inaccurate—the grenade went through the open window, hit the wall adjacent to it and exploded with a loud bang, mortally wounding the terrorist inside. The thatched roof was immediately engulfed in flames.

I instructed Edwin to retrieve the terrorist while I went with two of the other TTs to look for the terrorist I had shot earlier. He was not lying where he had dropped and instead of a body I noticed some very heavy blood spoor. We followed it for a few metres until I saw that it was leading into some long grass. I could see exactly where he was hiding—lying in the grass behind a contour ridge, mere metres from us. We went to ground—he still had his rifle and, if 'hard-core', he would fight bitterly to the end. I knew he was mortally wounded but I did not want him to die. If we could get to him then there might be a slim chance he could be helped. We called to him in Shona and English, telling him repeatedly that he would not be harmed, all the while watching the spot where he lay, and hoping for some movement which would indicate his surrender. The response was a sharp crack, the detonator of a terrorist F1 grenade being activated. In seconds the main charge in the grenade would ignite. There was a muffled explosion. His body bucked vigorously and then flopped to earth like a rag doll. We went to him but it was all over. While in training his political masters had convinced him that if captured by Rhodesian security forces then the most unimaginably horrific punishment would be meted out. This was nonsense but it certainly served its purpose by hardening the terrorists into fighting to the death.

The body of the other terrorist was dragged from the hut before it burned down completely.

Three kills in one contact was good going for a day's work. When we got back to Gatooma everyone made a point of insisting we retrace the gory details while offering their congratulations, which I accepted with some humility. The country was now rid of three more terrorists, but with 'peace' supposedly a few short weeks away I questioned the relevance of it all. I do not take any personal satisfaction from having killed a man. Yes, the man was my enemy and had I not killed him he would have killed me or one of my men. I looked upon him as another combatant. He and I were equal in all ways except in the final analysis where, to paraphrase Wilbur Smith, the final outcome is determined in the milliseconds of mortal combat. On the battlefield no one wins. The outcome is decided by those who have lost the least. I managed to walk away from that contact having lost nothing. The three guerrillas lost their lives. I vacillated between pride and an emptiness I couldn't quite identify.

Heat exhaustion was always a problem in the summer months. Once, when I was making my way to a relay station on the top of a *kopje*, I was suddenly overcome with dizziness and nausea and collapsed. I was only fifty or so metres from the relay station so fortunately one of the signallers climbed down to me, gave me four salt tablets, lots of water and I recovered within seconds.

On another occasion I did not do too well.

I had been on patrol; it was midday and the truck had arrived to pick us up. I plonked myself down in the back. We'd just got going when I noticed a group of locals on the side of the road. As a matter of course I told the driver to stop so I could talk to them. I noticed that one of the women had a calabash balanced on her head. A calabash is a hard-skinned fruit; with the pith removed and the outer shell dried, it makes a perfect water receptacle. Assuming this particular calabash contained water and being very thirsty I asked the woman whether I could have a sip. She graciously gave it to me and I took a small sip. What I tasted was not water; it was more like a fruit drink. It was very nice so I took another sip, then another before eventually downing about a litre of the liquid. The next thing I knew I was waking up in my base camp with a pounding hangover. I had drunk the best part of a litre of marula wine. The fruit from the *marula* tree is delicious but when fermented has an incredibly potent alcohol content—elephants have been known to keel over from its effects. I suppose I got what I deserved—the poor woman had made the wine and had carried it for miles before I came along and greedily drank most of it, and without paying.

As our presence in the area was consolidated we gathered much valuable intelligence. But in spite of our successes terrorists continued to pour into the neighbouring TTLs, almost at will. The numbers of those infiltrating the country, in spite of the thousands killed in external raids, had increased to the point where the country was quite literally in danger of being overrun. For my part I desperately needed any troops I could lay my hands on.

I appealed to some ex-regular Selous Scouts I knew in the area. They had all been regular Scouts at one stage but had returned to civilian life and were now doing TF call-ups as required (normally six weeks in the bush, every six weeks). Because my request would assist with the safety of their families, they all willingly obliged, conditional to their being able to kill a few terrorists!

I had information to the effect that three ZANLA sectoral commanders were gathering for a meeting in the Chakari area. I did not know exactly where or when but was sure that by infiltrating a specific area and doing a snatch we could find out where the meeting was taking place and then plan accordingly.

With the Scouts I got the best of the best.

Carl was acknowledged as one of the Scouts' best trackers. He put together a stick of three other Scouts—Ian, Rick and Dave. Christopher, my TT, would be attached to Carl's stick. The plan was to walk in under cover of darkness from well outside the target area, base up in hiding the following day and over a ten-day period carry out clandestine observations to suss things out and formulate a plan of attack. With their combined experience we were guaranteed success.

On the day of the start of the operation I gave them a briefing prior to their final preparations. I was in my office when Carl came in and said that Dave had a stomach bug and could not go. He wanted me to take his place. I had by then well over four years' operational experience and was confident enough, but I felt way out of my depth with these veterans. I told Carl as much. In response he told me that he'd been quietly observing me on ops and felt I was as good as any one of them and that he really *would* like to have me on his team.

It was one of the proudest moments of my life. I could not, and did not, refuse the offer.

We were going in dressed as terrorists and carrying terrorist weapons, so if we were sighted, at first glance it would not be obvious that we were SF and valuable seconds would be gained in any ensuing contact.

We were deployed from vehicles just after eleven o'clock that night and began the walk-in, in single file, with Carl leading. It takes one or two kilometres to get into your rhythm and nine or ten kilometres before fatigue sets in.

"Listen!" Carl hissed as he brought the patrol to a halt.

We all stopped and listened intently but I couldn't hear a thing other than the usual sounds of the night.

"No listen, did you hear that? Is that a dog barking?" he persisted.

Still nothing.

"Okay," he said, "let's move on."

This happened two or three times until we got to a spot where Carl decided we'd lie up for the night.

Much later I asked Carl what he had heard.

"Nothing," he said. "But because I heard one or two of you starting to drag your feet, I knew you were getting tired ... and careless. Every time I stopped you thought I'd heard something so your senses were heightened and you were alert again." A truly magical bit of bush wisdom.

We lay up for the last few hours of darkness in very thick bush where the ground rose away from us. Early the next morning Carl and Christopher went to recce the area ahead of us. They came back in a hurry.

Carl urgently called us together. "There are terrs all over the place and they are looking for us. They know we're here. Forty plus," he whispered with the faintest trace of alarm.

This is not what you want to hear. Somehow we had been compromised on the walk-in and now over forty determined terrorists were hunting the five of us! We had now become the hunted. It was most unsettling.

Carl told Rick and me to move fifty metres away onto higher ground while he, Christopher and Ian would stay put. His thinking was that the terrorists would soon find us and that contact was inevitable. He wanted us split up so when they did find us we would not be in one concentrated position. Rick and I left our packs with the others and moved off into position.

And then we waited, in nervous anticipation, adrenaline pumping. I had absolute confidence in Rick but must confess that as I lay there waiting for the contact to break, I was scared. Carl, Ian and Christopher watched the terrorists sweeping towards them with Carl waiting for just the right moment to open fire. While he waited another section of terrorists had appeared at our rear and began sweeping up to our position—directly in front of Rick and me.

When Carl was sure we were all committed and ready and that contact was inevitable he sighted on the lead terrorist and fired a single round, effectively initiating the contact. Gunfire erupted from every quarter and the bush was alive with bullets cracking and zinging through the foliage above. Rick and I held our fire, waiting for a clear target to appear. Then a terrorist, for some insane reason, broke cover and ran across our front, ten or so metres from our position. I fired twice, a double-tap, hitting him with both rounds in the chest. At the same time Rick opened up with a burst from his RPD machine gun, hitting him in the abdomen. The terrorist came to an instant stop. It looked like he had run into an invisible brick wall, before he slowly toppled over, dead.

From a position of no more than six or seven metres in front of us a section of terrorists opened up on us with a terrifying fusillade. One of them had a PKM machine gun, easily identifiable among the mass of AKs. The firepower was so effective and they were so close that the long grass around us was being mowed down as if an invisible scythe was slashing maniacally above us. The tree next to me was taking hits, causing leaves and debris to shower us like confetti. Never before had I endured such intense and such sustained enemy fire. There wasn't even time to think that I might get hit. Literally hundreds and hundreds of rounds were being directed at us. Fortunately, because of the incline, the enemy fire was high; still, it was too close for comfort.

The terrorists started spreading out in an effort to outflank us. We could sense them re-positioning themselves through the thick bush. It was just a matter of time before we were comprehensively routed. Waiting for the *coup de grâce* was a sickening feeling. Carl, on his belly, suddenly appeared from the rear, with Christopher and Ian in tow, crouched low, eyes wide and hollow, lips bloodless and drawn. There was so much noise that we could barely hear Carl speak. He said something to the effect of "Let's get the hell out of here." I understood—loud and clear. There was no way that we were going to fight off the terrorists. Hopelessly outnumbered and outgunned Carl had chosen the only option available—to get out. Rick and I turned, leopard-crawled a few paces and then altogether, with Carl, Ian and Christopher, we ran. We ran and ran and ran, waiting every second for that bullet in the back, stumbling breathlessly over rocks and gullies and bushes, thorns tearing at our skin and clothing. And still we ran, interminably, until at last the firing behind us suddenly seemed to diminish and peter out, with only the desultory crack of an AK round whistling harmlessly overhead.

We slowed down to a steady trot, catching our breath and regaining some composure, until we came to small *kopje*, with excellent defensive positions. We staggered up the slope and collapsed, exhausted, in the shade of the *mopane* trees, our camo paint streaked and smudged, almost gone. We dragged on our water canteens, long, hard, gulping swallows.

Carl got onto his radio and tried to call for air support but the signal was poor and it was unsuccessful. He re-positioned himself higher up the *kopje* and eventually managed to get a garbled message through to base to arrange vehicle uplift. We warily made our way to the agreed RV point at the nearest road and, in all-round defence, nervously waited for that heart-warming sound of vehicle engines approaching in the distance.

When the trucks finally arrived, Carl told the soldiers on the vehicle to stay where they were while we went back to sweep the contact area to look for any terrorists we'd shot—also to retrieve our packs which we'd abandoned during the flight. I doubted they'd still be there but amazingly they were. We arrived back at the scene of the contact. The terrorists had long since departed, fearful of air strikes and follow-ups.

We found the body of the terrorist that Rick and I had shot, stripped of his weapon and webbing, but there was no sign of the terrorist that Carl had clearly shot. He placed Christopher and me on either side of him and with Ian and Rick bringing up the rear, off we set, dog-legging to cut spoor.

After forty-five minutes of intense tracking Carl raised his hand, signalling to us to halt as he pointed towards a thick bush. We went to ground, crouching low, our rifles aimed at the bush. At first glance I could not see anything. But then I saw him. Carl's round had hit the terrorist low down in the abdomen. Mortally wounded the other terrorists had taken his rifle from him and placed him in a sitting position, hidden in the thick bush where he had been left to die. He had only recently died. We left the bodies where they were and returned to the vehicles.

It was getting dark so we drove to the nearby local Tilcor estate where Rick worked as a mechanic and lived with family alongside several others in a large housing compound. (Tilcor was a Ministry of Agriculture initiative to open up new farm lands in the TTLs for the locals' ultimate benefit.) We'd spend the night there and return to Gatooma the following morning. We had a shower and collapsed onto the bunks provided in the guesthouse but were woken shortly thereafter by the Tilcor staff who insisted we join them for a braai, a barbecue. Being Saturday night, as was the norm, they'd hired a movie. The projector was placed on a table in the bar and aimed at a white wall as everyone gathered round. With a few beers under my belt and the satisfaction of knowing I had managed to survive the fiercest fire fight of my life and, more importantly (to me anyway), stand as an equal alongside men of the calibre of Carl, Ian and Rick, I could not have felt more content.

The projector whirred into action, slightly out of focus, but that didn't matter. The movie was *A star is born* with Barbara Streisand and Chris Kristofferson. It's a feel-good movie. The key moment is when Barbara Streisand sings the song *Evergreen* with the sort of passion that is unique to her. It absolutely rounded off the evening for me—those scenes are forever burned in my memory. (When Janine and I got married the song we chose for our wedding was *Evergreen*, the lyrics as moving to me today as they were then.)

One of the Tilcor employees was a man named Johannes who was the estate agronomist. The fact that Johannes had done little in the way of operational work did not prevent him telling all and sundry his fictitious 'war stories'. He was such a good storyteller that rather than cut him short we let him ramble on. I would sit and listen to him while he told his stories and mutter to myself, "You *do* know I am in Special Branch?"

And still the farm attacks on innocent civilians continued.

Neighbours heard shots coming from a nearby farm homestead. The reaction team was called out and I followed. Terrorists had cut through the security fence, walked up to the window of the lounge and shot the farmer and his wife as they sat watching television. The farmer's wife was killed instantly. The farmer, mortally wounded, tried to make his way to the bedroom where he kept his rifle. With blood pouring from his wounds he stumbled against the walls of the passageway leading to the bedroom, his blood-stained palm prints imprinted and smeared along the wall where he tried to steady himself. He died at the foot of his bed reaching for his rifle.

The farmer and his wife died a few short weeks *after* the official end of hostilities.

Chapter twenty-four

Imphi iphelile, Comrade Ukuthula

Many Rhodesians, with the forthcoming demise of Zimbabwe–Rhodesia and fearing retribution from the incoming Black Nationalist government, were leaving the country in droves. This was called 'taking the gap'. The route from Salisbury via Beitbridge into South Africa became known as 'the chicken run'. Security-force resources in terms of personnel were becoming increasingly depleted and yet some of us remained. I have often been asked why I didn't leave then. For my part I had no illusions about either ZANU (PF) or ZAPU taking over the country. I knew it was going to happen. The reason I stayed is that ZANLA and ZIPRA terrorists continued to infiltrate the country in their thousands and their merciless attacks on the civilian population were continuing unabated. Some of us decided to stay to the bitter end, and beyond, to protect our families, many of whom were unable to leave due to a variety of reasons and circumstances, often financial. It was as simple as that. There were also many whites who held out the hope that "maybe it won't be so bad".

Contacts continued apace. The 'dissident' terrorists, i.e. those still not in the assembly points, had a go at us at every opportunity and we retaliated whenever we could. A *modus operandi* to deal with such incidents had been formulated between the various protagonists; in the event of a contact a representative from each ZIPRA, ZANLA and the security forces would travel together to the contact area with a Monitoring Force representative in tow. In our case this was a British Army colonel who acted as the neutral party or arbitrator. The representatives would fly to the site in question in RAF Puma helicopters with big white crosses painted on the fuselage. On arrival they'd investigate the contact area to try and ascertain who had initiated the contact—in other words try and figure out who was the guilty party.

I got to know these people quite well. As they disembarked from the helicopter the ZIPRA and ZANLA reps would invariably start arguing. With final victory in sight and, being bitter enemies with an election still to contest, each was determined to discredit the other in front of the Monitoring Force representative. While they argued I'd be questioned by the colonel and give my version of events. I was always the epitome of virtue, expressing my anger at the senseless terrorist attacks, and naturally regretting any terrorist deaths. The colonel hardly ever said a word, the security force rep generally backed me up and the ZIPRA and ZANLA reps would continue arguing, not paying the slightest attention to anything else. Eventually the colonel would calm them down before each of the four reps made his own way to the contact area to conduct his own private investigation. The whole thing was a complete farce.

After such contacts the terrorists would normally run away, leaving the security forces to mop up, usually with assistance from one of my team. It would be perfectly plain to all that an unprovoked attack had been launched against security forces who, forced to retaliate, had done nothing more than defend themselves.

The British Monitoring Force soldiers weren't fools; it was more than clear to them who were the 'good guys' and who weren't. However, they were in an invidious position—politically they had to appear neutral, so inevitably the colonel would return from his contact-site investigation with the comment "Nothing conclusive has been established", before boarding the helicopter with the petulant ZANLA and ZIPRA reps, the SF rep and return to their base in Gwelo.

Where the Brits were perhaps a mite gullible was when we'd be waiting with the RAF crew at the LZ for the Monitoring Force to complete their investigation. The pilot and technician would inevitably do what Brits do best—set up 'a brew'—have a cup of tea. We'd wander over and engage them in conversation; usually a bunch of 'war stories' kept them interested. The RAF crew were good people who were keen to chat and either didn't notice, or turned a blind eye as one of my men sneaked into the back of the helicopter and rifled through the RAF ration packs, pinching all the wonderful sweets and chocolate that we hadn't tasted since before sanctions in 1965 when UDI was declared.

Bob said he was a chief inspector with the Lancashire police and had been sent to the SB offices to monitor our movements. This didn't make sense as a chief inspector from a traffic department didn't really fit with an intelligence unit. Sure enough, a phone call from Neville confirmed that Bob was in fact from MI5. We therefore decided that if Bob, who was a nice-enough fellow, was going to be deceitful, then so would we. When I wanted Bob out of the way, which was all the time, I would tell him that I wanted to investigate a possible arms cache. When we arrived in the area I would find some excuse to leave Bob, usually suggesting he accompany Constable Zhou to the site of the supposed arms cache, promising it was only a short distance away. With that Bob would keenly set off on his trek and five or six hours later return exhausted, having been taken on a long, circular walkabout through the bush with Constable Zhou, the fittest member of my team. I, in the meantime had returned to base for a few beers. Bob was not stupid and must have known what was going on. To his credit he never moaned or said a thing. I wish him well.

Those early months of 1980 were surreal. Only weeks before we'd been at war with ZANLA and ZIPRA—now we found ourselves in an apparent ceasefire situation where not only were we forbidden to shoot the enemy but we actually had to interact with them. Rounding up and escorting terrorists to assembly points, without any display of hostility, was indeed a difficult thing to do.

This is where the Monitoring Force Commonwealth military units came in.

While on a patrol I was told that a group of terrorists had gathered at Vaneji business centre under a flag of truce. I drove to the business centre and saw them partying at a bottle store. Most were drunk, full of alcohol-induced arrogance and spoiling for a fight. When they saw my Land Rover with several constables on the back they started brandishing their weapons at me which, to say the least, did not endear them to me. When one laughingly raised his AK to his shoulder and aimed at me, I realized that perhaps I was not the best person to enter into negotiations with them.

A radio call to Gatooma had a Kenyan Army unit arriving at the scene in two brand-new Land Rovers kitted out with all the latest climbing and wet-weather gear. The commander, a captain, looked towards the terrorists who were still shouting and *toyi-toying* (dancing). In their state there was no way anyone was going to get any sense out of them.

"I will handle this," the captain said confidently and approached the bottle store with three of his men. I watched him trying to reason with the terrorists but he was clearly taking a lot of abuse and getting absolutely nowhere. The terrorists were full of bravado and looking for a fight, and the captain knew it. He promptly turned about and returned to the Land Rovers, any second expecting a volley of AK bullets in his back.

The captain was now very angry—he had been humiliated in front of his men and could not back down. The situation was very tense and it really was just a matter of time before one of the terrorists opened fire. My men were in position ready to return fire if and when this happened, but with all the locals milling about, it would turn into a massacre. I did not want a repetition of the earlier incident in Filabusi and was determined to avoid it at all costs. The captain and I agreed that he would ask the terrorists to move away from the bottle store into the open bush, away from the locals, and try again to negotiate with them. If he had no success he would make some excuse to leave and that we would come back another time.

While the captain and his men were busy negotiating with the terrorists my men and I took the opportunity to strip the brand-new Kenyan Land Rovers of everything we could, replacing such items we had 'mobilized' with our old parts. Everything, including wheel spanners, batteries, mountaineering gear, even the seats, were removed and replaced with kit from our vehicles. I rationalized that the Kenyan Land Rovers were going to be left behind when the Monitoring Force eventually left the country (I had decided) and as our needs were greater than theirs it was only perfectly reasonable that I should do what I could to help my own people.

When we were done with our plundering I turned my attention back to the negotiations at the bottle store, which were clearly going nowhere. A fire fight was surely about to erupt and the Kenyan troops were in danger of all being killed. So I called for an air strike. My idea was to get the Lynx overhead and circle the business centre in a threatening manner, waiting on my command to initiate the strike. From many years of war the terrorists had learned to recognize the distinct sound of a Lynx. When they heard the aircraft approaching they cut short their drunken negotiations and immediately fled into the bush. A very relieved Kenyan Army captain and his men scuttled across to us, oblivious of their cannibalized Land Rovers, and we all sped off with the Lynx still circling overhead.

Not all our meetings with the enemy were fraught with danger. Another large section of guerrillas had gathered at a business centre prior to making their way to Assembly Point Romeo. On this occasion I was driving past Digavi BC when I saw them gathered outside a store.

I was travelling in my Land Rover with Gordon who had joined me for a six-week call-up. Following was a Kudu mine-proofed personnel carrier with eight troops on board. I stopped my Land Rover, got out and stood for a while with my rifle in hand at my side, adopting a posture that was neither aggressive nor fearful. I wanted the terrorists to see that although prepared to talk I was still armed. As I stood there a guerrilla stepped away from the others and took up exactly the same stance. I handed my rifle to Gordon who had stepped out of the Land Rover. Likewise, the guerrilla handed his rifle to one of his men. With a deep breath I started walking towards him and he to me.

It was to be one the most memorable moments of my life. We met, simultaneously raised our arms and shook hands.

"I know you," he said.

That was a given; I knew him as well. I was shaking hands with a fellow combatant whom I had chased around the Gatooma TTLs for several weeks. Short and built like a bodybuilder his name was Ukuthula (perversely isiNdebele for 'peace'). A ZIPRA sectoral commander, he and I had been in many contacts where we had tried to kill each other and where we had both lost men. He told me that he was making his way to Assembly Point Romeo and as it was a good seven hours' walk asked if I could arrange transport for him and his men. That was no problem. Gordon, overhearing the discussion, had radioed ahead and had organized four APCs to rendezvous at the business centre.

My men, sensing there was no danger, alighted from the vehicles and started chatting with the ZIPRA guerrillas. The atmosphere was relaxed as the former enemies mingled and laughed together. It was gratifying.

During the two-hour drive to the assembly point Ukuthula and I sat together in the back of one of the personnel carriers. After an initial period of awkwardness and clumsy probing we started talking more freely and within a very short time we were struggling to get the words out fast enough—there was so much we wanted to tell each other. I learned much from him and I think he from me. He told me that much as guerrillas feared helicopters they knew that the mere mention of a landmine had us halting all vehicle movements, calling in mine-detectors and effectively delaying further security-force operations in the area. He said his men would tell locals they had planted a landmine on a section of road but were never specific about its exact location. When the information filtered through to us we would avoid travelling along that particular road for at least a day or two, with the result that the terrorists would be able to move unhindered into the adjacent areas.

Ukuthula told me that on many occasions he had seen me in BCs and recognized me by the distinctive way I wore my webbing. What prevented him shooting me was the habit I had of mixing with the locals. To have opened fire on me would have undoubtedly resulted in civilian casualties. Thankfully it was not in his character to do such a thing.

We discussed contacts we had been involved in together and we talked about how each of us had behaved under fire; how we had come so close to killing each other yet somehow hadn't. Yet there was no animosity between us. We were simply two soldiers forced into fighting a war not of our making and now, having fought against each other, were talking as men before us, our elders, should have done a long time ago.

dagga: mud (Shona) e.g. pole and *dagga* (wattle and daub) hut

dagga: marijuana (Afrikaans)

DC: District Commissioner

DI: Detective Inspector

donga: ditch (Afrikaans)

doppie: expended cartridge case (slang)

doro: alcohol, drink (Shona)

D/P/O: Detective Patrol Officer

D/S/O: Detective Section Officer

ek sê: I say (Afrikaans)

Fireforce: airborne assault group

GC: Ground Coverage (grassroots intelligence-gathering arm of the BSAP)

goffle: derogatory sland for a coloured, a person of mixed race

gomo: hill or *kopje* (Shona)

HE: high-explosive

hondo: war, conflict (Shona)

int: intelligence

Intaf: Ministry of Internal Affairs (abbreviation)

jesse: thick thorn scrub

JOC: Joint Operations Centre

kak: shit (Afrikaans)

KIA: killed in action

kopje: hill (Afrikaans—pronounced 'copy', also *koppie*)

kraal: African village (South African corruption of the Portuguese *curral* meaning a cattle pen or enclosure) lemon: term for an aborted or botched-up call-out/operation (Rhodesian Security Force slang)

loc: location or position

locstat: positional co-ordinates

MAG: *matireurs à gas*—gas-operated, belt-fed section machine gun, manufactured by Fabrique Nationale (FN, Belgium) and used by Rhodesian security forces

mapolisa: police (Shona)

meneer: mister (Afrikaans)

mielies: maize cobs (Afrikaans, also mealies)

mombe: cow (Shona)

mtagati: 'bad medicine' (Shona)

mujiba: young civilian guerrilla supporter, the guerrillas' 'eyes and ears' (Shona)

munt, muntu: a black person (Rhodesian slang, from the Shona for 'a man', sometimes derogatory)

murungu: white man (Shona)

NCO: Non-Commissioned Officer

NS: National Service/man

NSPO: National Service Patrol Officer

OC: Officer Commanding

oke: lad, guy (from the Afrikaans *ouen*)

OP: observation post

ops: operations

PATU: Police Anti-Terrorist Unit (BSAP paramilitary specialist unit)

PF: Patriotic Front (ZANU/ZAPU alliance)

PGHQ: Police General Headquarters

povo: people (Portuguese, and now commonly Shona)

P/O: Patrol Officer

PRAW: Police Reserve Air Wing

pungwe: a large meeting, a political rally (Shona)

PV: Protected Village

R & R: Rest & Recreation

RAR: Rhodesian African Rifles

RBC: Rhodesia Broadcasting Corporation

RF: Rhodesian Front, white political party headed by Ian Smith

RIC: Rhodesian Intelligence Corps

RLI: Rhodesian Light Infantry

RPG: rocket-propelled grenade

RR: Rhodesia Regiment (white Territorial battalions)

RV: rendezvous

SABC: South African Broadcasting Corporation

SAP: South African Police

SAS: Special Air Service

SB: Special Branch (of the BSAP)

SF: (Rhodesian) Security Forces

sitrep: situation report

SLA: Sabi-Limpopo Authority

S/O: Section Officer

stick: four- to six-man unit or battle group (originally from a 'stick' of
  paratroopers)

SWAT: Special Weapons and Tactics

'take the gap': Rhodesian Security Force expression used to denote a rapid exit
  from a location

terr: terrorist

TF: Territorial Force

TT: tame/turned terrorist

TTC: Teachers' Training College

TTL: Tribal Trust Land/s (Rhodesian Land Tenure Act)

UANC: United African National Council, headed by Bishop Abel Muzorewa

UDI: Unilateral Declaration of Independence

veldskoene: rough suede bush shoes (Afrikaans)

vlei: swampy, open grassland (Afrikaans)

ZANLA: Zimbabwe African National Liberation Army, ZANU's military wing

ZANU: Zimbabwe African National Union, headed by Robert Mugabe

ZAPU: Zimbabwe African People's Union, headed by Joshua Nkomo

ZIPRA: Zimbabwe People's Revolutionary Army, ZAPU's military wing